From Student to Professor

Other Titles of Interest by
Rowman & Littlefield Education

From Student to Professor

Translating a Graduate Degree into a Career in Academia

Carol A. Mullen

ROWMAN & LITTLEFIELD EDUCATION
A division of
ROWMAN & LITTLEFIELD PUBLISHERS, INC.
Lanham • New York • Toronto • Plymouth, UK

Published by Rowman & Littlefield Education
A division of Rowman & Littlefield Publishers, Inc.
A wholly owned subsidiary of The Rowman & Littlefield Publishing Group, Inc.
4501 Forbes Boulevard, Suite 200, Lanham, Maryland 20706
www.rowman.com

10 Thornbury Road, Plymouth PL6 7PP, United Kingdom

British Library Cataloguing in Publication Information Available

Library of Congress Cataloging-in-Publication Data

Mullen, Carol A.
From student to professor : translating a graduate degree into a career in academia / by Carol A. Mullen.
p. cm.
Includes bibliographical references and index.
ISBN 978-1-61048-903-4 (pbk. : alk. paper)
1. College teaching—Vocational guidance. 2. College teachers—Employment. I. Title.
LB1778.M85 2012
378.1'2—dc23
2012014261

☉™ The paper used in this publication meets the minimum requirements of American National Standard for Information Sciences Permanence of Paper for Printed Library Materials, ANSI/NISO Z39.48-1992.

Printed in the United States of America

Contents

Foreword

Imagine for a few minutes that you have decided to enter graduate school, perhaps in pursuit of a master's degree requiring a thesis and/or research papers, or a doctorate with a more demanding dissertation. You dream of being immersed in student life, eventually walking across the graduation stage bursting with excitement with degree in hand. Your intentionality gives you vitality. You begin to plan, knowing full well from your master's-program experience that a secret to your success will be allowing your vision to unfold to achieve your goal.

It is at this point that Carol Mullen's research and writing, as realized in this book, comes into play. Drawing on her own experiences as a master's and doctoral student, and in particular her award-winning supervision of graduate students and collaboration with them and beginning professors, she guides you through "doors" of opportunity.

This prolific writer vividly describes those doors (e.g., specialists) already in place to assist you in ways big and small, and she helps you construct other doors on your own terms that will ensure your success. She also places you in the seat of ownership so you will be better able to not only recognize but also proactively address problems and challenges associated with doors that are closed or only slightly ajar.

A major theme in this enterprise is building relationships with one or more mentors, notably professors and peer leaders, who share their talents with you and care for you. It is this connection with mentors that will make your journey less lonely and give you access to academic, social, emotional, and practical skills that will last throughout your career and life. You will learn how to navigate the norms of the academy from the inside out.

Professor Mullen gives you an overview of *From Student to Professor: Translating a Graduate Degree into a Career in Academia* in her preface, so you will want to take the time to mull it over. I am excited about sharing with you what makes this book special and how she contributes in unique ways to the literature on graduate-student success, with a special emphasis on the mentoring process.

First, Mullen brings to this book an authenticity based on the marriage of scholarship and practice. Not only has she established herself as an accomplished researcher and writer, but she also demonstrates the value of leadership and collaboration in mentoring with graduate students, junior faculty, and even seasoned faculty and practitioners. On a daily basis, she actually does what she writes about and is a living expression of what it means to mentor, coach, network, and assist others in succeeding and realizing their vision.

Mullen was a highly successful editor of the prestigious international journal *Mentoring & Tutoring: Partnership in Learning*. In this role, she opened doors for graduate students and colleagues from many different countries. I was one of many recipients of her largesse, as she published my essay, "Cherishing the Memory of Seymour Sarason—Public Intellectual, Mentor and Friend," and she paved the way for the reviews of my coauthored books *Why the Principalship? Making the Leap from the Classroom* and *Advancing Your Career: Getting and Making the Most of Your Doctorate*. Such generosity in the service of others and their impact on the field and world is the measure of a true scholar-practitioner, colleague, and friend. Mullen continues to open doors for others as the 2012–2013 president of the National Council of Professors of Educational Administration. The point of all of this is simply that the chapters in her book are deep with lived experience; they bring to life how you, the reader, can engage in your own learning and reciprocity in the mentoring relationship as a graduate student, master's or doctoral graduate, or beginning professor, and in the process learn how to pass this torch to others as a mentor.

A second thing that makes this book special is how Mullen draws on her rich background and experiences in the humanities in general and literature in particular as the basis for storytelling. Case studies animate the chapters and take readers backstage into the professional and personal lives of graduate students and their mentors. As with the best writing in the humanities, Mullen's prose conveys compassion and sentiment without being maudlin or insipid.

Mullen's mentoring stories are riveting and they will make you think. The descriptions of her WIT (Writers in Training) are vibrant and will place you in the role of writer, student, faculty member, practitioner, and leader. As you read this book, you will find yourself living the curriculum of academia, not simply mechanically taking courses.

In short, this book is invigorating, and stimulating in contrast with too many leadership books that are simplistic, "paint-by-number" monologues that insult the intelligence of the reader, lack depth, and fail to promote thinking or transformation. Mullen's writing has precisely the opposite effect, for which I give thanks. It recognizes, indeed celebrates, the complexity of persons and contexts in the mentoring process. By doing so, her writing honors the tradition of such giants in education as John Dewey, George Counts, and Maxine Greene, examples of those who have resisted certainty and the quest for it.

A third characteristic of Mullen's book that makes it unique is the excellence she brings to writing. I recently had an opportunity to experience what she refers to in this book as "practicing observational learning." In 2012, she participated as an invited member of a panel of three professors at The University of North Carolina at Greensboro, sponsored by the graduate school, who focused on practical strategies for dissertation research and writing. The bane of question-and-answer sessions that followed is wanderlust. Carol was not a party to this diversion. Her comments were concise and deeply reflective, the result being that graduate students in the audience found her ideas intriguing and easily understood.

She brings these same precise as well as penetrating communication skills to this book. You will find a clear map for learning, and her word choice makes the complex worlds she describes understandable and moving while not robbing them of their magic or mystery. The book has coherence in its presentation, structure, and flow, and readers will find it compelling, beneficial, and practical.

A fourth and final characteristic of the book is that mentors, sometimes stuck in their routines, politics, and patterns of academe, are reminded that the conditions we desire for our students (selected mentees) must also exist for ourselves. There are examples throughout of veteran leaders and professors coming to life and being inspired by their students and the mentor–mentee relationship. The memories of our own graduate-student days help us see from the eyes of our students, empathize with their struggles, and move forward as understanding mentors. This is the essence of authentic and focused collaboration, as well as productive, trusting mentor–mentee relationships.

Mullen's writing illustrates the idea that the learning settings we create have their own personalities, and it is our challenge in a culture that primarily focuses on the personalities of individuals to consider how relationships, such as mentoring, are influenced and changed in a variety of contexts. For example, the student and advisor must carefully choose thesis and dissertation committees. As you read, you will see that student mentees are being alerted to how professors might want to handle such situations and have them handled by their students, another example of how conditions we want for our students must also exist for ourselves.

A few words about this book being a second edition will end this foreword. The first edition gives an author the opportunity to try it out with a variety of audiences, in this case mentees and mentors. Professional-development experiences and graduate-school courses, programs, and informal learning situations are the contexts in which this takes place. Mullen has adopted a more informal, even more accessible writing style in this edition. Indeed, it now reads like a conversation between author and reader. Tech-smart and culturally up-to-date examples also invoke this revolution in communication.

A new contribution (see Chapter 10) on the digital learner and entrepreneurship in and beyond graduate school is geared toward academic careers, again taking the book to the next level. Case and case analyses using electronic learning among digital participants and innovators in changing graduate-program contexts are a welcome addition to the original. These and other changes were initiated because Mullen recognized the need for a more digital and entrepreneurial edge, and to know her is to see that she lives the change she describes.

This second edition has an open invitation to students and faculty outside education. Readers from professional schools, the humanities, the social sciences, and religious studies have found common ground in Mullen's writing. Professors in advanced writing courses have recommended this book to their students. Chapters in the book that prepare graduate students to enter the world of research and writing after graduation are of special interest, as are sections that give advice on academic career preparation, selection, and advancement.

My vision for Mullen's second edition is that professors and students, mentors and mentees, and others will collaborate in a variety of learning settings using this guide as a kind of map for realizing their personal and professional goals. With this book in hand, readers will feel more empowered to take ownership over their own learning and preparation, mentoring and engagement. Using the tenets and practices of this book, I bet you'll feel inspired to generate frameworks for learning, collaborating, and mentoring that can enrich your own present and future. These new beginnings will emerge for you as you flip to the preface and immerse yourself in the entire book. Take this step forward. Invite this change in your perspective and life. This is precisely the kind of book that can make all of this happen.

Dale L. Brubaker, Professor Emeritus,
University of North Carolina at Greensboro

Preface

OPENING THE ACADEMY'S DOOR

Newcomers to graduate school often feel like outsiders looking through a window. Such an activity-filled life seems remote and unfamiliar. This book is your doorway inside. Enter. Experience graduate-school life from the point of entry as a student to the point of exit and reentry as a professor. Immerse yourself in the spaces described to assist your adaptation, development, growth, success, and sustainability. Learn how to navigate everything from initiation rituals to mentoring relationships, scholarly writing to career preparation.

From Student to Professor: Translating a Graduate Degree into a Career in Academia brings graduate school to life, animating it from the inside out. This is not a how-to manual, even though various tools are provided. This is more a thoughtful, lived account that taps the perspectives of graduate students and professors who describe healthy relationships, productive networks, smart ideas, community involvement, clear communications, writing dissemination, digital presence, and market sensibilities. They also share obstacles and potential pitfalls that prevent progression in graduate school or career development.

The big idea is that you will be learning about obtaining a graduate degree and translating it into a career in academia. Hidden and complicated dynamics reside in this culture—these go well beyond formal study and what can be observed on the surface, which is why a book on this subject is needed. I am your guide. A thriving insider, I have been in academia my entire career, transitioning from student to professor. I am a first-generation college graduate who was raised in poverty in a steel town in Canada, who got my doctorate in Toronto, and who reentered academia as professor in the United States.

As you flip through these pages, you will move from outside to inside the academy. Tune in to your responses: What resonates with you, and what are you excited about? Discover more about yourself as a learner and an emerging scholar, leader, and activist. What ideas and practices do you find meaningful or motivating, and what actions might you take? How will you transfer what you are learning in graduate programs to a career in the academy? Do you know what it takes to nurture a career as a professor, researcher, or administrator?

This book will focus attention on you and your personal study of developmental learning. Doing well in courses and having study goals are important, but there is much more to be gained. Think bigger, deeper, and more strategically about how you can penetrate academic cultures. With this book in hand, you will have a snapshot of life in graduate school as you progress and prepare for the job market.

The stories are from graduate students, thesis and dissertation writers, beginning professors, and seasoned professors from different institutions of higher education. Graduate students identify pitfalls to watch out for, such as delayed and weak communication with faculty advisors, mentors, and peers. They have generously shared roadblocks and ways to overcome them through lively descriptions of problems and breakthroughs. Whether mentoring structures are in place for facilitating information flow and connections, they recommend that graduate students, everywhere, take responsibility for your own learning.

Professors and peer leaders feel closest to students who exhibit a commitment and willingness to actively participate. Opportunities for learners to engage include informal and formal mentorships, team-based projects, and networked learning spaces. Insiders value their own enrichment and yearn for mutual learning opportunities and rewards. These include authorship and other roles in disseminated works, leadership and participation in learning communities and grants, and spearheading and supporting humanitarian projects.

Some higher-education graduates work in partnership think-tanks with schools, districts, and regions. They want to influence high-need, low-income areas, possibly to empower employees, such as teachers and principals working in poverty conditions with struggling families. Another focus is educational and employment opportunities for disenfranchised children and youth.

Engaged professors who are relationally oriented want to learn alongside their best students, coach you and be coached by you, and collaborate on projects. Many faculty members gravitate toward funded, high-profile, and multidisciplinary efforts, while others maximize their freedom with scholarship on their own terms.

You do not have to have all the ideas yourself. Tap into and build on ideas being communicated in cafes, seminars, webinars, cyberspace, and elsewhere. Invitations to webinars abound! These include free access to such topics as university–district–school partnerships and leadership preparation for aspiring teachers and principals. Listen for others' nuances as you engage in observational and collaborative learning. Take notes, keep a video diary, or draw your thoughts. This way you'll avoid "brain freezes" that come from facing a blank page/screen and "brain drains" that ensue from writing exhaustion. "Plugged in" students keep a running record of their conversations, breakthroughs, and ideas that, in turn, enhances the quality of their thought process, interactions, and scholarly works.

The people in this book read as characters darting in and out. But, you are the main character—your stories, reactions, and interests are central and they thicken this graduate-school plot. Get in touch with your deepest desires, personal thoughts, and profound feelings. Make meaning out of the ideas and advice simply by recording your spontaneous associations and reflecting on what transpires. Maybe create a to-do list of questions to ask advisors, events to find out about, networks to research, communications servers to subscribe to, causes to join, and so forth. Absorbed in the book and in your graduate life and goals, you'll be making the shift from student to professor. Become an insider. You can choose to start now.

As a student or professor, you will transform in graduate school and potentially change learning situations for others. Shed the role of witness as your observational antenna matures. Become a passionately engaged creator by committing to life-changing work. By surfing the Internet and reading current uploads, books, and articles, you cannot help but see that some students and professors are not just studying ideas; much of the work carried out in graduate programs reflects the human impulse to create and make a difference in the world.

Do Internet searches to find professors' and students' blogs, videos, and discussion groups that interest you. As you'll see, some people in graduate school are educator-activists who are, as examples, struggling for rights and freedom in cyberspace; there is an outcry against the aggressive actions of some countries to censor Internet content. Other researchers are taking a humanitarian stand against child exploitation and violence, speaking out against the suffering of children living in war zones. Still others have joined communities united in a spiritual effort to serve as role models and resource generators for disadvantaged populations.

Spearheading innovation, graduate-school teams are demonstrating that ingenuity has no bounds in this era of digital revolution. One group of researchers has developed electronic chips that trace disease at the molecular level for cancer detection. An entrepreneur, a former graduate student in social work, trains service dogs to assist special-needs families and children with impaired learning and disorders. Citizens enjoy the dogs' playful antics. This attraction sparks community by bringing people together. A university team of digital entrepreneurs collaborated with a department of education and school districts to transform high-needs schools with twenty-first-century technology. Students living in poverty can accelerate by having state-of-the-art teaching and learning experiences. What do you believe in? What will you try to influence through your academic pursuits and career?

The inner world depicted is your raw script to imprint with your ideals and aspirations. *From Student to Professor: Translating a Graduate Degree into a Career in Academia* is for graduate students with special emphasis on doctoral students, specifically dissertation writers. Master's thesis writers should also find it useful. The primary student audience is graduate students in education and related fields of study, such as the social sciences and humanities.

Entering the **doors** of your graduate programs, literally and figuratively, through formal admissions, orientations, and other means, you encounter the academy's culture. Perhaps you know what courses to take and what degree program to pursue and where, but what about the inner life of academia? What about how advisors, mentors, and students learn together? What about how professors transmit ideas, expectations, and values? How will you go about becoming an insider yourself? In what ways might you direct the learning you wish to cultivate through your academic work and relationships?

Reclusive people doing public work inhabit the academy's densely hidden worlds. As mentioned, many professors and students are doing innovative work that reflects their beliefs and commitments. More and more people have a strong digital presence as well, which is a conduit for students seeking opportunities in areas of personal and political interest. Despite the public interface that academia is cultivating, graduate-school life seems mysterious. Even insiders often feel this way. One alumnus, an academic journalist, revealed, "It always struck me—in college and even after—that graduate students were engaged in a magical, mysterious quest" (Toor 2004, B5). What is this mystery and how can one make sense of it?

DIFFERENT TYPES OF GUIDES

Learning means moving beyond the known to accepting new guides in one's life and in turn accepting being a guide to others. With curiosity, anticipation, or excitement, one enters a new world; and with vision and commitment, the person is slowly transformed, exiting profoundly changed. This book is about taking this journey—learning about and becoming immersed in opportunities that foster research, networking, socialization, camaraderie, enrichment, and career development. People, procedures, and processes sometimes permit, and at other times prohibit, the very opportunities graduate schools mean to support. Guides can help you foresee and even navigate obstacles, as well as fully participate in your newly found professional home.

People's concerns, worries, and fears can obstruct movement, intelligent decision-making, and success. As Toor (2004) fittingly writes, "No one outside of the U.S. government is more adept than graduate students at coming up with conspiracy theories" (B5). So we must become very aware of our own mental states and personal issues and closely monitor them. Vigilance filters personal insecurities, defenses, jealousies, and neuroses that can be consuming. Remember, doors are not only encountered but also manufactured. When you are uncertain what something means or someone is thinking, don't assume or fret—it may be best to go directly to the source. In online contexts, communication lacks nonverbal cues and often the subtlety necessary for understanding someone's intended meaning. So reach out.

Your **selfhood** matters. The self you are—and the self you are becoming—is often the invisible force that shapes your experience of "doors" (e.g., virtual advisor). This intervening reality, your self, is a major influence in the quality of your experiences with different people, courses, procedures, policies, programs, causes, and so forth. What you gravitate toward or steer away from may differ from your peers, and the same door, such as a person or program, attracts varied reactions. No door has static meaning or value. Get to know doors. Know that you yourself are a door.

Doors have personal meaning and cultural significance: "The styles of doors evolved by a culture reflect the concerns of its people through time" (Rowland 1982, xiv). Doors, and how they are designed, framed, and used, are not merely functional but reflect the culture in which they are created. Examples include Indian doors, in actuality massive city gates designed to keep out elephants; Persian mosque doors, made from precious metals denoting spiritual aspects of this culture; and Dutch doors, wooden structures closed at the bottom to bar small intruders. Some spaces in the academy have no doors, inviting participation, engagement, and collaboration.

Some doors are private spaces enclosed within public spaces. Within these interior spaces, absorptive focus is on resolving unforeseen complications with programs, advisement, and supervision. We cannot overlook those unstable doors that reside on a shaky foundation where help is conditional or unreliable. Doors that are closed, like some people, reverberate "Do not trespass" without even knowing it. Visual cues, such as a frown or furled brow, cannot be taken at face value. It is just that some people seem sealed off or unapproachable when they are absorbed.

Many doors in academia (including those in websites and blogs) have signs or notices that communicate what the person, entity, place, or organization stands for—causes, for example—or upcoming events and activities. Note the welcoming signs.

The doors you come across on your journey will have different shapes and functions and will take on new meanings as you interact with each. No one door will give you all that you need in the way of guidance, illumination, and mentorship. You are your own best resource—make the best of hospitable doors or systems, and when possible, remodel unwelcoming ones.

WINDOWS OF OPPORTUNITY

Past doors and inside the academy, find good mentoring. Quality mentoring is a sign of excellence in learning and education. It is crucial to the satisfaction, retention, and accomplishments of students in advanced degree programs. Take the example of doctoral program completion. Statistics vary on this point. Only up to 50 percent of North American doctoral students in education may be graduating (Dorn, Papalewis, and Brown 1995; Ogden 1993), although retention and completion are higher for students in cohorts (Horn 2001). Generally speaking, racial minority populations have not been terribly satisfied with their college experiences. Low morale negatively affects performance and graduation. Isolation, compounded by low self-esteem, interferes with student progress and career progression, notably for faculty of color (Johnson-Bailey 2012).

What makes the difference? As described in this book, social integration, participation in campus organizations and activities, and purposeful interaction with peers and faculty widely benefit student groups (Johnson-Bailey 2012; Lamb 1999).

Graduate students have a window of opportunity as never before for being shepherded through their degree programs. The environment of graduate school is, no doubt, high pressure. Students make profound sacrifices as they progress through high-quality, knowledge-based communities. These incorporate such crucial elements as regular attention, online networking support, and mentoring across disciplines and races (Lamb 1999; Mullen 2009). For motivated digital entrepreneurs who thrive in social networking contexts and for some cultural ethnic groups, virtual and communal possibilities are welcoming—signaling affinity.

Inside academia, diversity and mentoring go hand-in-hand in other ways too. Quality mentoring does not depend on one method, approach, or style. Students can thrive in **traditional mentoring** or **alternative mentoring** contexts. **Mentorship** historically involves apprentices learning information, skills, and habits from experts. In contrast, alternative mentoring is about respecting that professors and students are equal but different partners who serve a higher aim of changing fundamentally flawed systems (Darwin 2000; Mullen 2011b). When people decide that power, authority, and negative bias are subjects of critique, regardless of the subject of study, alternative mentoring is at work.

Traditional mentoring overlaps with **technical mentoring** (Mullen 2011a) or functionalist mentoring (Darwin 2000). This process of socialization can cement boundaries between teacher and learner and also subjugate students' selfhood, rights, experience, and voice. A closed-life system keeps the door shut on a fairer, more enriching relationship dependent on a level playing field.

Alternative or progressive mentoring is not somehow magically flawless. It has distinct drawbacks, too. Nontraditional mentors and students, and the interventions they spearhead, function within macro-systems hindered by external mediators, such as uninformed public opinion, legislation that devalues education, and economies of deep recession. Also, more interpersonally, if a mentoring relationship is too friendly or overly informal, the student may not learn the necessary skills at the expected pace or even progress. In life-changing alternative mentoring relationships, biases concerning gender, race, disability, poverty, and other differences are addressed. Systemic inequities that subtract from fairness and opportunity are confronted and they can be changed. *How* students are learning is no less important than *what* they are learning (Griffin and Reddick 2011; Johnson-Bailey 2012).

While graduate students complain about the mentoring and supervision they receive (Toor 2004), others speak highly of it. Waterman (2004) reasonably speculates, "Satisfaction is not, of course, universal, but mentoring seems to be what doctoral programs do best, even though many stories that get widely recounted are about poor mentors and failed mentor–student relationships" (B18).

This tension in student perspective is real, and it needs study. To this end, responses were elicited from professors and graduate students about their experience of the academy. Students and faculty members were asked to consider graduate mentoring relative to their personal and professional goals, experiences, and aspirations. They were also asked to share ideas and practices that support student growth, faculty engagement, and program success. I have added personal stories.

DOORS THAT TRANSFORM IDENTITY

Self-empowered, seize upon mentoring and networking relationships as an opportunity for "identity transformation, a movement from the status of understudy to that of self-directing colleague" (Healy 1997, 10). Self-directing does not mean feeling disconnected even if you are living alone (Klinenberg 2012). Graduate students, especially younger ones, have fluid, multiple selves that take shape in high-energy networks, mostly online (Bauerlein 2011). They are using such tools as Skype, Twitter, Facebook, iPads, smartphones, voice-activated software, and other technologies (English, Papa, Mullen, and Creighton 2012). Unlike the graduate schools of the recent past, many adults belong to online learning communities and also work and play in virtual worlds. They feel comfortable communicating at chat sites and they surf the Internet, use browsers, personalize websites, customize software, befriend electronically, and more.

Even when digitally adept graduate students are networked and globally connected, many still feel disoriented and confused. In one such instance, a doctoral student (respondent to this book) received departmental assistance upon entry into his program but later felt lost. He shared,

> There is no good way to meet other graduate students in the department. I have many other unanswered questions, such as how one gets to know the students in this degree program, what kinds of topics they are researching, and how they find literature sources online. While the department chair has been helpful in e-mailing me back, I have yet to be connected with other students and learn from them.

Recall a situation when someone's involvement in your initial foray made a difference. As this student revealed, feeling that you belong and are making academic success depends on interactions with peers who provide coaching on real-life situations. However, realizing this need early on, like this student, and actually reaching out for help are different levels of adaptive response.

Finally, this leads to the question: what strategies do new students have for coping, connecting, and collaborating? Acknowledging that disorientation and confusion are inevitable states of mind when acclimating to graduate school and even when progressing through it can ironically help with navigating spaces and resources. Truth-telling about these uncomfortable issues and overcoming difficulties, not just merely coping, are uncovered in these chapters. Importantly, student survival necessitates a commitment and willingness to seek advising, support, coaching, and even counseling. Everyone can benefit from mentors, allies, and learning alliances, says Clutterbuck (2001), a leading researcher of mentoring.

Mentors, role models, peers, and other supports are crucial for a life-altering experience of academia. The students, professors, and administrators who populate these pages reflect the power of this statement. The students benefitted from or could have benefitted from "intentional mentoring" structures, scaffolds, and relationships throughout their programs and careers (Mullen 2012, 12). Online and networked, graduate students are being called upon not only to collaborate within worlds in great flux but also to remake the academy for students around the corner.

GLOSSARY

alternative mentoring. A democratic process of faculty–student comentorship built upon power-sharing professional relations and egalitarian structures (Mullen 2005, 2011a).

doors. A metaphor for people, processes, and systems, more specifically mentors, peers, specialists, committees, groups, support systems, traditions, customs, mores, practices, procedures, and policies.

mentorship. An educational process, the focus of which is "teaching and learning within dyads, groups, and cultures" (Mullen 2005, 25).

selfhood. Having our own identity, personality, and character and personalizing our worlds in ways that reflect our value and self-worth (*Merriam–Webster* 2012).

technical mentoring. Power-based educational training that reifies managerial efficiency, hierarchy, and authority (also functionalist mentoring) (Mullen 2005, 2011a).

traditional mentoring. Relationships and systems that transmit skills or knowledge top-down, preserving or heightening power differences, cultural deficits, and opportunity gaps (e.g., resources) within stratified systems.

Acknowledgments

The backbone of *From Student to Professor: Translating a Graduate Degree into a Career in Academia* is dozens of anonymous contributions from graduate students, as well as nontenured and tenured faculty members and university administrators. Data were gathered through e-surveys that expanded into elaborated exchanges with some contributors and from my own mentoring support groups. I thank everyone who took the time to respond to my questions about personal mentoring experiences, processes, programs, and structures in higher education.

I appreciate the creative contribution made by Dr. William A. Kealy ("Bill") and Christopher L. Kennedy ("Chris") and who collaborated on designing Figure 1, "Mentoring Map for Navigating Graduate School," after reading this book and reflecting on its content.

Dale L. Brubaker, Professor Emeritus of Educational Leadership and leading author in doctoral education, wrote a thoughtful Foreword and was encouraging throughout.

I also thank Sharan B. Merriam, Professor Emeritus of Adult Education and renowned scholar in mentoring and adult development for her book endorsement. Her work is phenomenal.

Thomas ("Tom") G. Nelson, Professor of Curriculum Studies and Qualitative Research, also endorsed this book. His commitment to doctoral student development is an inspiration.

Rowman & Littlefield Education's publishing team gave personalized attention to this project and their assistance was exceptional. Dr. Thomas Koerner, vice president and editorial director, and Mary McMenamin, assistant editor, oversaw the book production stages.

Introduction

INSIDE THE ACADEMY'S DOORS

This book is about succeeding in graduate school and applying your graduate degree to a career in academia. The focus is on learning how academics orient themselves, network, mentor, interact, communicate, write, create, and think. Securing an academic position and thriving, not just surviving, is the goal.

Dale Brubaker, a widely recognized author of the doctoral education process who graduated dozens of successful students, is the foreword's messenger.

Special features of *From Student to Professor: Translating a Graduate Degree into a Career in Academia* start with a visual map of the entire graduate-school experience (figure 1); this is followed by cases in the words of students and professors, discussed with the support of extensive analyses; points to remember about what you've read; navigational prompts that exercise understanding; and end-of-chapter glossaries (the special terms are bolded in the chapters). Specific examples, real anecdotes, and data-driven narration are highlights. References and resources supplement the material and prompts. Nine appendices serve as practical documents for thesis/dissertation writers seeking assistance with program responsibilities, writing demands, and job searches.

HOW TO READ THIS BOOK

Using the Mentoring Map

Figure 0.1, "Your Mentoring Map for Navigating Graduate School," is an original artwork depicting salient reading cues (i.e., icons). These include clipboards (i.e., writing), clusters (i.e., networks), and light bulbs (i.e., ideas). This figure resembles a map and functions as one too. Not literally a Google map with routes and driving directions, this imaginative depiction is of the graduate-school experience from start to finish. The route is interpretive rather than linear, and it is a graphical depiction. As you look at figure 1, you might want to anticipate some of the content before settling in to read the book. The visual map forecasts expanded ideas and narration.

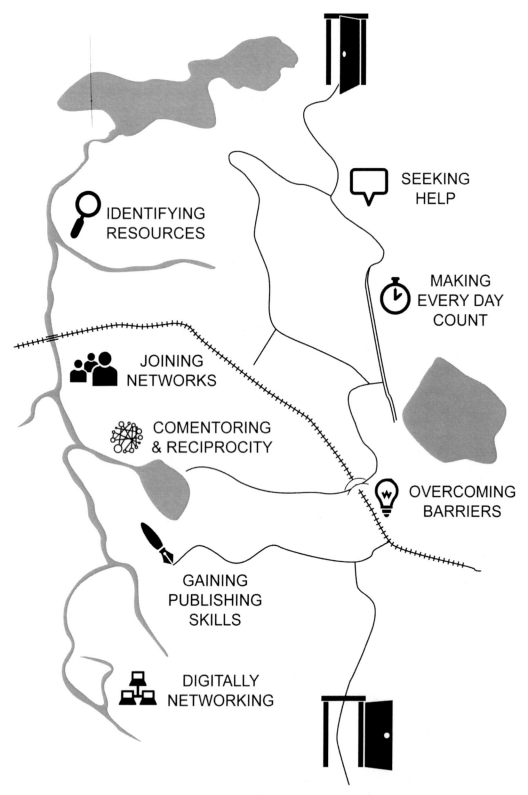

Figure 0.1.   Mentoring Map for Navigating Graduate School

The map, codesigned by a professor and doctoral student in education, represents the entire book (and table of contents). The icons fit the text. This list reflects the student's spontaneous, meaning-making associations with each chapter's key idea:

- *Door* (top of the map). Invites campus and program entry.
- *Speech bubble.* Represents "seeking help" and "making contact." Even before you get to graduate school, you will be a sleuth, figuring out what people's passions are and the tone and feeling of a place, thoroughly considering the community and physical place you will be a part of; expect a lot of correspondence.
- *Magnifying lens.* Helps you locate places and platforms of connectivity and figure out how to practice connecting and collaborating; walk around the place, neighborhoods, and streets. Leave the formal classroom and find things around you that can invigorate your research interests. Have coffee with people and make them a part of your organic living community.
- *Clock.* Reminds you to make every day count while paradoxically learning how to pace yourself and be fully present in your body and context. Through this process come awareness and a robust sense of identity. Living in this way makes every day meaningful, facilitated by experiential engagement and an ongoing negotiation of value. Making every day count also means being attentive to your own wellness. This requires you to be healthy and take time for yourself, to have spontaneous and meaningful experiences, and to reimagine wasting time as generative.
- *Networks.* Refers to joining networks that attract you. Find institutional frameworks that you can participate in and learn from.
- *Cluster.* Signifies comentoring and reciprocity. This is about being generous and open, finding ways to reimagine the value of our work beyond capitalist paradigms, and figuring out how to barter with each other by doing work that is mutually engaging. In this process of being vulnerable we become mentors to each other.
- *Light bulb.* It takes good ideas to overcome constraints, such as isolation or financial debt. Associated with big challenges is an overwhelming uncertainty regarding what attracted you to graduate school in the first place. A kind of "overcoming" of constraints emerges from finding others to identify with, tapping into numerous resources, and developing strategies for emotionally and physically managing the burden of cost and the sacrifice of pursuing graduate degrees.
- *Pen.* Focuses on gaining publishing skills by, for example, being the author of your own life. Think about sharing your stories and developing an awareness of how best to tell these stories within sociologically mindful contexts. Submitting to journals for publication review can result in failure, but submitting again means you are resilient and making progress.
- *Computer.* Refers to networking in a digital age. People are harnessing technological resources and using blogs and websites to coauthor ideas, catalog strategies, and visualize and make the ideas real through media and shared experience. The Internet and digital databases, software and hardware are being used as a research tool. We all need to be aware of the limitations and pitfalls of too much technology. We also need to realize that technology can be inaccessible to some people and populations.
- *Door* (bottom of the map). Connotes program exit and reentry into the academy for graduates hired in academic positions.

Starting with Other Parts

Another way to plunge into this book is to start with the index and work backward. Simply select topics of interest (e.g., mentoring) and read the corresponding pages. Or, you can consider where you are in your own graduate school journey—early, middle, or end—and go directly to the section of the book that best reflects that phase or the one you are eager to know more about (e.g., orientation, immersion, and preparation, parts I, II, and III, respectively).

For example, if you've already been oriented to your program, begin with part II. Learn about immersion in graduate school and some ideas and tools for enriching your experience. If you've already been on your way for some time, try part III to access tips on publishing, marketing, and job searching. If you want to know more tech-savvy ways for being as productive as possible, consult this last section.

Like figure 1, this book has three overarching parts. Part I, "Getting Started: Strategies and Options," describes the early phase of graduate school. Chapter 1 takes you through orientation and socialization and shares faculty, administration, and student outlooks on these essential learning steps. Navigational prompts are activities that readers can pursue on their own to ensure a thorough and successful adjustment period. This early phase serves as the foundation for the other two developmental phases, immersion and preparation.

Readers are then strongly encouraged to make connections with insiders, specifically faculty members and peers at all levels of their program (chapter 2). Making inroads with faculty advisors involves subtlety, grace, and perseverance for the adult learner. This complex interchange is described from the perspectives of students and professors alike. A checklist guides you through selecting insiders with whom you want to align and get to know better. Ideas are presented for how to approach them as allies through your research efforts, participation in venues, and development of contacts.

You will most certainly need to find out about resources and opportunities, which is why an entire chapter is devoted to this topic. Salient sources include relationships, role models, knowledge of hidden rules, and mental resources. A list of resources both external and internal to graduate school is provided. You will want to consider closely those described, as the graduate students and professors who wrote about these resources underscored their importance for supporting their progress and supplementing costs. Premium resources available within and outside your programs include people, opportunities, events, associations, groups, and tools.

In part II, "Becoming Immersed: Relating and Learning," the lens shifts. You'll now be immersed in the academic life through relating and learning exchanges. Making every minute and day count is the mantra of chapter 4, with emphasis on strategies for academic immersion, including establishing cultural affinity, practicing observational learning, joining peer groups, and choosing program advisors or dissertation chairs. Regular scholarly productivity is a habit of mind being formed, but constant separation from others is to be avoided. Navigational prompts will help you map your experiences: Record communications with select individuals and study the documents included to "get the scoop" on next steps.

In chapter 5, informal and formal network types are described along with their shared elements and functional differences. Try out the strategies for creating your own groups. The exercises included invite readers to analyze peer-group discussion and practice analysis, discourse, and negotiation.

Consult chapter 6 for more information about mentoring scaffolds, networks, and programs. Here, you will be exposed to adult learning philosophies and the relational ethic of comentoring and reciprocity. The idea is for all involved in the education enterprise to gain from it and for students to make their learning relationships successful. The Mullen Mentoring-Based Reciprocity Gauge pinpoints how relationships can have very low or very high benefits for the parties involved, whether one-to-one mentorships or groups. Navigational prompts help readers think about their own growth from this perspective and gauge the success of groups.

In part III, "Emerging Prepared: Networks and Markets," you will gain knowledge about disseminating and publishing skills (chapter 7). You have access to writing and publishing advice, tested strategies, and publishing trends involving student writers. Navigational prompts help with developing manuscripts for publication review and using specific writing aids.

You will likely have to market yourself while overcoming job market obstacles (chapter 8). Serious decisions will be made about your career in academia and/or other domains of work while learning what is involved in academic career preparation. You will be taken through this complex decision-making process, and for this purpose you are given insider tips to consider as you progress. Navigational prompts foster awareness of professional development in digital contexts and proven job-search strategies.

Even while thinking about your future, you can consider how to cultivate two-way, mutually beneficial mentoring agendas (chapter 9). Dispositions and behaviors in this phase include adult learners' reflection on the capacity being developed for modeling, nurturing, and giving. Lifelong learning and reciprocal mentoring are essential elements of learning relationships that students will want to foster. You will be encouraged to initiate or join networks that benefit all who belong, psychologically and career-wise. Navigational prompts help readers think about win-win mentoring efforts, with ideas from respected faculty leaders and mentors.

Digital networking as an entrepreneur is the last chapter. In chapter 10, the reader encounters a changing academy in which hybrid (face-to-face and virtual) environments command an adaptive set of dispositions. These manifest as new concepts of presence, accessibility, and productivity. Digital immigrants and digital natives are reshaping the academic environment around you. Cross-generational learning and comentoring practices are energizing organizations and you have a vital role to play as a self-starter. The tips shared extend to publishing and linking with virtual others. Reflective exercises attune readers to networked learning and Internet-savvy strategies that include collaborative sharing tools.

The book's postscript takes the reader in a loop, closing and then reentering the academy's door.

THIS BOOK OPENS UP

Chapter 1 and the chapters that follow have an aperture on significant mentoring issues for students and professors alike. These include productive learning within groups, developing effective marketing and networking strategies, and creating flourishing student-centered programs. Together the chapters provide a broader perspective on the professoriate and access to spoken and unspoken requirements for advancing your studies and career (see also Brubaker and Brubaker 2011).

Readers are guided through the process of becoming mentored and mentoring effectively, largely by entering into viable learning relationships in which giving, not just receiving, is a healthy norm. See how a meaningful and productive writing life can grow out of a robust networked existence with others. As you will see, you do not have to write alone all the time or be insulated to get ahead, or for that matter, only participate in sponsored events or mentorships.

Various mentoring formats invite your consideration and experimentation. These demonstrate the value of learning within highly variable one-to-one systems and group contexts. In some cases, the source for knowing what graduate mentors expect and what values they stand for is the graduate student him- or herself. In other instances, the source is the dissertation produced by a **doctoral candidate** on the topic of doctoral education and complex issues of adult learning (e.g., Bennouna 2003; Stripling 2004). Other sources of authority cited are researchers and formal studies, as well as scholars and writers. The learning concepts and practices were tested in face-to-face and virtual settings. Furthermore, the chapters' cases and analyses are supported with data from multiple sources—documents, surveys, interviews, and studies. Dozens of graduate students in education, as well as faculty and administrators, openly but anonymously contributed their views.

For clarification before continuing, the **bold** words throughout this book are glossary terms, clarified at the end of each chapter. All names of respondents (the students and professors who contributed statements through e-surveys and e-mail) are pseudonyms and their specific contexts have been protected.

GLOSSARY

doctoral candidate. A doctoral student who has completed all of the requirements for the doctoral degree, typically consisting of coursework and comprehensive or qualifying exams, with the exception of that major work—the dissertation.

I

Getting Started

Strategies and Options

Chapter One

Creating Mentoring Maps of the Academy

If you are a new graduate student, you must have "a song that longs to be played." What is it? How does it sound? Play it. Let family, friends, and colleagues know you've arrived and are ready to begin. Committed to taking on a new challenge, you might find yourself humming, "Make me some room, you people up there / On top of the world, I'll meet you I swear!" (Previn and Previn 1965).

Allow me to introduce Andrew who, for two decades now, has been a professor of educational psychology who hums as he works. This graduate professor remembers his demanding, eventful, and ultimately successful transition to doctoral education. This is how he described his survival and orientation:

> I admit that my life had become entirely too comfortable in the Californian city I grew up in. One day—in my late thirties, not too old to make a change but too old to make a mistake—a buddy of mine suddenly showed up. Peter had just graduated from a **top-notch university** in Nevada with a PhD in education when he met with Ralph, his other best friend, and me. With unstoppable enthusiasm he urged us to move out of state to attend his **alma mater**. Not only were many more potential mates available, he exclaimed jokingly, but also the learning opportunities were phenomenal. Ralph and I got caught up in Peter's "rush" and applied to the "desert" school, only to hear that my friend was rejected and I had been accepted, having exceeded the requirements for the minimal GPA [grade point average]. Regretting my friend's loss and our separation, I soon jumped on a plane and moved to Nevada. Before leaving, I sold my old car, resulting in a mere four hundred dollars to settle in a strange land and prepare for a new life.
>
> Because the fall semester was a scant two weeks away from starting, I had to get cracking—so much to do in so little time! I worked frantically to get myself set up and worried that I was already behind in my studies. But this would simply have to wait, as I did not have a place to live or a job. After scanning the daily newspapers, in over one-hundred-degree temperatures I knocked on one door after another, apartment hunting. I also dropped into the university to get information about my new teaching assistantship. Because the money for this position was modest, I took out a substantial bank loan (an annual occurrence, I would eventually discover). With the first week of classes already underway, I had just landed an apartment. Relieved but exhausted, I was nonetheless feeling out of sorts—I had not obtained any of the required course readings, read through the syllabi, or even met any of the professors or students. This school, noted for its academically rigorous standards, would no doubt demand a much higher level of excellence than I was accustomed to.

While throwing together my apartment, I prayed that I would be able to perform in line with what was expected of a full-time student in educational psychology. I waited for an invitation to a graduate orientation, retreat, or social but received none. As an independent but highly sociable person, I soon adjusted to this somewhat foreign climate. Almost two decades later I am still enjoying the study of psychology and being employed in the field.

CASE ANALYSIS

Does Andrew's case bring to mind Maslow's (1962) classic hierarchy of needs model? Adults, no different from children in the blueprint for living, have basic needs of food, shelter, and safety. Applied to Andrew's transition to graduate school, Maslow's model of human development—physiological, safety, social, and esteem—has potency. Andrew could not be expected to learn, teach, or interact meaningfully and excel intellectually until he had obtained food (a job with a paycheck) and shelter (an apartment and place for study). People must fulfill their personal, physiological, and psychological needs, and academics are no exception.

Andrew's graduate story resonates in the lyrics of "You're Gonna Hear from Me" (Previn and Previn 1965). The huge investment he made quickly consumed his entire existence. He took admirable risks, enrolling in a top-notch university and moving to another state, without any social or financial capital. In retrospect, Andrew wishes that he had had access to a faculty **advisor** and student inductees to get his feet wet. No doubt counsel, direction, and assistance would have helped him move forward, mitigating loneliness and isolation. Yet he persisted, creating a survival plan and, though apprehensive, he remained optimistic.

As we know, Andrew did not receive invitations of any kind from his program. Apparently, he did not even know to whom he had been assigned as an advisee. In the same way that he had taken it upon himself to learn more about his teaching assistantship, he could have benefited from communicating with the key personnel in his program in other respects. For example, he waited to learn whether an **orientation** or retreat had been planned but did not inquire. It is worth noting, however, that while the delay in Andrew's intellectual and social adjustment could have initially stalled his progress, his growth was not impeded.

Andrew shared that he grew tremendously as a teaching assistant (TA), becoming familiar with "such areas of instruction as assessing, grading, managing the class, designing and organizing lessons, resolving student issues, and encouraging active learning." Having taught a course prompted intellectual interest in "how students learn from text and in groups," which later formed the basis of his dissertation topic. And through his graduate courses, he managed to single out which professors he wanted to serve on his doctoral committee. The ongoing dialogue, writing, and research probably helped Andrew become a respected member of a scholarly community and, eventually, a role model.

As this story illustrates, a foundation should be laid at the outset of one's program for supporting the increasing complexity of academic life. Teaching and research assistantships are significant experiences, or markers, that propel acclimation to a graduate context. Meetings with advisors, faculty, students, and alumni; orientations, retreats, and seminars; and impromptu connections are other key features of **mentoring maps** that aid in the socialization of new students.

Participant Groups and Research Questions

This chapter focuses on creating mentoring maps in graduate school that incorporate orientation, acclimation, and adjustment, as well as the realities of survival, challenge, and growth. Specifically, education students from different states responded to questions about orientation and transition:

1. How are you being oriented to your doctoral program?
2. How are you orienting yourself (e.g., advisement, mentorship, formal orientation, networking, researching, or publishing)?

Doctoral and master's students who responded to these electronically distributed questions received this explanation: "A brief response to this two-part question, with examples, would be most appreciated. Or you can tell a story instead. I am tracking student experiences and keeping all responses anonymous."

Similarly, for the same time period, education faculty members and doctoral coordinators, also representing various states, were asked about orientation and transition in their context and function. They addressed these questions:

1. How are you currently orienting students in the master's or doctoral program (e.g., advisement, mentorship, formal orientation, networking, researching, or publishing)?
2. How were you oriented in your own doctoral program, and how did you go about orienting yourself?

To the professors, I explained, "I am tracking faculty reflections for my new book and keeping all responses anonymous. Your written input would be most appreciated. Please write a brief statement, complete with examples, to either question. Or you can tell a story instead."

For part I of this book, the data collected and analyzed primarily consist of 315 electronic responses obtained from faculty members and 378 from students. The definition of "orientation" was not presumed or provided to the respondents to solicit as many understandings as possible. A few of the participants openly grappled with the meaning of orientation but most simply replied using their own thought processes as the starting point.

Student Outlooks on Orientation and Socialization

Kathy, a second-year doctoral student, identified her dissertation chair and cohort as the mainstays of her program. About her **cohort**, she shared, "My support group orients me all of the time, as those students who are further along in the program give me advice and direction." In addition, her chair had helped her feel anchored:

> Having my dissertation chair on board from the outset has made the difference. She helps all of us navigate treacherous waters; for example, she saved one of her student writers from making an embarrassing methodological blunder. Knowing this about her is the only thing making me feel okay about this journey right now!

When asked, "How are you being oriented to the doctoral program?" Satish, an American immigrant, said he received no formal orientation. However, he also explained how "several faculty and students have spoken to me about how to become oriented and on various levels, and I have initiated some of these conversations too." Satish might have been similar to Andrew and Kathy in taking responsibility for his **induction**, socialization, and success, regardless of whether **mentoring scaffolds** had been put in place. Satish's sense of self-efficacy, combined with a positive attitude and a proven capacity for self-direction, helped him find his way.

Sean, also new to the doctoral process, demonstrated similar self-efficacy and resourcefulness. Because he had switched doctoral programs, he could "discern differences in the orientation patterns." While Sean's experience in his new doctoral program was not as focused or directive as in the previous department, his conclusion is not at all what one might expect. Ironically, he claimed to be "receiving more information from informal and semiformal meetings with my current faculty advisor than I ever did with my previous program." Playing with the meaning of "orientation," Sean referred "to the level of official communication between the doctoral program and myself." From this standpoint he declared,

> The level is low, but the paucity of communication is not a negative reflection on the usefulness of the information received. Although I have to pursue answers from faculty members to my questions, the responses I receive are complete with recommendations. Further courses of action are also identified for me.

Defining "orientation" another way, Sean added, "If you're asking, 'Do I feel that there is a set method of indoctrinating students into the doctoral program that I am enrolled in?,' I would have to say 'no' based on what I've seen and heard thus far."

The mentoring maps that Sean drew suggest a healthy adjustment to his new environment. Mentorship was coming from several external sources—informal meetings, relevant information, and pertinent recommendations. He spent time "asking individual students how they dealt with certain aspects of their educational plan and instructors how they thought the challenges students identify should be addressed." Concerning his internal resources, Sean recognized that he is orienting himself through student-generated questions, self-initiated interactions with faculty, question posing, active listening, and policy review.

In contrast with the aforementioned perspectives, a handful of students concluded, "The university does not attempt to help us." Maureen cited the university's disregard of its student population—upon receiving an important letter months late, she discovered that the administration had been losing vital information from her file. She also complained that a workshop that the Institutional Review Board (IRB) office had sponsored was canceled without advance notice. This action prevented those who attended from satisfying the mandatory requirement set by the IRB, sending the attendees off to complete one of the online options in order to "stay in the research game." As a former legal secretary, Maureen found such institutional actions "upsetting" and "unprofessional."

Fortunately, Maureen, who came across as particularly at odds with the university and emotionally disconcerted, had a lifesaving orienting experience: "My main gateway has been my doctoral cohort. I depend on information from my peers. I also try to help others." In this support group, another student became a major source of **synergy**:

> Since Don defended his dissertation proposal, he has been giving me great feedback. I'm gearing up for mine next semester. I've been worrying about Don, though—he's in a rut lately with the changes he has to make on his proposal. He was planning on coming to our last meeting but did not show up. A session with us would have lifted his spirits.

Through her scholarly support group Maureen gained a feeling of stability and a sense of belonging. Even though she was not as far along in the program as her friend Don, she nonetheless was helpful as peer, making efforts to intellectually and motivationally kindle his fire. She sent a vital message: "Without the support of my professor and group, half of us wouldn't make it. It is such a lengthy process. If doctoral students knew what they were getting into beforehand, and if they were urged to take steps early on to join a cohort, more would probably finish."

Sammy, an out-of-state doctoral student who had just arrived, also showed that he could be resourceful and independent, exhibiting research skills and proactive mentee skills:

> The day after I received my acceptance letter, I visited campus to "get the lay of the land" by going to the bookstore, university center, and library. I learned from the university's website the things I needed to do (establish a Net ID, get a student ID, get vaccinations, establish a login account, etc.) and quickly accomplished everything. Once classes started, I continued to orient myself by spending time on campus (especially during the day, even though my classes are at night) and by asking questions of fellow students further along in the program.

This student thought it was a good tip when the program coordinator advised him to "choose a dissertation chair soon." Sammy was relieved that he had not been locked into the coordinator's matchmaking; instead, he was given the freedom to select a dissertation chair by "meeting each professor in my program." However, Sammy was given a fairly tight timeframe to make his decision. Some departments allow students to get to know the professors better—through courses, assistantships, orientations, retreats, and socials—before having to choose.

Sammy raised none of these concerns. Instead, with relief, he exclaimed that he had "quickly found a dissertation chair with whom I felt comfortable and established a dialogue, someone who periodically asks me, 'How are you settling in?' and 'Do you need help with anything?'" Sammy's satisfaction with the early development of his new **mentoring dyad** was extended through membership in the program's graduate student listserv. He regularly receives useful information, such as "the news about a half-day orientation activity for newcomers."

While some students do not flinch over finding a dissertation chair soon after they are admitted to their doctoral program, others understandably find this a hindrance. Of course, this expectation varies from one university and program to another. Not all students get the opportunity to work with an advisor on their **program of study** and other important matters *before* selecting their **major professor**, also known as dissertation chair, doctoral supervisor, and permanent advisor.

In some institutions, the program of study is to be completed with the dissertation chair. This means that a student's third-party assignment to a professor, typically by a program coordinator or department head, will occur, unless students are given license to choose. This kind of decision-making activity happens behind the scenes; students should find out if they can find their own dissertation chair and, if so, work even harder to make contacts with faculty members. Students generally want to meet all of the professors in their program so their choice can be informed and lasting.

In concert with this, research in mentoring suggests that third-party assignments tend to be less productive and successful overall than naturally occurring mentoring relationships or dyads (Mullen 2007a). This makes sense, as mentees and mentors can more easily thrive in dyads of their own making. Students who proactively network and make meaningful connections on their own often fare better than those who simply accept their lot in life. The match with a high-quality dissertation chair whom graduate students have widely characterized as collegial, available, comprehensive, professional, career sponsor-oriented, productive, and current (Johnson 2007) is one of the most crucial doorways of any graduate program, so approach this reality with the utmost seriousness and resourcefulness.

Faculty–Administrator Outlooks on Orientation and Socialization

Orientation systems that socialize newcomers to their new academic life are standard practice in some universities and programs but certainly not all. It appears that program leaders are giving more thought about how to orient students, not only at the outset of their programs but also through the duration. In this spirit, I have developed an overview statement that applies to all who write a **thesis** and dissertation, given that there are university policies to follow (see appendix A).

One faculty program coordinator of a curriculum studies department, Dr. Might, described in list form the mentoring scaffolds he had developed for moving master's students from one semester to the next:

> At the very beginning: (1) Early in the program, I meet with each student to discuss career objectives and write out a program of study. (2) My campus organizes a general graduate student orientation, which I attend. At the end of the session, I hold a breakout group meeting to introduce myself as the program advisor and answer questions, get them correctly registered, etc.
>
> In the first or second semester: (1) In an introductory course, Dr. Bushley guides students in drafting an ethical statement that is developed throughout the program, especially in the practicum. (2) In a course on principles in the field, one of us guides students in drafting their educational philosophy, which is refined throughout the program, again with emphasis on the practicum.
>
> In the second or third semester: In another course, students undertake a personal assessment and change/improvement project specifically designed to strengthen their communication or related skills as a leader.
>
> In the last semester: Late in the program, I support each master's student in the development of a professional portfolio that includes personal and educational philosophy, code of ethics, professional goals, self-assessment of their strengths as school leaders, and an overview of their growth as a school leader, with evidence from both course learning and professional leadership experience.

The same day I received this response, another came from a student in Dr. Might's program. Rachel raised doubt, not about the master's program but rather the doctoral program: "While the master's advising function works well in my unit, I have been struggling to find a dissertation chair." This doctoral student claimed to have "asked Dr. Might several times and others on my campus. So far, no luck." Feeling frustrated, Rachel approached several professors who teach on other campuses but still had not found anyone willing to take her on.

This single instance of faculty/student dissonance is not intended to contradict what the faculty leader shared and perceived to be quality programming. However, the issue of doctoral mentoring, particularly the availability of qualified doctoral supervisors and exemplary **cohort mentoring**, might need review. According to Rachel, the doctoral faculty, "while competent instructors and advisors, place serious limits on their mentoring role."

Maria—who was employed as a master's advisor at a different college—revealed that, from her perspective, the doctoral orientation had been "pretty nonexistent":

> I know that my program usually hosts an orientation and retreat for its doctoral students each year, but I'm in the dark about what it entails. Here I am going into my third semester of the doctorate and have not received any communications. Since I have yet to be assigned to a professor, advising has been a piecemeal affair at best.

A troubling allusion to a faculty/student divide was also provided by two other testimonies. One student had been doing his doctorate in this program for three years but had never been to an orientation or a retreat:

I'm not sure how routine these events are for people like myself who did not get placed into a cohort upon entering the program. Besides, I tend to pay less attention to the formal orientation procedures and operate on a need-to-know basis. What you're asking is a good idea, though.

Clearly, Tommy identified a hole in the orientation process but saw the problem as mutual, without casting blame on his program.

Within another unit, coordinated by Dr. Blighte, a faculty member reported that an orientation and retreat are held annually. In the meantime, a second professor within the same unit responded, "We haven't done an orientation for the last few years." Signaling a further breakdown in communication in this education unit, yet a third professor e-mailed that "our planned events for helping students to get oriented have been suspended lately, as the folks in charge are in tenure-earning positions, which places undue stress on them." But Dr. Blighte mentioned that student volunteers, not faculty members, had taken responsibility for organizing the events: "Over the last several years our graduate assistants have done the bulk of the planning for the retreat, and they've done a great job."

Dr. Blighte further explained how the mentoring program works: "This annual event is organized much like the orientation in terms of being a full group session where everyone's together, followed by breakout sessions, lunch, and a final group session." According to Dr. Blighte, the department's recent retreat sponsored a student panel that, importantly, represented the coursework and dissertation stages of a doctoral program: "Students presented their observations on the program and their advice for their peers. That was a fun session!" In addition, each year the department chair "holds one session where students give feedback that sometimes get folded into program improvement." For the orientation, "We finish up by breaking the students into small groups. A faculty advisor goes through the program or plan of studies and handles individual questions."

Students are expected to make social gains as they connect across various program stages. Specifically, Dr. Blighte shared that the students "express huge appreciation at the opportunity to get together outside of class and hear the advice of faculty and other students." Those who are "at the dissertation stage have a chance to see students from their coursework and reconnect—they love this!" And doctoral students "who are beginning their coursework have a chance to meet students who've been through much of the program." Clearly, such opportunities should not be devalued or missed. Each potentially provides a scaffold for induction, socialization, networking, and development.

In yet another department, the major way new doctoral students were oriented was through a beginning seminar with an accomplished **dissertation supervisor**. The syllabus for this course, which was provided in its entirety, is summarized here (without identifying information). The course is introduced as an intensive induction into doctoral studies emphasizing scholarly inquiry, professionalism, collegiality, and the doctoral process. The course objectives, which overlap in content, highlight key milestones in the doctoral process, the basics of scholarly inquiry, collegiality in doctoral education, transition into and successful completion of the doctoral program, and the aftermath of the doctorate. Students are evaluated based on their performance in preparing a research study, analyzing a research article, submitting a critique of an approved dissertation, and attending a minimum number of proposal and dissertation defenses.

The professor who forwarded the course syllabus deemed it "unique" within his discipline. Based on the feedback I received from numerous faculty and coordinators, this might be the case even more broadly, as only one other unit mentioned an entry doctoral course, but it is only in the early stages of planning. However, this is not to imply that such pivotal orienting courses do not exist within many up-to-date student-centered programs.

In one education department, the doctoral orientation event has been a rare occurrence, along with the retreat. Students are not connected except through the convenience of a cohort structure. As faculty coordinator, Dr. Falstaff revealed,

> Currently, we rely heavily on the program advisor and supervisors to satisfy these functions with students on an individual basis. Also, whenever we admit a newly formed cohort—which occurs far more frequently at the master's level than the doctoral level—we rely on this structure for preparing new students.

In the past this department offered a daylong Saturday orientation at the university, but without annual consistency. In addition, "It has been five years since our program faculty organized a department-wide orientation for incoming students." The format used at that time appeared to be standardized, at least with respect to the data received from program coordinators from Alabama, Florida, North Carolina, and Texas who described their events. The orientation or retreat typically featured

> an introduction and icebreaker session, breakout sessions, lunch, and meetings with advisors and their advisees. The breakout sessions are in tracks for people early, middle, and late in their programs, and each track has at least one session per breakout period. Examples include developing a program of study, effective writing, how to study for comps, how to pick a dissertation topic, and a panel of doctorates who have just finished their dissertations.

The department chair in a different unit said that four orienting activities occur once a year or more frequently: "a department-wide social event held in the fall for all of our students; program area mentoring and socialization; brown-bag seminars held monthly to which the college is invited; and social gatherings that the students organize for themselves and faculty." On the day of her response, Dr. Sonnet had given a brown-bag seminar for doctoral students on the topic of job searching in higher education. On her own initiative, she also held "Saturday seminars for the doctoral students every semester. We meet over lunch and share our work, talk about conferences and presentations, discuss our writing, and talk about the nature of teaching in higher education."

Currently, members of her group are working with her to put together a book proposal, and each plans to contribute a chapter: "We are excited about launching this project, but it is slow going because every one of us has many obligations." Certainly, this degree of commitment to group mentoring is somewhat unusual for a faculty member, let alone a department chair whose assigned responsibilities emphasize administration over teaching.

In Dr. Sonnet's large department, there were multiple programs. The faculty coordinator of one of these sent a detailed e-mail. Dr. Creswell explained that, for his K–12 school-based unit,

> the program of study is carefully designed to optimize opportunities for mentorship. Students are admitted as part of a cohort. All of the students' major field courses are completed with this cohort, and many individuals find it advantageous to take other required courses, such as statistics and research courses, with cohort members.

Beyond coordinated course registration, the faculty members in this program plan activities for cohorts. Students network with colleagues at other institutions, conduct research and scholarly activity, author articles for publication, and make presentations at professional conferences. Dr. Creswell added that "the cohort is a unique and important part of the PhD option in this area."

Each student is assigned a doctoral advisor who provides guidance during the initial program stage. The task of the faculty **mentor** is to ensure that students have college teaching experience, have some research experience prior to the dissertation, and participate in the affairs of (state and national) professional organizations. Furthermore, Dr. Creswell claimed that "many of the students receive teaching and research assistantships and tuition waivers."

These opportunities not only provide financial support but also give students "experience with research, writing, and editing of publications; development of grants; and creation and maintenance of websites." Moreover, the student's thesis or dissertation committee also helped with professional networking and targeted development. Participating faculty worked with students to select courses, develop their qualifying exams, and supervise the planning and completion of their research.

Not all education colleges, however, offer campus-wide orientations and retreats. Some have decentralized this practice, shifting the responsibility onto individual departments. An associate dean for academic affairs (who is part of a university's listserv of graduate program coordinators) wrote this explanation: "Many moons ago we had a college-wide orientation for our doctoral programs in education but discontinued this practice, as departments have preferred to arrange their own orientations and retreats. Most of our units have successful programs in place."

Decentralization can work well. Notably, in one such college, a department in the combined areas of second-language acquisition and instructional technology provides ten mentoring opportunities. Most of the mentoring scaffolds listed, formal as well as informal, are elaborated on elsewhere; for example, chapter 3 covers the topic of student resources, specifically seminars (workshops and brown-bag lunch series), associations (student association), and mentoring structures (cohorts).

1. *Faculty mentoring.* Students shadow faculty in their courses and coteach with faculty members; faculty present at conferences with students and mentor students through the dissertation process with weekly meetings.
2. *Senior student and incoming student mentor program.* Incoming students are paired up with senior students who mentor them throughout their studies.
3. *Cohort system.* Students enter the program and are automatically placed in a cohort; the members mentor, support, and assist each other in various ways.
4. *Annual doctoral reception.* Informal mentoring takes place at the annual dinner for the PhD students hosted by the faculty of the doctoral program.
5. *Annual meetings.* Faculty meet with students once annually to discuss their progress and plans.
6. *Workshops.* Given by faculty and senior graduate students, these assist students with qualifying exams, job searches, research innovations, and the dissertation.
7. *Brown-bag lunch series.* A collaborative effort between a language education unit and an English-language institute where faculty and students present on state-of-the-art research.
8. *Preparing for the profession.* Students have diverse experiences that assist with preparing for the profession and in securing jobs upon graduation, including shadowing faculty, coteaching with professors, serving on search committees, supervising interns, and working on funded research.
9. *Listserv.* Students electronically share ideas and seek input from peers and faculty members.
10. *Student association.* At the start of each semester students gather in an orientation meeting organized by the student officers; workshops are given at these sessions.

Adopting a broad view of orientation, one established professor shared that her doctoral education program has an unusually high completion rate—at least 85 percent. This success was attributed to "seminars in place that support student progress through the program (such as a literature review class and a proposal preparation class)." Also, the program faculty

> require our PhD students to write an article and submit it to a journal in order to be admitted to candidacy. We have a seminar on writing for publication that is required late in the students' program (when they have something to write about!). The major professor mentors advisees through this process. The article does not have to be accepted, just submitted. Study/writing groups form informally, but we probably could do more in that arena.

POINTS TO REMEMBER

It seems clear that adjustment and success are largely dependent on the willingness of students to make the most of mentoring and the willingness of faculty members to serve them. Students who have committed not only to graduate school but also to the mentoring process take advantage of both formal and informal opportunities and, by doing so, likely fare better as learners, mentees, researchers, teachers, and employees. Faculty and administrators who have committed to the mentorship agenda by creating a range of strategies and options will have done much to help orient, socialize, and prepare students for life within and beyond academe.

Orientation occurs throughout the stages of the graduate degree. Proactive guidance on the part of faculty and their units ranges from impressive to lacking. The most successful programs offer a variety of interconnected, ongoing activities that students are informed of and participate in, and where appropriate, assume leadership in their developing roles as organizers, presenters, authors, researchers, and professionals. Students help ensure their success by reaching out within and beyond their units.

Dissonance between faculty and students can occur based on perceptions of the availability of quality programming—entry-level and ongoing support structures. Because some departments cannot rely on their colleges to organize annual events for their own doctoral students, they must take this leadership step. At campus-wide events, although students can meet many faculty members from other departments and units, few valuable connections are sparked. However, they are rarely exposed to faculty outside their own unit when orientations and retreats are organized from within. Regardless, all students should take it upon themselves to knock on doors outside their unit by reaching out—participate in campus events and associations and look for ways to interact.

Each story and response presented herein is a "peep hole." As such, everyone (e.g., student, professor, or administrator) provides only a partial view of the mentoring process. The roles of faculty member and student inevitably create some tension due to differences in perception, expectation, experience, status, values, and goals. The contradictions that surfaced across some testimonies of faculty members and students suggest an untapped source of further study.

In addition, a mentoring intervention (e.g., early or preassignment of the permanent advisor or dissertation chair) that suits one student may not work well for another. Personalized forms of mentorship are essential for strengthening doctoral programs in particular. In an effort to further close the gap between the perceptions of students and professors, systematic and ongoing evaluation of graduate programs are necessary. Mentoring in higher education is attracting attention in ways that reorient people to exciting possibilities for learning in globalized contexts, networked spaces, and digitized environments. Students will find that many people in different places can offer helpful advice, but they need to "show up" to benefit from these various contacts—tapping student advisement offices and writing centers for assistance are examples of unofficial orientation outlets.

On a philosophical note, deeper learning does not happen all at one time or in a single setting. Becoming oriented to an unfamiliar place is itself a cultivated aesthetic you will want to develop. This "domain of consciousness" is outside our immediate reach (Greene 1971/ 2004, 141). As students struggle to become oriented to a new place or group of people, it is common to experience frustration. Stick with it, as more satisfying and unified connections can emerge.

As adult learners, we internalize new ideas, integrate the old with the new, and develop understanding over time. Just as you will want to receive structures of knowledge for orientation throughout your program or academic career—much like a map showing the stranger in town where one is in relation to where one wants to go—you will want to be resourceful.

So instead of hoping that everything will magically fall into place with your program, advisor, or workplace, take the steps yourself. Fill in the gaps in student and faculty handbooks, for example. Generate the critical structures that are missing and join or create the networks that you want to see. Ethnic minorities have been turning to one another and generating their own support groups for years.

Graduate students are customizing services and opportunities for themselves that are sometimes available in person but typically at a distance. Those possessing a great capacity for learning have a high acceptance for strangeness and create order out of upheaval, disruption, and dislocation. As networked insiders, they facilitate their own orientation while enriching the quality of life for others, which in turn fosters learning cultures in academia and elsewhere.

SUMMARY

This chapter encourages graduate students to benefit from researching opportunities for induction, socialization, and advancement, which can occur before they apply to a program. While some manage to thrive without having attended organized events, they cannot know with any certainty what they would have otherwise gained.

Students with a larger picture of doctoral education will be guided by a more holistic view than that afforded by the peephole; conversely, those who rely too heavily on one system or way of doing things (e.g., meeting with their advisor) will see far too little of academic life. A more comprehensive picture unfolds through no single incident, act, or person but through ongoing exposure to orientations, retreats, cohorts, courses, seminars, gatherings, and meetings.

Importantly, conversations with faculty members, administrators, and peers can shed light on the various stages of one's program and the steps that follow. The stories and advice of others—invaluable as a socializing source—are the soul of mentorship. Networks maximize this effort across multiple people and different places. Expedite the time it takes to bring out the best in your collaborations.

Navigational Prompts

- *Examine doors in your graduate school* (first literally, then figuratively). Guess at their significance—are these open or closed to mentoring?

- *Write down/record your experiences for review later on.* Who is saying what to you, and what information is helping to fill the gaps in your knowledge? What do you still need to know in order to get started?
- *Contact others*, even if you are having difficulty formulating questions or do not yet know the academic jargon. Talk regularly with your advisor, faculty members, and other students in the program, including alumni. Overcome any nervousness or fears by talking them through with trusted others or by recording them.
- *Create a mentoring map.* What are the opportunities for mentoring in your program? No one person will have all of the facts, so count on surfing the university, college, and department websites and talking with every available individual. Depending on your interests, find out who the faculty mentors are and obtain their profiles—which ones might be the best fit for you? Who are the peer leaders in your unit whom you can contact and from whom you can seek **coaching**? Also seek information from advising offices and about such areas of interest as organized orientations, retreats, and cohorts; teaching or research assistantships; stipends and conference travel funds; and awards. Again, assume that no one person, including your advisor, knows everything—reach out.
- *Analyze the **vitae** of departmental and college faculty.* What do these vital documents tell you about the profile and reputation of faculty? Look at their lists of presentations and research publications—are they current? And do any of the listings include students on conference presentations, publications, grants, projects, or editorships? Ask around to identify the names of potential students on the curriculum vitae; based on this effort, infer the status of students as collaborators relative to different faculty. Also consult with the department chair or program coordinator to learn about unit-sponsored student activities and opportunities; volunteer to take the lead where appropriate and solicit feedback concerning the mentoring strengths, talents, and availability of faculty.

GLOSSARY

advisor. Assigned faculty or staff member who gives advice to and counsels students.

alma mater. A school, college, or university that one has attended or from which one has graduated.

coaching. Faculty, administrators, and others who instruct, direct, or prompt and assist with intensive training in an educational process.

cohort. A group of individuals with a common statistical factor (e.g., age or class) and goal.

cohort mentoring. A collaborative faculty–student support group through which a knowledge community is constructed and reciprocal learning is practiced.

dissertation chair. A doctoral supervisor or permanent advisor responsible for overseeing a doctoral student's program and dissertation; students can be assigned to this key person or select this person through negotiation. *See also* major professor.

induction. A challenging experience of being formally initiated into the role of student or professor and, more broadly, academic life.

major professor. *See* dissertation chair or supervisor.

mentor. A trusted counselor or guide; Mentor was a friend of Odysseus entrusted with the education of Odysseus's son, Telemachus.

mentoring dyad. An educational or professional relationship consisting of two persons, the mentor (teacher) and the mentee (student).

mentoring map. A literal or metaphorical representation of the whole or a part of an educational area with clarity suggestive of a map (e.g., proactive orientation to a new place; recording of pertinent information).

mentoring scaffold. A framework (e.g., cohort structure) that supports educationally oriented processes and student goals.

orientation. Becoming acquainted with the existing situation or academic environment involves "the act or process of orienting or of being oriented"; usually involves a "general or lasting direction of thought, inclination, or interest" rather than a quick introduction to a new place or process.

program of study. A planned sequence of courses outlined by a department, typically preset for master's students and more flexible for doctoral students; choice and complexity in the planning of this critical document increase for doctoral students who are not in cohorts, which receive a structured course calendar and timeline.

socialization. The process of becoming acclimated or "fitted" to a new situation or academic environment, as well as "participating actively in a social group."

synergy. "A total effect beyond any individual's particular contribution" (Mullen 2005, 99).

thesis. Master's students produce original scholarship or research referred to as "the thesis," a significant component of their program typically followed by a defense. The document, required for an academic degree or professional qualification, presents the writer's scholarship or research. A typical thesis has chapters (introduction, literature review, findings, etc.), and a reference section, but these vary in their structure in line with the discipline and committee preferences (Thomas and Brubacker 2008). (Some master's programs have alternative requirements, such as capstone portfolios and defenses.)

top-notch university. Refers to the Carnegie Foundation for the Advancement of Teaching's classifications of higher education institutions (consult the organization at classifications.carnegiefoundation.org 2012).

vita. An indispensable document used for job searching and promotion, highlighting personal history (e.g., address, contact information); scholarly history (e.g., areas of specialization, educational degrees, presentations, grants, publications, honors, and awards); and professional background (places worked, leadership experiences, appointments, community involvement, etc.) ("Writing Your Vita" 2012, psych.hanover.edu/handbook/vita2.html; "Sample Template for Creating a Vita" 2012, www.socialpsychology.org/vitatemplate.htm). Used by candidates seeking college and university teaching positions, as well as for applying for fellowships and research jobs (Heiberger and Vick 2003, para. 16). Also curriculum vita and résumé.

Note: Where a source is not cited, the term is from the *Merriam–Webster*, 2012; quotation marks around words within these terms denote verbatim citation; the terms presented were all rewritten for the graduate education context.

Chapter Two

Seeking Help from Program Faculty and Peers

Jesca, a twenty-seven-year-old master's student entering doctoral study, recounts how she made the admissions process work. Eliciting support from key decision makers and determining a program fit, she launched her academic life.

As a hopeful PhD student (now applying and anticipating acceptance), I've already found some direction for my doctoral study. I wanted to become informed about which programs might best fit me and my interests. From university websites and Internet searches, I've been learning which degree programs are aligned with my research interests and are "job friendly."

I'm also noting what I admire—faculty research interests, books, journal articles, and so forth. After e-mailing the graduate-program personnel listed on the university's website, I inquired about their programs. I'd say, "I'm wondering if I can share my academic interests and the topics I might like to research and whether you can let me know if your department is the right place for me." As you can imagine, this caught people a little off guard (smile)! But what can I say: I was sincerely clueless about where I belonged. And I wasn't getting any closer to this answer the "old-fashioned" way, by applying to a college and department that might fit me and waiting to hear back, hoping for the best.

One contact with childhood education's PhD program in reading resulted in an invitation from its coordinator for a face-to-face meeting. "Dr. Burney" proved to be very kind and accommodating. I said that I wanted to work with adults to increase their critical literacy skills. I explained that the idea came from my work in an educational leadership program, and I saw connections to the reading area within my master's program.

I went on about how K–12 students in the nation's schools are being pushed toward uncharted levels of critical literacy in response to business needs and demands while entire generations of young to middle-aged adults lack these skills. I also said that a crisis would undoubtedly ensue in the United States and that I'd like to be ready to contribute when it does. Furthermore, I expressed my belief that one of the major problems facing schools today is that many teachers and leaders have not been taught how to think critically. Inevitably, a gap exists among curricular goals, decisions/actions, and outcomes.

This strategy of sharing one-on-one with a faculty coordinator worked. I simply disclosed what was on my mind and possible directions for my doctoral program and waited for a response each time. And guess what? Dr. Burney exclaimed, "We can help you get on board!" Since then I've been signed up to take courses in adult education, even though this reading program has never promoted a focus on the adult learner—but Dr. Burney is game if I am. Childhood education is already feeling like a good place for me.

CASE ANALYSIS

University Admissions

Making contact with and seeking help from faculty and peers matters for advancement, success, and well-being. Consider Dewey's (1938) famous principle of habit—capable people form habits and attitudes in a way that is fluid and responsive to the conditions they encounter—in this case, in graduate school.

Jesca brings to life this Deweyian principle by approaching doctoral admissions in an inquisitive way, not succumbing to blind hope. Dr. Burney was so impressed with Jesca's preparation, intelligence, and personality that she accommodated her desire to work outside the box. By doing so, Jesca was empowered to create a hybrid program for herself that incorporated courses in higher education, an area not customarily associated with childhood education. She "learn[s] by easy stages," is "courageous," and "work[s] like a soul inspired / Till the battle of the day is won," and her personal mantra just might be "I'm gonna learn to dance or burst" (Fields and Kern 1936). You, too, will want to find a door like Dr. Burney, one welcoming your entry into an academic world that you find exciting.

Jesca did not contact any department or person until she had some of the necessary facts available online. Within the admissions context, those skilled at answering your questions are typically faculty (or staff) program coordinators and advisors with decision-making authority. Jesca not only located the names and contact information for the relevant parties but also did some background research on the program and faculty. She left herself plenty of time for this often-overlooked exploration, not rushing anyone with a compressed deadline. By using all of these strategies, in addition to being prepared to discuss her research passions and even the direction these might take in the program, Jesca made a favorable impression.

The issue of references is also relevant to Jesca's story. In an extended commentary she discussed using professors from the same college of education and to what effect. When appropriate, faculty members who work within the college or unit that one is applying to can be used as references; in fact, this sends the strong message to application committees that their own colleagues are invested in you. Of course, this approach works only when graduating students are continuing at the same institution. However, this scenario can be problematic: although common in higher education, the practice of doing one's doctorate at the place all previous degrees were awarded tends to be frowned upon, especially by premier institutions that expect candidates to be equipped with a multiplicity of scholarly experience. Consult informed parties, such as faculty coordinators or admissions committees, about this matter (see chapter 3).

When giving careful thought to possible references (primary supporters you will identify who are sometimes letter writers), choose faculty members and employers with good reputations and solid records. In addition to the necessary materials, always supply your references with an updated vita and outline relevant details concerning your association (e.g., leadership and other critical qualities, demonstrated capacities, assignments undertaken, performance, and evaluations or grades).

In other words, requesting a letter without providing the required information to the nominating party may produce a form letter with poorly substantiated accolades, something conspicuously generic and perhaps even erroneous. Supplying a vita is helpful, but very few students supply evidence that the nominating party can build upon. (Appendix B provides a nonidentifying example of a supporting letter that a professor wrote using input from the master's student.) Give yourself the competitive edge. Speaking as a member of advanced graduate admissions' committees in programs at different universities since 1998, applicants who submit impressive packages obviously have an advantage. Quite simply, they provide materials that are complete, they have followed the instructions, and they make themselves known by a decision maker. Determine whether Facebook and other social-networking tools will foster or hinder your chances to secure that desirable position, especially as potential employers have been known to consult these sites to make decisions about applicants (Rosen 2011).

The outline can cite the length of your association with your personal reference, as well as context, location, and relationship. Areas that you can highlight are (1) leadership credentials (e.g., certification or certificate programs, relevant training, activity coordination); (2) noteworthy achievements (e.g., graduate degree[s], special awards, honors); (3) commitment to the profession (e.g., coach, leader, publications); (4) community involvement through volunteerism (e.g., tutoring, youth clubs, charity events); and (5) innovation as an entrepreneur (e.g., creation of new opportunities; digitalization of antiquated systems).

Incorporate the vision or mission statement of your institution, department, and/or program to frame the context of your work. This is a good strategy for better informing references of your values and ideas. You could also benefit from drawing attention to your program or institution's banners of excellence, such as accreditation, certification, membership with national organizations, partnerships, funding agencies, and scholarship donors.

Remember, your references will likely not know a great deal about you, or at least not all of the relevant particulars, so help them out. Also, select wisely those you know through coursework, committees, employment, and other avenues. Avoid approaching people you do not know well because this inadvertently signals problems. Just because someone has cachet in the academy in such roles as program coordinator, director, department chair, dean, or provost does not mean that person is prepared to respond to questions that necessitate firsthand knowledge about the applicant's character, dispositions, habits, and trajectory for success. Nominators (also known as "references") must know your work and habits so they can confidently respond to questions asked about your fit for academic positions.

Areas probed about job finalists (pre- or postinterview) include whether the candidate can hit the ground running, secure tenure and promotion without difficulty, readily ease into the dissertation supervisory role, obtain external grants, successfully teach online, enhance the reputation of the institution, be active in national organizations, be a leader and team player, and so forth. These are the some high-stakes questions I get asked about candidates I nominate for whom I write letters of reference. Search committee members make contact out of the blue and want information quickly. No doubt, those giving references must have current working knowledge of their nominees beyond the letters they write.

Go online to learn about the graduate admissions process at your targeted institutions. Avoid submitting applications that are incomplete or exhibit weak communication or writing skills. It is surprising how common these flaws are. Have astute readers go over your application before submitting it. Again, give yourself enough time to accomplish all of these tasks without unduly rushing anyone. Applicants are responsible for the timely arrival of the supporting letters, so send a friendly reminder to your reference writers if necessary.

Planned Programming

Whether she was aware of it at the time, Jesca's conversation with a program coordinator initiated an early process of planned programming. As previously established, the program of study can be completed early on or after a certain number of credit hours. In some research institutions, the program of study must be submitted within the second or third semester of the student's program, along with an additional document (supervisory committee form) requiring doctoral committee names and signatures. One's committee might need to form quickly and, because of this, the dissertation chair or advisor will need to be relied upon more heavily to assist with the selections.

Regardless, you will not want to select courses without the input and approval of an informed party—the program advisor or dissertation chair. That person will help with mapping out courses that make sense given your academic and professional interests and goals and in what sequence. Student advising centers can assist, but your faculty advisor will have a deeper, more comprehensive understanding and thus can best guide you. Generally, because the program of study is more fixed for master's programs, the risk factor increases at the advanced level. So take courses that will count toward your planned program and fit with the program's cycle of offerings—not always communicated to students. Be prepared for all advisory communications or meetings, having researched the calendar and other relevant materials that are likely available online. If possible, locate a recently approved student's program of study (and relevant documents) from your unit and refer to this template when completing your own.

The business of the cognate in doctoral programs is also relevant, but students and new faculty can find it confusing. The official language of handbooks does not necessarily help because it can be vague. According to graduate catalogs I have consulted, a **cognate** is an area of study that is outside, but supportive of, the major emphasis area. While descriptions of cognates can be more specific in graduate or program handbooks, this is not usually the case. Information examined from eleven different programs confirmed this: Explicit statements advised students to select a cognate area for (1) extending their area of expertise in a particular discipline and (2) supporting the research problem or focus their **dissertation** will address. Since even the available examples are not terribly precise, ask advisors and graduates.

After e-mailing supervisory faculty at several premier universities in the United States, I asked how they understood "cognate" and "program of study" in general and as related to their own discipline. A typical response was: "In many instances, the cognate is a reflection of the student's life experience, personal interests, or occupation." Concerning his own discipline, one faculty member wrote, "Students in educational leadership programs choose, as their cognate, cultural foundations, corporate management, exceptionalities/disability, or another." Another characteristic response was,

> For a doctorate in instructional technology (IT), the possibilities for cognate areas include cognitive psychology, industrial psychology, measurement and statistics, management/business, computer science, communication/information studies, human factors, engineering, cinematography, and even military science.

Good news—this small sample shows that the faculty's responses were all consistent with and more detailed than the descriptions provided in the graduate catalogs from their own institutions. One could see that their capacity as advisors and mentors was intact. This is the kind of detective work that students seeking clarification can do for themselves.

Making Inroads with Faculty

For this book I also contacted faculty located at American schools personally known by me for their high-quality mentorship as doctoral supervisors. Although my decision to select only proven mentors obviously introduces a bias, my goal was to exhibit, through best-case scenarios, the mentoring and networking possibilities for motivated students who reach out and plan well. I asked five professors to forward me all of their communications over a twelve-month period involving one entering student who became their protégé. Accordingly, the narrative selected for discussion involves two major players: Sam, a student new to an instructional technology doctoral program, and Dr. Goya, the professor.

As you will see, Sam went the extra mile, demonstrating qualities that might remind us of Jesca's self-directed but connecting style. From his Texas hometown he made contact with a professor in Georgia. Similar to Jesca, Sam proved flexible in his use of cell and e-mail for effectively soliciting a response to his questions.

Because Sam, unlike Jesca, focused on a university hundreds of miles away, he had to have good grounding of support from the outset. Otherwise, it would take longer than necessary for him to adjust psychologically, intellectually, and socially to the new environment. In fact, unlike some of the faltering that is familiar in new circumstances—"I'm as awkward as a camel, that's not the worst / My two feet haven't met yet" (Fields and Kern 1936)—Sam was able to adapt well even though he was operating at a distance and was disadvantaged in that respect. Not only the selected faculty member but also a few other professors and staff members promptly got on board as helpers, satisfying his various requests. They proved indispensable to his induction. The self-reliant, respectful ways in which this new inductee approached others, in addition to his talent and drive, drew them in.

The mentoring correspondence that enabled a potential breakthrough for Sam occurred one Friday, when most students are gearing up for a relaxing weekend. Whether Sam realized it, his action is perfectly aligned with the graduate handbooks I studied that encourage doctoral students to take the first step in contacting potential permanent advisors and dissertation professors. Selected from more than forty electronic letters that Dr. Goya sent me, the following exchanges (in chronological order) have been edited for anonymity and excerpted, as well as paraphrased.

> Hello Dr. Goya:
>
> As mentioned in my voice mail, I'm a just-admitted PhD student in instructional technology eagerly anticipating the start of fall classes. My immediate goals are to (1) find a major professor, (2) determine which classes I can/should/must take this semester, and (3) register for courses.
>
> I've reviewed the material published on your institutional faculty page and found your background and research interests to be both impressive and interesting. It was while reading one of your articles on faculty members who establish networks and lineage through research-oriented mentoring that I said to myself, "Wow, now this guy would make a great major professor!" Therefore, if you have the available "bandwidth," I would be honored if you would serve in this capacity.
>
> Here is some info about me: I'm probably not a typical PhD student, as I have fifteen years of professional experience in [a technology field]. I've also been teaching part-time for over five years at [a top American university]—this is how I discovered that I enjoy teaching undergraduate students, a rewarding experience that led me to pursue a doctorate. My resume is attached for your review.
>
> Assuming you're able to serve as my major professor, would you please let me know when you're available to meet? I can connect almost any time this week. As you've probably guessed, I'm eager to register for classes soon.
>
> Thank you and best regards, Sam

The same day, the faculty member wrote back:

> Hi Sam:

Thanks for your e-mail. Your vita is very impressive, and I think that you and a doctoral student of mine would have much to discuss regarding the proliferating field of instructional technology. I have time tomorrow afternoon to meet. Will you be at a number where I can reach you?

Let's say I'll serve as your MP [major professor] for the time being, and we'll see if there's a good fit as time goes on. I like your "hit the ground running" style and welcome assisting you in building the momentum you desire. Attached is the latest program of studies form. (I created it after being fed up with the clunky stuff that passes for administrative forms.) Take a shot at completing it, and give some thought as to a cognate area for yourself.

For your information, my research interest in the IT field includes innovative technologies for solving problems in real-world settings. [He gives a descriptive overview of three distinct lines of research.] Each of these has been presented annually at conferences, including [a national meeting] this year. Life will be hectic for the rest of the month, as a few of my students have joined me in completing several studies for this upcoming conference. There'll be opportunities to participate in this research, if you're interested.

Let me know how many courses you expect to take this fall. Congratulations on your new journey in the doctoral program.

R.G. [Dr. Goya]

Later that day, Sam responded that he planned "on taking a full load this semester, which means three or four courses." He mentioned having "no obligations outside family right now other than school." To generate some income, he planned to work no more than twenty hours per week on an assistantship or teaching at his alma mater.

Three days later, Dr. Goya wrote back. He followed through on all of Sam's queries, advising him which courses he might consider taking in the fall and spring semesters. Dr. Goya also mentioned the possibility of Sam doing a "cognate in cognitive psychology (or even, for that matter, industrial psychology) so that [he] can start to build a network with the psychology department."

After reading the description of the undergraduate IT course he was hoping to teach, Sam saw that it was similar to one he had taught. Realizing this advantage, he texted Dr. Goya, providing evidence for the claim that he would be a good choice for the teaching assistantship. Backing up his statements, Sam outlined elements that the two courses shared, among these "an overview of information technology, including hardware, software, applications, and systems design." With these tangibles in hand, Dr. Goya recommended Sam for the job. Just two days later, the professor texted Sam the good news that he had been approved to teach the course, adding, "This much sought-after graduate assistantship, normally reserved for advanced doctoral students, will provide you with a tuition waiver."

The student then Skyped "Dr. Vincent," the professor of record for the undergraduate course. Sam showed that he was already ahead of the ball, explaining that he had met with the unit's staff member responsible for managing certain aspects of the course. From this contact, questions had arisen, which he itemized for Dr. Vincent. Sam introduced himself as "a 'low-maintenance' person with some housekeeping questions to ask." Among these he inquired as to why the course had not yet been entered into the university system for student access and enrollment—the professor thanked him for the news about the omission. Sam asked about graduate teaching space. He then purchased all of the required texts for his courses from the online bookstore of his choice in order to save on the shipping costs. And he joked, promising to "stay within his five-question limit in all e-mail messages." Sam had wisely cc'd Dr. Goya on this correspondence (and on all future messages), who, along with Dr. Vincent, was able to act on his behalf.

Unexpectedly, Sam was offered a second assistantship for the fall, this time on a very attractive, high-profile grant project. Because he was torn, he turned to Dr. Goya, his hoped-for dissertation chair, for advice. Dr. Goya aptly responded,

> Like the saying goes, "when it rains, it pours." Now, although you're smart, motivated, and energetic, I'm wondering if you might be biting off too much too soon. I suggest either quitting the teaching assistantship or accepting the present offer but not doing both in the same semester. My concern is that as a new student you might burn yourself out or get misdirected.

Several exchanges ensued about this issue, so Dr. Goya decided to communicate relevant aspects of his educational philosophy and values. He took a risk knowing that Sam was inclined to accept both assistantships for the fall semester. Quite simply, he did not want to be the bearer of bad news. Hence, he offered a long view of the problem that was an honest reflection of this own thoughts and experience:

> Along our academic path toward achieving a goal, tempting offers arise that have the potential to lure us away from our main objective. Some folks never finish the doctorate because, by the time they've taken all the required courses in their program, they might know enough to get a good-paying job without the degree. This is what happened to Ronnie, a friend who took a big-income job while still ABD ["all-but-the-dissertation" status]. He never did get the doctorate and soon felt stuck in his job, an outcome he later regretted bitterly.

Reassuringly, Dr. Goya said that the faculty members expressing an interest in Sam would likely continue to show interest: "Successful people get lots of practice turning down offers that others view as attractive in order to stay on course." He elaborated, explaining that "the PhD is a research degree with important foundational courses in research, which you'll need to nail down this semester in order to do well." The culminating point was secured with this statement: "If you want to do well academically, learn how to do outstanding research and become a prolific writer." The student decided to decline the research assistantship, primarily because he had already promised the school that he would teach the course. Expressing appreciation for the sage advice, he thanked Dr. Goya for "the ABD guidance, which [he'll] always try to keep in mind."

Several major initiatives soon emerged from the ongoing, layered communication that characterized this mentoring dyad. Through the positive synergy and trusting relationship that developed, within the first year of Sam's program he experienced research projects, conference presentations, and coauthored publications. Dr. Goya encouraged Sam to knock on the doors of others professors and work with them as well—a mentoring mindset that does not belong to possessive program advisors and dissertation chairs. Sam also enjoyed the benefits of peer mentorship by joining the professor's study group.

The particular phases of first-year mentoring that Sam experienced functioned at cultural, institutional, technical, interpersonal, and intellectual levels. They were expressed in a movement from program investigation to course registration, to assistantship opportunities, to dyadic bonding, to research development, and, finally, to project teamwork. Every doctoral student who steps up to the plate and is being effectively mentored should expect to experience these themes, albeit in variation.

POINTS TO REMEMBER

Graduate students who approach their programs as eager mentees, have professional styles, and exhibit leadership potential tend to get noticed. Through the advanced graduate admissions process, coursework, cohorts, committees, and other means, students will make meaningful contact with faculty and peers. By doing background research about people and places and negotiating their needs, entering students will be well on their way. Think positively in your interactions with busy faculty and potential mentors, and persist in reaching out for advice. Push past any fears. As the song goes, "Nothing's impossible I have found / For when my chin is on the ground / I pick myself up / Dust myself off, Start all over again" (Fields and Kern 1936).

As a final point, Jesca, the new doctoral student whose narrative initiated this chapter, advises graduate students to become familiar with the publications of the faculty members with whom they have interest. In her own spirited words,

> Avoid entering a program—and especially doing an entire course, program, or dissertation—without intimate knowledge of the relevant faculty's writing, past and present. I think we should be conversant about who they are and what they stand for.

Jesca wrote this addendum: "Obviously, the ideas of faculty members will more than likely influence your own, so you will want to be open to this." This advice extends beyond potential dissertation chairs to the doctoral committee. When relevant, you might even cite your committee members, as they can be legitimate research sources. This acknowledgment, where appropriate, can build **reciprocity** and **integrity** in the work relationship. Professors can be cited (as either published or interpersonal sources) when their feedback is foundational to the student's thinking or influential in shaping and crafting the work. Make your scholarly shapers visible.

Students who strive to understand the graduate-school and faculty cultures will have greater leverage for "decoding" its values and systems. Those who take ownership of their education read and internalize their institution's graduate academic policies—know the responsibilities and rights of both faculty members and students. Carefully follow the policies that pertain to you and regularly look these up. Graduate student handbooks provide an invaluable overview of all campuses and programs from an institutional and legal perspective, covering such programmatic issues as graduate admissions, programs of study, advisor and dissertation chair responsibilities, committee formation, qualifying examinations, and defenses. (For more information about graduate catalogs, see chapter 3.)

Concerning the mentoring roles of dissertation chair and committee member, as chapter 3 (and others) illustrates, there is wide variance regarding the philosophies, commitments, values, and habits of faculty members. Take the time to get to know your program and the faculty members who teach in it and your college. Also become familiar with the forces and trends governing the mentoring habits, attitudes, and skills of faculty members. Examples include eroding personnel-support systems, including technology staff, in some places in addition to heavy advising and mentoring workloads and lack of compensation. Be a leader among your peers and a service to your advisors by reaching out, sharing information, and managing upward.

SUMMARY

Making contact with faculty and peers is a significant part of socialization, so much so that it extends well beyond one's orientation to a new place. In fact, interacting and networking dynamics influence the phases leading up to entry into a graduate program, inform the duration, and shape one's career.

Dewey's (1938) principles of habit and experience come into view here: "Every experience both takes up something from those which have gone before and modifies in some way the quality of those which come after" (35). In other words, growth for growth's sake is not enough, as the experience of growing can be educative or miseducative. Establish and nourish academic connections and networks as a reflection of your own developing scholarly habits.

Navigational Prompts

- *Research graduate programs of interest, as well as the background and achievement of selected faculty members.* Examine the mentoring profile of professors or infer it. From this process, determine whether there is a potential fit for you, not only with an advisor and/or dissertation chair but also with committee members.
- *Develop a cultural affinity chart for yourself.* List all of the areas of life and facets of a person that strongly attract you. See if the result can help you find solid mentoring matches.
- *Create a mentoring checklist for gauging your own academic and professional goals.* Track your interests and desires and the corresponding actions of your mentors. To do this, create two columns, one identifying your academic and professional goals (self) and the other itemizing opportunities that come your way (mentor). To illustrate this setup:

Desired Activities (Self)	*Invited Activities (Mentor)*
Develop as a peer leader	Facilitate a group
Write conference proposals	Codevelop a proposal
Learn to write for publication	Coauthor an article

After you have gathered a sufficient number of entries, do a basic comparative analysis—to what extent is there an overlap between your desires and the invitations received? Use a plus (+) sign to denote agreement and a negative (–) sign to signal disagreement. Over time, work toward creating matches between the columns. The idea is to increase your level of satisfaction, morale, skills, networks, and competitive edge.

GLOSSARY

"all-but-the-dissertation" (ABD) status. Candidates who have accomplished all of their course requirements for the doctoral degree but have not completed the dissertation (Stripling 2004); coined "no-man's land" (Heiberger and Vick 2003).

cognate. A thematically unified cluster of advanced courses listed on the doctoral program of study; includes a minimum number of courses and credit hours.

dissertation. This is an extended written treatment of a subject that demonstrates scholarly competence and significance. It contributes original work to the student's discipline (e.g., behavioral sciences, humanities, social sciences). Doctoral students' scholarship or research is the hallmark of one's program, typically followed by a defense. The document, required for the Doctorate in Philosophy and some other advanced degrees, has chapters (introduction, literature review, findings, etc.), and a reference section, which vary across disciplines and committees (Thomas and Brubacker 2008).

integrity. "Clarification of a personally valid set of beliefs that have some internal consistency," which involves examining the values of one's family and culture (American Psychological Association, www.apa.org) as well as the academy and workplace to see if there is a fit.

reciprocity. "Mutual dependence, action, or influence"; a two-way exchange of privileges (*Merriam–Webster* 2012).

Chapter Three

Finding Out about Resources and Opportunities

Just what makes that little old ant / Think he'll move that rubber tree plant?" (Cahn and Van Heusen 1959). Graduate students (that little old ant) who effectively tap into and use **internal resources** and **external resources** have more success in their programs (that rubber tree plant). This idea, raised in chapter 2, is elaborated on here where resources and opportunities are outlined to further guide readers.

Meet Cassandra, who has worked as a professor in education since the 1980s. Ever since she was a doctoral student, she has been viewing people as her "best resources" for moving forward, finding fulfillment, and growing intellectually. Most importantly, she has reciprocated, being available as an expert resource for students and her program. She has vivid mentoring memories from her graduate student days, which are influencers on her advice giving today:

> In my own doctoral program, I saw the people around me as my best resources. Because of their encouragement and faith in me, I was employed as a research assistant, a teaching assistant, and a research intern. As a result, I worked closely with my professors on research projects and cotaught with them. I learned about rules and requirements by asking my interim program advisor direct questions and talking to other graduate students—two other major resources of mine. My major professor [not the advisor] included me in proposal writing, presenting at conferences, writing, and publishing—all opportunities that I acted on. At the American Educational Research Association (AERA), this leading researcher introduced me to the top folks in the field. Thus I was totally involved in and oriented to becoming a successful professor and researcher/writer.
>
> Other professor mentors emerged as critical resources, too, nominating me for leadership roles in AERA, advising me on which journals to send my manuscripts to, and even eventually connecting me to editors. Through this networking I became a member of prestigious journal editorial boards. I learned how AERA works by asking lots of questions of people in specialized leadership roles (e.g., committee and program chairs) and by doing all sorts of service. I volunteered for roles on committees and was nominated by faculty members from within AERA and the academy.
>
> Over the last several decades I have been returning these gifts to my outstanding doctoral students. And in my master's classes I give advice and act as a resource in a variety of ways. For example, I get them thinking, reading, and writing about the future in a doctoral program, say, at a top research university that has a specialty that interests them. I encourage all students who want to pursue doctoral studies to go elsewhere in order to broaden their life experience—no one should get all three degrees from the same institution. As an exercise, they find the top three programs (nationally and internationally) in their field and then make contacts. I also urge them to join professional organizations in their area of study. If they wish to become a professor or researcher,

they should be surfing the websites of prominent professional associations to come up with good matches for their academic and career interests. By presenting at conferences, they get more of a handle on academic issues and the professions.

I see my role in the classroom as advice giving. I share methods for promoting student growth as part of every seminar I hold. After having had a great doctoral experience, I only later realized how lucky I was to have such dedicated, informed, and passionate teachers and role models. I was blessed and can only hope that students who study with me will one day feel the same.

CASE ANALYSIS

Payne's (2003) classic *A Framework for Understanding Poverty*, while applicable to families living in poverty, is also pertinent to students and graduates. The framework makes a connection between capital (economic and human) and eight essential resources: financial, emotional, mental, spiritual, physical, support systems, relationships/role models, and knowledge of hidden rules. As Payne reveals, impoverished guardians must use most of their resources for economic survival, often leaving human capital (and their children's needs) undernourished. The relative luxury of being able to focus on human capital makes the academy special.

Given Payne's framework of resources, what are three salient ones from Cassandra's case? I would list, in order of importance, relationships/role models (e.g., professor mentors), knowledge of hidden rules (e.g., unspoken rules of conferences), and mental (e.g., thinking, reading, and writing). Notably, there's no mention of economic capital by Cassandra, only human capital.

Obviously, higher-education institutions are a place of privilege for many, exposing the flip side of Payne's portrait of poverty. However, among us are graduate students making more sacrifices than others to obtain an advanced degree; some work side jobs and spend a great deal of energy just trying to survive. They might come from what Payne refers to as "generational poverty" or "situational poverty," the latter resulting from a major life event, such as divorce, death, or illness. Two doctoral candidates in education who researched student productivity ended up encouraging students to seek good mentoring in order to better navigate "the emotional, social, and personal issues associated with graduate school" (Rendina-Gobioff and Watson 2004, 17).

People like Cassandra make the most of internal and external resources, first as students and then as professors. In an extended account, she described her internal sources of strength: lifelong commitment to yoga, meditation, and travel (spiritual resources); ongoing love of reading, particularly novels; writing on the artistic and critical engagement of students (mental resource); and educational philosophy ("Give your life energy to positive people and things and avoid getting stuck in the past"). Moreover, she also found support beyond the program chair and committee. In fact, throughout her career she made good use of expert support and guidance.

MENTORING-BASED RESOURCES AND OPPORTUNITIES

Resources External to Graduate School

Support structures for graduate students include knowledge of and access to academically relevant associations, foundations, networks, and clearinghouses that facilitate mentoring relationships, research opportunities, and scholarly grants and awards. Along these lines, a list of current resources geared toward the various stages of the doctorate, including the dissertation and other projects, is included (see "Nonprint Resources" [covers websites] in "References and Resources").

Resources Internal to Graduate School

Resources internal to one's university vary depending on academic context, so this is a snapshot only. I invited professors to list resources supported in their own programs—below are some graduate-mentoring resources and opportunities:

- A cohort model structure that absorbs and orients entering students
- Assignment of doctoral advisor aligned to students' research interests
- Active participation in regional and national professional organizations
- Attendance and presentation at annual conferences and special events
- Sponsored reception for doctoral students at national conference
- Opportunities for professional networking and development
- Coauthorship on scholarly publications and joint presentations
- Opportunities for research, editorships, and web development
- Experience teaching, reflecting on teaching, and peer collaboration
- Funded scholarships and fellowships, tuition waivers, and allocations
- Grant-writing assistance and involvement in established grants teams
- Special workshops on graduate student success and academic careers

These mentoring elements are relevant to any graduate program in education and other fields. It does not matter what programs this list is from for a few reasons: (1) the best practices mindset is the broad takeaway message, and (2) the information submitted from different programs, while less comprehensive, offered a few or more of these initiatives. Clearly, this generic list can function as a handy checklist: faculty and administrators can use it for generating an impressive palette of mentoring opportunities and resources or for assessing the quantity and quality of current offerings. Students do not need to wait for information and invitations to come their way: ask questions, seek out information, and initiate prospects.

Next, I discuss mentoring opportunities and resources that account for the data I obtained for this book: Catalogs, seminars, events, associations, groups, collaborations, scholarships, and defenses are all vehicles of socialization facilitated by the education college culture. Students and mentors alike can use this list as a rough but iterative sequence for their programs.

Catalogs

The topic of graduate catalogs (also known as handbooks) is briefly covered in chapter 2. Notably, these documents do not always stand on their own: you will probably need to turn to various additional resources (i.e., a faculty member, administrator, staff member, or peer leader) for interpreting the multiple rules and policies, especially for your own program, as well as interests and goals.

One doctoral student found the catalog he was expected to follow helpful as a source of and catalyst for targeted mentoring: "I read about my program in the handbook and on the website and then used what I learned to have informative conversations with my advisor, confirming the best courses to take."

Unlike Wilson, after completing this process Jamie experienced sustained confusion. Because she had a one-hour drive from her college, she felt hindered. Although Jamie accessed more than a single internal source—catalog, online materials, advisor—for answers, she did not have all of the critical information she wanted. Feeling depleted and lost, Jamie revealed some of the dynamics behind her struggle:

> I've been trying to understand the handbook and other online program information. However, these materials are not very helpful or explicit in some areas. For example, they do not clarify the difference between a thesis and a course project. Additionally, while the core classes for the EdS [educational specialist] are similar to the EdD [doctorate in education], I still don't know which ones will transfer to the doctorate. I bug my program advisor via e-mail and phone but rarely hear back and have nowhere else to turn.

Jamie is not alone; however, I did get responses from students who seemed more proactive and strategic in their problem-solving approaches. Doug is one such instance. This digital immigrant, generationally speaking, started his doctoral program *before* university websites existed:

> In those days I had to pick up the handbook from the graduate office and refer to it a lot during my coursework. I found that I often had a better understanding of the program deadlines and expectations than some professors and committee members in the department. I gave them forms and pages from the handbook to clarify the rules when discrepancies arose.

Experiencing a setback with his qualification examinations, Doug was transferred from the initial program. He added, "Recently my advisor informed me that changes made in the procedures could affect my graduation date—actually moving it up one semester—so her guidance reminded me to get current on the vital information."

The doctoral students who contacted me also mentioned deviation in the governing policies of their institutions. Some were unaware of any course, workshop, or professor that focused on orienting students to the doctoral program: "I often meet deadlines and expectations by following the handbook and by persevering in order to get anywhere." Others presented a more hopeful picture, especially when they had done their "homework" and reached out to more than one party, securing the necessary assistance. However, simultaneous communications with people, separately contacted, can create confusion and even deplete personnel resources. It can work best to "cc" all relevant parties on the same communication.

Contrasting with the student testimonials, faculty leaders shared that they were on top of the handbooks, procedures, timelines, program sequences, and so forth as pertaining to their departments. While most faculty advise students to draft the program of study for their review, some partner with them from the outset, increasingly online (at a distance) with groups of advisees (not just individuals).

Some faculty advisors and mentors are more labor-intensive and personalized when guiding students. One of them presents her advisees with a program sequence that starts off with "the graduate handbook as the main resource in my first meetings with incoming doctoral students." Personally meeting each student one-on-one, she "prepares a program of study that takes into account the institutional parameters and the individual's academic and career objectives."

Seminars

Take advantage of seminars, webinars, and workshops. Teaching centers, institutes, departments, programs, and professional associations all support professional development; geared toward the needs and interests of students, many are free, low cost, or value-added (for paying members). These focus on technology skills, electronic referencing, first-time publishing, academic and grant writing, student-centered teaching, job readiness, research compliance, and much more.

Brown-bag lunches, off-hour seminars, and advisory boards are also a welcoming door in the academy. Students, faculty members, and specialists present at such events and interact in a more relaxed way. These sessions range in purpose, audience, and focus and are sponsored or cosponsored by organizations, schools, departments, or offices. As presenters, doctoral students share their research and rehearse formally defending their work.

A different type of seminar is the research compliance workshop. Instead of simply uploading your Institutional Review Board (IRB) documents and hoping for the best (these usually come back with requests for additional information and stated concerns), prepare ahead. Attend the workshops at your college, many of which are available online along with the certification process. Even if your research project is not yet under way, you will learn a great deal about how to compile an IRB application to the satisfaction of the institution by becoming involved. Turn every challenge into a learning and networking opportunity, and search for resources that will assist you. By familiarizing yourself with the IRB process, including the administrative point person, grant specialists, and faculty experts, you'll empower yourself to produce a strong application while defusing any fear.

Listservs

Join the university's graduate student associations or another forum and subscribe to listservs. You'll need the information that typically comes via different listservs to the student community from your program, school, and university, as well as from individual faculty members and student groups.

Watch for important announcements regarding IRB notices, thesis/dissertation tutoring sessions, and more. Be in the know and up to date. Students who are members of listservs can more readily register for workshops that have limited seating and high mentoring value.

Public examples from Internet websites include:

> Graduate students and faculty members are invited to a research compliance workshop entitled "Mentoring New Researchers: What They Need to Know about the IRB Process." The focus of the workshop will be how faculty members can best work with doctoral students, including the appropriate development and use of consent letters. Attendance fulfills IRB requirements. (sponsor: Research Compliance office)
>
> A new workshop on "Innovative Uses of Technology in your Thesis or Dissertation" is being offered. Digital scholarship can be so much more than making a PDF of a (print) document. This workshop provides valuable skills in creating a thesis or dissertation using technology, based on award-winning examples from across the United States. Learn about the $1,000 award for an outstanding example of innovative use of technology in a thesis or dissertation. (sponsor: Graduate School office)

Events

Become connected. Combat feelings of isolation. Attend and organize as many relevant, timely, and inspiring events as you can manage without being distracted from your academic and professional obligations. This includes not only socials but also conferences (regional, state, and national), defenses, seminars, celebrations, ceremonies, exhibits, and more. Avoid being in a situation where you are about to graduate but have no conference proposals or publications, especially if you're seeking an academic appointment or highly competitive practitioner position.

Does your program, department, or school have institutional membership or accreditation with a professional association? Such affiliations give students a foot in the door. Professional associations provide opportunities for qualified doctoral students to participate in such venues as preconference sessions, targeted mentoring programs, and career events. Also, attend public events as early as possible in your program in order to meet faculty members outside your department. You will need close affiliation with course professors, committee members, sponsors, and advocates. The members on your committees should not be selected exclusively by your dissertation chair and hence unknown to you.

In the 1990s, as a doctoral student in Canada, I organized several events, one of them a yearlong seminar series for well-known faculty members from different provinces and countries. I enjoyed the fancy meals with articulate, fascinating scholars and had the chance to discuss cutting-edge scholarly ideas while honing an interpersonal academic style.

As it turned out, one speaker later served as the **outside chair** for my dissertation defense, another wrote the foreword to a student-generated monograph I organized, and a third invited me to write a chapter for her book. Looking back, this experience reinforced how one action or event in the academy can serendipitously yield another, producing an unexpected but desirable chain reaction. Become involved, assume leadership, and adopt the long view.

Associations

Graduate-student associations can function as very active branches of their colleges and departments. Some even network with such governing bodies as research councils, senates, and central administration, including the university president's office and community-based organizations. These associations sometimes incorporate faculty advisors and provide visibility to student-driven approaches, ideas, and concerns. Grassroots bodies sponsor such activities as internal conferences (e.g., panel and poster presentations), student projects involving grants, various leadership initiatives, and awards. And these associations sometimes have financial resources—budgets that support travel funding, research allocations, dissertation expenses, and more.

In some of the colleges I have worked in, the graduate-student committee has had an administrative structure complete with its own president. These link with governing bodies to share planning and financial responsibilities, and provide advocacy for student issues (e.g., conference and research funding support) through college-wide membership and activity.

A doctoral student symposium is one of such success. The idea for a scholarly event of this nature was presented at the College Research Committee, which I chaired that year, and it was endorsed: The education dean and an institute gave matching funds. Through a publicity blitz, the graduate student association managed to attract a good number of students, who turned out as presenters, attendees, and even reporters. Two colleges cosponsored the event. Faculty members and administrators provided funding, ideas, and support, and some reviewed the student proposals. As is evident, internal resources (e.g., funding) and external resources (e.g., cosponsorship) can be creatively combined to support graduate student involvement and development.

In my education college, we are constantly offering opportunities for graduate students around scholarship, writing, partnerships, mentoring, and cultural topics of interest. Our advisory boards, consisting of program graduates and leaders, help guide our decision making as a whole body and our current students in their academic and career goals. The graduate-student associations, an activist arm of the college and university, navigate resources, resolve concerns, and manage upward.

Groups

Groups are usually an underutilized resource for graduate students, including those in candidacy who are eager to obtain feedback on the dissertation process and their own work. Although student–faculty dyads are the foundation for one's development, progress, and completion, they cannot satisfy all of a student's intellectual and emotional needs and are not meant to. Students have benefitted greatly from creating a **mentoring mosaic** that cultivates academic, intellectual, and political capital, and that leverages opportunities for networking and professional and career development. Within these groups, students interact with colleagues and collaborate in **comentoring** relationships with selected faculty members or peers (Fletcher and Mullen 2012). (See Part II for a detailed elaboration on different types of groups.)

Invite experts to speak to your groups. Also include graduates from your program or successful IRB applicants. Sometimes it's best to make personal contacts first with key personnel, such as with knowledgeable insiders in a research compliance office. Talk with them about your projects and their procedures and systems. As you build rapport, you will have buy-in with insiders who may be willing to go to your group to share vital information. Proactively build your community, organize your work, progress toward your goals, and manage upward.

Collaborations

As described in "Resources Internal to Graduate School" and chapter 2, some students form collaborative partnerships with faculty members in teaching or research. Although not articulated as a national goal, more and more students and faculty members are calling for opportunities to collaborate with specialty experts on research and teaching (Mullen 2005). While faculty–student collaboration exists in different programs, it is telling that Rendina-Gobioff and Watson (2004), who investigated an education department's productivity, found that conference presentations are a more popular medium of partnership than publications, which involve more time and effort. The doctoral-student participants in this study, while appreciative of the opportunities they had, desired more coauthoring experiences with professors and an overall increase in collaboration. Consciousness-raising about student desire, combined with institutional support, can help create a shift toward the nontraditional role of scholarly comentor and coach.

Rendina-Gobioff and Watson's (2004) seed study of faculty–student collaboration and my insider knowledge discern a trend: education departments generally support joint presentations with far greater regularity than shared publications. By advising graduate students of "the importance of mentoring and how to become good candidates for mentoring," they will become educated about the value of forming collaborations with professors that they find desirable (17). (For more information about faculty/student collaboration, see chapters 4 and 5 and Part III.)

In her first semester of the doctorate, a hopeful student described the newly forming collaborations she was experiencing: "I've already put together my committee after establishing who would be my major professor. I also corresponded with and met all of the members." In addition, she has "also had the good fortune to interact with professors and students who are willing to share relevant information with me." She "already managed to coauthor an article with a professor from a different discipline—it's been accepted for publication!" If all of this seems too good to be true, consider that she had networks in place that she was building on, benefitting from "a head start due to my completed master's degree at this university and contacts in elementary education."

Scholarships

Different types of scholarships and fellowships are available for graduate students, possibly within their own program or campus, as well as professional associations and networks. Professors get solicited to identify potential recipients who have financial need, a good grade point average (GPA), outstanding achievements, innovation or other talent, particular demographics, and more.

Stay alert to great opportunities by having mentors act on your behalf. Also contact your school and graduate-student association. If you think that you qualify for an award (or something else) but have not been contacted, just take the initiative—folks are busy. Make your desire known, especially to an advocate. Check out your graduate school's website, surf the web, join listservs, and make it a habit to seek out opportunities for which you qualify and ongoing support.

Take advantage of teaching or research assistantships in your own locale. This applies to part-time students and especially full-time students. Hit the ground running, even prior to program admission. Make contact with people, such as faculty coordinators, and learn what internal resources you qualify for and the eligibility criteria for various awards. For example, the universities I work in and the associations in which I have membership annually grant graduate assistantships. These are for students who do outstanding teaching and research, while others support competitive entry-level students, productive dissertation writers, and members of disenfranchised populations.

For some awards, students engage in teaching, research, and service activities and collaborations with designated faculty and peers. I have personally seen the benefits of assistantships and scholarships for those who are selected by prestigious organizations for significant professional development and networking opportunities (e.g., David Clark seminar, Holmes Scholars Program). Awardees join national think tanks that spearhead critical and collaborative developmental activities. They conduct research studies, prepare scholarly works, create pedagogical materials, present at conferences, publish with insiders, collaborate with groups, organize events, get desirable jobs, and more. Their new scholarly knowledge and skills manifest across the multiple platforms of writing, presenting, networking, and connecting with esteemed scholars and invigorating peers. Even a stipend that covers conference travel can be a breakthrough for recipients who channel the opportunity afforded to create more opportunities. Opportunity builds opportunity.

Defenses

Anyone preparing for either a proposal or dissertation **defense** should observe other students in action, especially those who are, programmatically speaking, one step ahead. Avoid going to your own defense without having had this exposure and time to reflect. Locate notices for student defenses, likely from your university server or administrator. One student e-mailed me saying that she would not have known about any of the defenses in her own college "if it weren't for my dissertation chair, who years ago created a listserv through which all such notices are forwarded to her mentees."

In order to derive greater value from any graduate defense you attend, read the candidate's document beforehand. Decide for yourself what works in the scholarship or research and writing and what might need improvement, an action that will enhance the quality of your own dissertation and presentation. Pass/fail is the typical assessment standard used, with "pass with revision" as the general case—meaning that students are commonly required to make simple corrections, modest changes, or even complex modifications to improve the quality of their work.

Empower yourself to produce the highest quality work possible by being immersed in your scholastic performance context. Defenses can communicate a lot of information in a short time. In a calm, centered state, put your keen observation and listening skills to good use. Closely watch this ritualistic event unfold. Note the structural and interpersonal elements at work: the organization of the discussion and space; the introduction by the dissertation chair or external party, including the procedures followed; the presentation content and style (formal versus informal, including technology use); the interactions among all parties; the types of questions being asked—are they speculative in nature or more narrowly analytical?; and, importantly, the candidate's responses—are they appropriate, complete, substantive, acceptable? Is the candidate controlling the space for dialogue? You be the judge.

POINTS TO REMEMBER

An important message underlying this chapter is that you are your own best resource. Your ability to tap into internal and external resources alike is key to making the most of mentoring. Just like a "little old ant," you will have to "move that rubber tree plant." Your internal resources will prove indispensable in accomplishing your purposes and realizing your dreams. Combined with this, your ability to reach out and attract external resources beyond your advisor, dissertation chair, or committee will also be essential for growth and success.

The "rubber tree plant"—your graduate program—is what you will find yourself pushing against from time to time, attempting to budge it. Because your program will exhibit some flexibility under your persevering hand, there will be movement and results. But if a program (or the people in it) is pushed too hard, it might snap back unexpectedly, just like an elastic band. In cases where students lean too hard, they might, for example, act rudely, aggressively, or even threateningly. Real-world situations include students who want to graduate by a certain date even though their proposal or dissertation is not yet ready; feeling upset and panicky, some might become demanding and obstinate. In such cases, the political resource known as "knowledge of hidden rules" is being depleted and faculty frustration rises.

Remembering this critical resource from Payne's (2003) book, except in extraordinary situations, the tacit cues of one's committee that safeguard scholarly standards are not to be challenged or dismissed. Committee members might become disgruntled or worse if they feel forced to prematurely hold a defense or if previous recommendations or changes have been ignored—believe me, I know. Students who refuse to make the changes that committees ask of them either before or after a defense are exhibiting unprofessional behavior; the unforeseen repercussions of acting unethically by dismissing faculty feedback can cost a student the investment or, even worse, the trust of their committees. Exercising control over one's destiny while also taking responsibility for one's actions is the fine line we all must walk. Everyone expects monitoring around stress levels, inner drama, and attitude.

Consider the actions of Jamie, narrated earlier. She was not acting inappropriately or aggressively—in fact, Jamie obviously deserved respect and assistance from her program advisor. However, one can see that her strategy for finding answers was not working and that tension was mounting: "I bug my program advisor via e-mail and phone but rarely hear back and so *have nowhere else to turn*" (my italics). Instead of continuing to push against the "rubber tree" (the program advisor), Jamie should have sought answers from other resources, such as the program coordinator, department chair, or a dean in charge of academic affairs. She should *not* give up. We all must rise to the occasion of being our own best advocate.

Anyone in an advising situation, regardless of the quality and satisfaction of it, should document the exchanges that occur; keep a log that includes all e-mails and other correspondence. This kind of record can prove invaluable as students are called upon to know particular dates and other facts about their program and progress. In thorny advising cases, a decision-making authority would have the record to consult, not having to rely on hearsay. Sometimes students have to take action to resolve conflicts: "When troubles call, and your back's to the wall / There's a lot to be learned, that wall could fall" (Cahn and Van Heusen 1959). How the ant goes about moving the rubber tree matters, just as how we act matters.

SUMMARY

This discussion focused on an array of mentoring opportunities and resources, including healthy, productive mindsets for working relationships. Catalogs, seminars, events, associations, groups, collaborations, scholarships, and defenses are socializing processes that universities and professional associations offer. Different types of resources (human and economic), particularly internal and external resources, are keys to opening more doors. One door opens another door. Success builds success.

Navigational Prompts

• *Develop a support tree* that is tailored to address your program needs and goals. In addition to your advisor or dissertation chair, what other support resources can you map onto your tree? As examples, add a program coordinator, technology specialist, admissions/registrar officer, a director or dean of student academic services, reference librarian, and administrative assistant. Who or what else should be included and relative to what specific functions? Consult web pages, graduate catalogs, and campus directories (and any other informational sources) to identify titles and duties. On your support tree, include services that you can personally use. Share this map with others and add to it during your program.

- *Conduct a program assessment of mentoring resources and opportunities.* Use the bulleted list of mentoring resources (e.g., cohort model structure in "Resources Internal to Graduate School"). Adapt it to your own context to see how well your program fares. Talk to students and faculty members when completing the list and use it to help build the success of your program. Make recommendations for changes that support students.
- *Custom design your own resource library.* Access virtual libraries for materials of interest and tag your selections, placing them into organized e-folders (right at the library website or another place). Also, from your Internet browser, go to databases–education–journals and search using academic databases of your choice. Visit the websites of publishing companies (e.g., Routledge) that provide journals of interest. Furthermore, find sources via professional associations of interest (for names and website links, go to "References and Resources" in this book). Use your preferred browser to search using descriptors (e.g., "educational leadership journals"). Compare results with peers or tackle this as a mentoring mosaic, with each individual accomplishing part of the task.

GLOSSARY

comentoring. Proactive engagement in reciprocal teaching and learning that aims to transform power structures to close opportunity gaps between individuals and groups and to honor equity, fairness, and the greater good (Mullen 2005).

defense. Final defense of the thesis or dissertation to a faculty committee occurs after the eligible candidate has completed the document; oral examinations (defenses) may also accompany other major summative projects, such as capstones and portfolios; requirements vary among programs and disciplines.

external resources. Sources beyond one's internal resources that are external to the self, such as guides, experts, committees, and specialists, as well as professional associations, libraries, clearinghouses, and websites (chapter 2).

internal resources. One's personal inner resources that range from the psychological to the spiritual, which may extend to close affinity with peers, groups, advisors, or mentors (chapter 2).

mentoring mosaic. Collegial clusters of mentors and role models expand beyond formal mentoring dyads; these are synergistic networks, study groups, or cohorts that offset traditional or limited relationships and that facilitate academic and career support and opportunities for ongoing growth (Mullen 2005).

outside chair. Selected or distinguished scholar from outside the program or department who may preside over the dissertation defense and who may function strictly as a facilitator of the discussion or as an independent evaluator of the work. (This role is not always required.) Also known as external chair and examiner.

II

Becoming Immersed

Relating and Learning

Chapter Four

Making Every Minute and Day Count

The collection of students and faculty members you are about to witness in action thinks and acts as a single entity. Meet the WIT (Writers in Training), a doctoral cohort of mine that was active for seven years:

Dr. Mullen (dissertation chair) [speaking to Mark]: I believe your text is workable but that you can take it to another level. You can accomplish this by making just one change throughout the work. A typical example appears on page 27: a whole paragraph revolves around a single source. You depend on solitary sources to create every paragraph of the writing, but you need to synthesize your key sources and scaffold the writing at a metalevel. Think of yourself as looking out at the educational leadership field, trying to make sense of a part of it in its entirety.

Mark (awkwardly): I see what you mean, but it's hard to grasp. Are you are saying that I have to speak in my own voice?

Mentor: No, not exactly.

Shirley: Let me help. I recently struggled with this issue at a WITs meeting. You have to figure out the main idea for what you want to get across. Ask yourself, what is my message? It will change somewhat in each paragraph. Back up your points by citing the key researchers that say the same thing.

Raymond: Right, for your writing you're depending on one source at a time, such as John Dewey—can you see that?—and on paraphrases of each to get by. But you aren't capturing the literature or even making any major points. You were probably feeling overwhelmed and so broke down the task into small chunks to manage it.

Kathleen: Yes, you just need to pull out the major themes from a number of key sources, say six or seven. Then cite the group of thinkers in parentheses, using the strategy that Dr. Mullen often mentions, after you've made your big point. It's a different strategy than what you're using, that's all.

Rhonda: There's another problem here. You have something like "the subject will be talked about throughout." Throughout what? Your life? Your career? This paper? What?

Mark: I'm missing a direct object. Got it.

Rhonda: You know what I mean, right? I just don't want your doctoral committee to jump all over this section.

Mark: Right. Yeah. Right.

Rhonda: I guess I'm playing devil's advocate. I know what you mean by that sentence based on your explanation here today, but the reader might not, so that's where I'm coming from.

CASE ANALYSIS

You have just observed a few minutes in the life-world of an informal doctoral cohort. This grassroots initiative was both student generated and professor guided. Once monthly, the WITs met at my home for five hours. Each session was student driven and had an agenda onto which individuals could add their work on a rotational, as-needed basis. Agenda items featured literature reviews, research instruments, and dissertation proposals and chapters. Because students were encouraged to join early, this support continued from program entry to graduation.

The peer group comprised EdD and PhD students (up to seventeen, including graduates) for whom I served in the dual role of permanent advisor and dissertation supervisor. Some were completing their dissertations, whereas others were early in their coursework, and most were full-time practitioners in K–12 public schools. These male and female members were a diverse group—they were financially strapped, although several made high salaries; they were single, divorced, and married, most with children; and they were African American, Latino American, and white American. Many had elementary or secondary teaching experience and aspired to become principals and district leaders, as well as professors. A few did not have clear career trajectories and immersed themselves in learning. Like the students themselves, the dissertation topics, all education based, covered a spectrum.

The excerpt that follows also resembles conversations from the years of Saturday sessions in my living room. When peers and mentors act in concert to support members' writing development and scholarly identity, inner awareness sparks. Positive synergy is also released, as this WIT demonstrates:

> Sometimes Dr. Mullen gives advice that I really don't know how to use without further help. At the time I think to myself that it sounds really good but feel stuck as to how the idea might transfer to my writing. Then one of the WITs adds to her advice, and then another does the same, which gives me processing time: The connection between the idea and the application starts to become clear. My professor reenters the dialogue, pulling the solutions from me, so it's not as though others resolve my issues or take control of my work.

Interdependence within vibrant mentoring contexts allows students to comprehend one another and sometimes more clearly than their mentors. Faculty mentors should rely on students as translators to be understood and when their feedback (e.g., articulation of an idea or word choice) is impenetrable or ambiguous. Students create meaning together. For example, in the opening scenario, the writer had difficulty understanding my feedback in regard to adopting a particular strategy for improving his work. The student had used an unacceptable format, which was not unique to him, and I tried to sensitively raise this point using the proverbial "but": "I believe your text is workable but you can take it to another level." It was not until his peers explained how every page of his text—a review of the literature in an area of educational leadership—had been revolving around a single source, without references to additional or multiple researchers who make similar (and dissimilar) points about the concept being presented, that he understood the issue.

Because the WIT cohort was intensely focused and the synergy positive, our rhythm absorbed misunderstandings, self-centered attitudes, and "ego rubs." An instance of ego bruising occurred between Rhonda and Mark when Rhonda implied that the writing did not meet scholarly standards. Mark, the writer, reacted defensively until she explained that her motivation was to protect him from committee objections in the future about the quality of writing (e.g., vague uses of "subject"). He seemed to understand her logic and conceded that more clarification would be good. The WITs shared their struggles with clarifying uses of "subject" in academic writing—a tricky word that can function as a noun, adjective, or verb.

All such dynamics are absorbed or overcome in one way or another and also worked into the totality of what we have become and are becoming. Indeed, the synergy of the WIT cohort helped students to persist with issues and to proactively address them. The dissertation is a daunting task and scholarly development entails a steep learning curve. The cohort bred confidence, generating a willingness to openly grapple with and resolve problems as a group.

The WITs strove for acceptance, connection, and affiliation, while also engaging in the push and pull of intellectual tension. The commitment of groups like the WIT is perseverance at scholarly work that can improve life for struggling schools and disadvantaged populations. Catalysts for realizing one's dreams are reciprocal learning, scholarly critique, and peer mentoring. Along these lines, Theodore Roosevelt, twenty-sixth US president, aptly said, "Far and away the best prize that life has to offer is the chance to work hard at work worth doing" (www.brainyquote.com). (Chapter 5 further explores cohort learning in mentoring programs.)

A fuller descriptive analysis of and longitudinal retrospection on the WIT cohort and its functions and outcomes are available elsewhere (see, e.g., Mullen 2011a).

STRATEGIES OF ACADEMIC CULTURAL IMMERSION

No one mentoring strategy is a panacea for student engagement, quality of work, and program success, but each is nonetheless a critical piece of the puzzle. The educational literature—and my own experiences as a dissertation supervisor, course instructor, educational researcher, and department chair—reinforces the value and potency of certain mentoring strategies, both personal and programmatic. These include establishing cultural affinity, practicing observational learning, joining **peer/cohort groups**, forming mentoring dyads, choosing advisors and dissertation chairs, selecting committee members, resolving misconceptions, and utilizing external resources.

Mentees and their supporters will benefit from adopting all such approaches that promote the progress, retention, and graduation of striving, talented doctoral students. These will also assist students in their own immersion process, knowing that it is "time to get it all together / Making every minute count" (Spanky and Our Gang 1967).

Establishing Cultural Affinity

Cultural affinity has been described as the comforting feeling that culturally ethnic minorities—the emerging majority population—experience when they look around campus and see others like themselves (Freeman 1999). Applying this insight to your own circumstances, ask yourself what defines you culturally or helps you feel at home. For example, do you identify more closely with other students from a particular ethnic/minority group? Are you more comfortable with one gender? How about a certain age group or religious affiliation? Does a particular attitude toward life, philosophy, ideology, or research attract you? Or what about affinity with certain career stages, such as practicing teachers aspiring to become school leaders?

Knowing yourself is only half the picture; the other half involves challenging your intellect by becoming as open minded as possible. From this vantage point, consider the learning potential of mentors who, while tolerant and fully accepting of you, are also quite different. Mixed viewpoints along these lines are presented in the literature, however. Do minorities and females in particular benefit more from having mentors who are a mirror of themselves? Some researchers say yes, others no. In Freeman's (1999) study involving high-achieving African Americans, students found their relationships with mentors from the same ethnic group "extremely important to their initial adjustment, in their stay there, and in their transition from their institution to graduate school or the work environment" (3). To foster diversity, both mixed-race and same-race configurations should be promoted and cross-cultural mentoring encouraged (Johnson-Bailey 2012).

However, in reality, a Eurocentric male ideology still confronts, even disarms, many female and minority students and faculty members (Johnson-Bailey and Cervero 2004). A related complication involves the extent to which white males should mentor nonwhite women (Mullen 2005). Some feminists argue that relational mentoring should remain open to white males, and that teachers should be paired with learners of both genders and all races. Others counter that the real issue is systemic, not relational, in that organizational access is a closed door for disenfranchised persons (e.g., Darwin 2000).

In fact, studies of historically black universities have found that women and minorities paired with white male mentors benefit from the open door that facilitates professional networking, employment, and success. Dreher and Chargois (1998) conclude that "cross-race developmental relationships" should encompass workplaces, not just academia (402). Societal institutions, including professional associations, still face the challenge of ensuring equitable access, opportunity, and salary for women and minorities, especially for the most coveted positions and rewards. The logic here? Any insider access to the power grid can prove advantageous for the mentee, not only those wanting careers in male-dominated fields but also those seeking an influential or activist role.

Practicing Observational Learning

Observation is a crucial step in learning and adapting, appreciating the historical context in which you're situated, and avoiding needless mistakes in relationships and decision making. One Latina graduate student astutely stated, in Weis and Fine's (2000) qualitative research text, that "the mechanism through which socialization takes place is observational learning" (102). However, as she also noted, traditional theories of socialization assume that the process is "unidirectional," meaning that we model ourselves by what we learn from others.

But, in actuality, this process can be "bidirectional." Some of the graduate students who contacted me for this book commented, unprompted, about the invaluable practice of observational learning. However, their individual statements revealed a unidirectional mindset, perhaps because two-way possibilities were just budding:

> I'm being directed informally by observation, seeing what people do in their degree programs and following their lead. I listen to the career aspirations of fellow students when they introduce themselves in my classes, and I record the names and particulars of those I find interesting.

Yet another student reflected on observational learning, this time as related to the mentoring received from his advisor, and again with a unidirectional tone:

> The university graduate department posts defenses that my advisor forwards to his students. He is an advocate of having graduate students observe others who are a step or two ahead of them in their program to see what's expected. That is helpful, but only when we act on it and see what we can learn and adopt for our own purposes.

Elaborating on the topic of peer mentorship though observational learning, students who attend dissertation proposals and defenses have a definite advantage (Mullen 2005). While the experience of cultural immersion in this context is one way, those who share what they have learned with their peers internalize the observations. By doing so, they engage in bidirectional mentoring, turning passive observation into active processing and engagement, and new directions.

Joining Peer/Cohort Groups

Early on, make contact with professors, administrators, and peers, and not just in technical ways. Seeking support from groups that provide support through and past the coursework phase and into the freedom/danger zone of all-but-the-dissertation (ABD) candidacy is crucial for many doctoral students (Mullen et al. 2007).

Although students in **doctoral candidacy** could conceivably start the search for a support group once their coursework and qualifying exams are behind them, they will not have benefited from the peer support and motivational coaching of ongoing membership. Those who desire this belonging late in their programs will have overlooked the stipulated **time to degree** and might well be left out in the cold. As Stripling's (2004) analysis of **noncompleter candidates** who are graduate school dropouts confirmed, "Candidates expected continued peer support and more peer support when they reached candidacy [but] any collegial help and support ended along with the classwork" (229).

Students and faculty members new to group-based mentoring should be keenly aware that ABD candidates have expressed "appreciation for any type of cohort group or the opportunity to associate collegially with other students" (Stripling 2004, 228). Furthermore, this group (in Stripling's study, minority and nonminority males and females, averaging forty-eight years old) stressed "the advantages of having an additional support structure to augment the institutional systems in place" (229).

Even noncompleters who consider themselves too independent to work with a group recognize that peers who were part of a cohort had gotten further ahead; for example, cohort members can be more "in the know" about the resources available to students and also have better coping strategies. Faculty-led cohorts and peer groups are extremely important for addressing the issues, barriers, and questions of each member and for passing along indispensable information (Stripling 2004).

Because programs vary in the opportunities provided to students for working in preformed groups, they can actively seek out membership within existing groups in their own or another program. Alternatively, students can create their own disciplinary or multidisciplinary group.

Students tell me that they become "charged up" from gathering with other writers in coffeehouses, homes, and online. Study groups led by professors may yield greater success than student-run groups, as the former has the sponsorship, investment, and guidance of committed faculty. This type of cohort enables groups to more readily function at regular intervals and over long periods of time (Mullen 2005), although "the jury is out," given the proliferation of peer-only groups.

Online cohorts and groups are flourishing in education and other academic disciplines in graduate schools around the world. Some of these are course and program focused with respect to meeting requirements for internships and portfolios electronically, through such new offerings as technology-based internships, web folios, wikis, blogs, and more. Other program innovations are aimed at a larger purpose beyond electronic adaptation of courses for group learning.

Learn about these innovations, including the preparation of practicing principals in a groundbreaking statewide fully online program. In it, graduate students explicitly function as change agents for improving the capacity of the low-performing public schools they lead through campus-wide technology integration, team-based professional development, and other interventions that target twenty-first-century school improvement. (For this wide array of online examples, consult the multiauthored e-book by editors Tareilo and Bizzell [2012]).

Forming Mentoring Dyads and Relationships

Students can excel by applying their intention and energy to viable mentoring dyads that are dependable as well as healthy. Permanent advisors and dissertation chairs with whom they feel comfortable but not complacent should be selected. Dissertation chairs should also have, among other qualities, a challenging intellect and the conviction to get students through. (However, some students decide to take calculated risks, selecting faculty members who are new to their institutions or who are tenure earning, typically because they feel connected to their student-centered approach or because there is a paucity of experienced faculty available.)

Interestingly, in Stripling's (2004) study of individual program attrition, the interviewed noncompleter candidates, perhaps surprisingly, had mostly found their relationships with dissertation chairs positive throughout their programs. Variance occurred within the mentoring dyad itself in accordance with student expectations. Worth remembering, some candidates complained they had not played a role in choosing the members of their committee. Do you have a say?

Deciding Dissertation Chairs and Permanent Advisors

A psychology professor at Stanford University says that mentors are more appealing if they are open to having a drink (or tea/coffee) with their student (as cited in Thorpe [2005]). Friendship—with one who accepts and relates to the protégé—has been recognized as an essential but not uncomplicated function of the mentoring role (Johnson and Mullen 2007). Furthermore, Gallimore, Tharp, and John-Steiner (1992) see attraction and attachment (i.e., intellectual and interpersonal chemistry) as underlying all effective mentorships. Alternative models of professional friendship, emotional intimacy, and authentic communication (Gallimore et al. 1992; Young et al. 2004) support this view.

Too few doctoral students select their mentors based on the individual's publications and expertise. In a study of seventy-nine doctoral graduates in education, only 10 percent selected their dissertation chairs with this in mind. The major reason given? The graduates believed their chair was personally interested in their topic (86 percent). Others selected their committee chair after completing a course with that person (47 percent) or upon receiving a faculty member's (30 percent) or another student's (19 percent) recommendation (Bennouna 2003).

As a dissertation chair who, from one year to the next, carries a heavy advising load of more than a dozen students (like some of my colleagues), this strikes me as accurate. Doctoral students generally do not know but should learn the scholarly history of potential dissertation chairs and use the information gained for assessment purposes before selecting them. Clearly, other pressing factors—particularly mentoring reputation, availability, willingness, disciplinary/topic fit, and interpersonal chemistry—will naturally be at work too.

Reading *one* article or even a book prior to initiating one of the most important and influential relationships of your entire life is wise. However, it is advisable to become familiar with and conversant about that individual's broader collection of works (and any changes in focus over time): Start with his or her vita. This is an area in which the scholarly prowess of students in general has yet to shine; knowledge of professors' as well as peers' significant work (e.g., presentations) is essential for helping them in many ways. This will help you build shared understanding and positive synergy, give you an intellectual frame of reference for your work, and orient you to understand your mentor's tacit values, advice, and feedback. Know the frameworks and approaches to scholarship invested in by your chair, peers, and academic learning community. Students who do are better poised to participate in teaching and research assistantships and, certainly, project collaborations.

Contrasting with this picture, *Scientific Elite: Nobel Laureates in the United States* (which arose out of Zuckerman's [1977] dissertation) describes the apprenticeship origins of the laureates who form the scientific elite. Zuckerman had learned from her interviews with forty-one (of the forty-six) Nobel laureates working at that time in the United States that, as young mentees, they had chosen their dissertation supervisors "before the master's important work was conspicuously 'validated' [by] a Nobel prize" and that they "had a discriminating eye" not only for seeking out "scientific stars" but also "for the major universities and departments doing work at the frontiers of the field" (108–109).

Just as these laureates-to-be took the time to assess the achievements of professors in their discipline, so too were the faculty members (also future laureates) searching to mine young talent. While education and science obviously differ in the systems of stratification and social elitism established, there are, nonetheless, lessons to be learned for education, particularly for those doctoral mentees whose intellectual curiosity is coupled with academic drive and an appetite for the professoriate. Tap into your own wisdom. Exhibit bravery by knocking at the doors of those whom you most admire and see as potential mentors and collaborators.

Search mindfully for mentors and influencers—get to know their work, how they think, and what they stand for and are invested in. Build on what you learn from one situation to the next. Dewey's (1938) idea is that your knowledge and skills gained in one situation will help you understand and deal with situations that follow.

Selecting Committee Members

Some colleges have democratic policies stipulating that doctoral students are to share in the decisions concerning their committee formation. However, they often do not know enough faculty members to offer informed suggestions, are unaware of who possesses expertise in particular areas, or see the selection process as their chair's responsibility. For these reasons (and others), the choices made might end up not being their own. Because this scenario is fairly common, especially for part-time students, you should contact your advisor or mentor to carefully decide each member selection and the criteria used, typically faculty expertise, skills, availability, and eligibility. This way, you are more apt to make your committee selection amenable.

Criteria for a dissertation chair's selection of faculty members are not always explicit or shared. These often extend to politics—who is able to get along with and trust whom—sticky issues that go beyond what students know or should know. From this perspective, some professors do not use "criteria," instead resorting to entrenched buddy systems, such as who they like, who they find reliable, or simply who owes them a favor.

At the other extreme end, when forming your committees, students know the graduate policies and tacit cultural expectations. Students have asked me to serve on their doctoral committees even though they have not informed their mentors of their wishes and, better yet, processed with them their choices for committee members. In some cases, students who do not yet have an advisor or mentor invite faculty members to serve on their committee. About their initiating interaction with me, students respond, in their defense, that they do not know any differently. They seem unaware that students do not solely form committees and that they are expected to consult with their mentor on who will be asked and what the next steps are.

Also, mentors may want to extend the invitations themselves to the selected faculty for potential service. If not, mentors let their students know how best to approach the faculty members and what to say. Commonly, students are advised to briefly introduce themselves and describe their research topic or interest and timeline for the program, defenses, or other areas. Despite the differences among professors and areas of study, mentors, like the mentees, must be comfortable with the decisions made; their agreements are crucial for student progress and success.

The timing of these crucial steps matters. This e-mail exchange demonstrates the need for greater specificity in university student handbooks, in addition to productive student networks and proactive mentoring communications that inform students and foster cultural awareness:

Dear Dr. Mullen: Thank you for the positive letter of reference you wrote for me. I hope to receive the [anonymous] scholarship. On another note, I would be honored if you would serve on my committee. You showed interest in my research paper and academic progress in your class and helped me a great deal. Is this a possibility? Daryl

Hello Daryl: It would be good for you to know that this decision usually gets made with your dissertation chair. Feel free to contact me later once you have selected or been assigned your dissertation chair and then together the two of you will decide who might serve on your committee. The invitations will be extended to potential faculty to serve based on the plan that is devised with your chair for who could serve and how that communication will occur. C. M.

Find out about how institutional policies and politics work in your own locale before taking any action—committee membership is rarely secured before the mentor–mentee match has been made. To compound this, chairs have idiosyncratic preferences for how work, decisions, and communications are carried out, so all of this will need to be revealed as well. Expect to fare better by closely attending your chair's advice: if you are being cautioned against choosing someone to serve on your committee but proceed, you might pay a price. Also, be forewarned that membership can change despite thoughtful selection, especially if writing progress is slower than expected. A member of faculty can become overloaded or ill and withdraw or leave for sabbatical, move, or retire. Changes can happen suddenly.

On a related note, a recently graduated PhD student from a premier institution shared an odd confession: as a student, against the better judgment of his dissertation chair, he played a game. He decided to bring together two long-time, warring faculty members on his committee just to see what would happen. Unsurprisingly, they butted heads—when one would approve a chapter, the other would adamantly block this decision. Eventually the mentor retired and a new one stepped in, immediately removing one of the faculty "warriors" so progress could be made on the dissertation. When I wrote to this graduate, curious to learn why he would put himself and his program at risk, he actually responded that he had not known at the time that his foolish gamble would cost him. Consequently, his program had been seriously delayed, and he expressed embarrassment over having subjected himself and others to the "gladiator blood bath" that erupted. Hopefully, this kind of dramatic tale is outside the norm.

In order to attract helpful committee members, you will need to understand how faculty members think. For example, some professors will only agree to be on a committee once the student has either taken a course with them and done well or at least agreed to an interview to explore a potential fit. Students assume that faculty members will likely serve on their committees once they or a sponsor have established contact, but professors tend to be much more cautious. We mostly share a "let's see" attitude—as perfectly characterized by how Dr. Gordon initially responded to Sam's request that he serve as his chair: "Let's say I'll serve as your major professor for the time being, and we'll see if there's a good fit as time goes on" (see chapter 2).

When interacting with faculty members, you will obviously want to make a good impression. Approach your coursework not as someone expecting unnecessary accommodations for an overwrought schedule or life situation but rather as a reliable professional capable of rising to any challenge. (Persons with disabilities should receive special accommodations.) Demonstrate strong leadership skills, produce high-quality work, and write and research independently. As established, it is not just your quality of work that matters when it comes to attracting potential committee members (and dissertation chairs)—students whose behavior strikes others as unprofessional, unethical, unreliable, aggressive, or immature can become isolated.

Conversations between faculty members about students occur behind the scenes, and rumors spread quickly, just as they do for students about professors. Students who cannot be trusted for one reason or another; are unreliable or taxing; are sarcastic, antagonistic, and hostile; or, even worse, are sexist and racist might be ignored, confronted, or even blocked. Faculty members commonly complete disposition assessments using rubrics, and they flag "problem students." Licensure-based graduate programs require that dispositions be assessed, not just the quality of work.

Also keep in mind that faculty members will be writing some of your most important supporting letters—primarily admissions, awards, and jobs. Graduate school is a "business" setting, no matter the college, program, course, or context. Let the faculty's image be uniformly positive.

Resolving Misconceptions

Professors and students engaged in doctoral mentoring develop misconceptions at one time or another—this is inevitable, especially as the mentoring process intensifies, tensions mount, and concerns surface. Students wrongly assume that faculty members are available around the clock to mentor, with only teaching responsibilities to worry about and plenty of free time on their hands. Several expressed the erroneous thinking that their dissertation chairs were probably being paid for their service, perhaps from their tuition dollars, which is not the case.

In addition, e-mail and social networking sites feed the illusion that faculty members are available for mentoring on weeknights, weekends, and holidays, but fewer than expected faculty members approach mentoring as an inherent part of their job. They are themselves struggling with their own research agendas and writing, and they must be highly productive to keep their jobs or advance.

Newly admitted and advancing students do not know about these realities or dynamics, so the hopeful "knock at the door" should be as informed as possible. Try not to go to the professor for information included in the student graduate handbook, written policies, bulletins, and databases. Be attentive and respectful. Work smart by not requesting information that has already been shared. Reach out to peers and build networks. Keep very organized files to track communications. Seek counsel from mentors for higher quality exchanges in which you are building on what is known and filling in gaps.

Students who are turned away by a faculty member, especially from someone with whom they have connected, will feel disappointed, even alarmed. But it might help to know about the politics behind such an action. The reason might not be personal at all; with each mentee assignment, professors cut into their own professional and personal time. Surprisingly, mentorship is treated as an "overload" responsibility separate from teaching, research, and service. It has been tagged as having an intrinsic, not extrinsic, reward. With great institutional variance, some senior faculty members manage to negotiate "assigned time" for their dissertation mentoring loads. They are rewarded for graduating students through workload adjustments such as course releases. However, this is not all that common.

Regardless, search for faculty members who have a reputation for valuing (and enjoying) working with students, have written graduate assistantships into their grant and editorial activity, want to engage in collaborative projects with talented student colleagues, or are simply inclined to provide mentoring assistance for its own sake. If you should encounter students who have taken on faculty mentors from unusual places, it might be that they had to reach further and deeper into the infrastructure. Just finding someone willing to serve on your committee, let alone as an expert in a desirable area of interest, is a "win" in the academy, particularly for those who have not entered their programs handpicked or with assistantships.

Essential to healthy mentoring, to the extent possible, correct any misconceptions in your own relationships and in a timely manner; otherwise, dissonance in the mentoring dyad can jeopardize your best interests. Keep the vigil.

Utilizing External Resources

Expert support and guidance does not always need to be ongoing for capable students to benefit. One-time or periodic assistance can make a world of difference, as in when students inquire of a qualified educator (someone not on their committee) how to perform a particular statistical analysis. Mixed-methods qualitative researchers are often asked for articles that demonstrate sound qualitative analyses.

Research institutes are generally much better equipped than academic departments to provide the resources that support students' scholarly development. According to Zajone, research institutes "house readily accessible experts in diverse fields who can offer graduate students knowledge and skills more congruent with the research problem that they decide to study" (as cited in Thorpe [2005, 3]). Students are strongly encouraged to establish affiliation with institutes in their area of research interest and seek opportunities for independent research.

Zajone believes that students do not sufficiently engage in independent research. This crucial piece of advice helps to explain why the vast majority of thesis/dissertation writers face a crisis when they move to doing independent research. Most candidates experience in-depth research or scholarship on their own topics only sporadically through coursework, without the guidance of mentors and other qualified individuals, including peer leaders. You can change this pattern.

POINTS TO REMEMBER

Mentoring mindsets, including bidirectional observation, should be promoted in the academy to guide student learning. Students: join groups early in your programs, especially those conducted by graduate faculty—and, where there might be a gap, initiate contact with professors, peers, and specialists. Also, establish cultural affinity in your academic environment to support your personal, professional, and political identity. While some students come from marginalized groups that are not part of the mainstream culture, others have multiple marginalized identities, such as their political/sexual orientation, for which alliances matter. Cultural affiliations that are organized foster campus awareness of key issues, opening doors for students.

Furthermore, the **hidden curriculum** of the academy suggests that student attitude, behavior, and ethics are at least as critical as quality work and academic performance (Pinar et al. 1995/1996). I inferred this after having conducted a thematic analysis of key documents from several higher-education programs that outline expectations for student behavior and performance. On the basis of the course syllabi and formal cohort contracts examined, the expected behaviors for advanced students include being a contributing member of the group who collaborates well with others and assumes peer leadership. Other standards include a willingness to help others, openness, honesty, a tolerance of differences, and patient, keen listening. It is assumed that this individual will be very well prepared, produce high-quality work, and come to class on time with all assignments completed—expectations basic to undergraduate education. This is especially applicable in teacher-education and educational-leadership programs where tomorrow's teachers and leaders are being prepared for public service.

Current studies of completers and noncompleters alike of the doctorate degree indicate that both of these populations can be usefully tapped for insight into mentoring issues (e.g., Bennouna 2003; Stripling 2004). Experiencing mentoring from their own legitimate, albeit partial, perspectives, these groups disclosed that expert support and assistance make a significant difference in the desire, competence, and completion of the candidate. On the other hand, careful assessment in selecting a mentor and committee can make a remarkable difference in your academic progress and contribution.

When you think about what *noncompleters* have to say, it confirms that mentoring interventions are sorely needed in higher education. These include designated personnel in academic units—qualified individuals whom doctoral students would feel comfortable speaking to about any issues that might surface in their programs and relationships. Also, all units responsible for doctoral education would benefit from providing students with formal orientation to the complex stages of research, writing, inquiry, individual program development, committee formation, and expected protocols of performance that include policy requirements.

Finally, doctoral laboratories that are positioned between the stages of formal coursework and dissertation writing can make an enormous difference in preparing candidates for the various apprenticeship skills they will need as independent learners and the emotions that many experience. Topics for these encounters via seminars, webinars, and hands-on workshops include practical writing strategies, library research, technology software, data collection and analysis, and document formatting.

Furthermore, avoid misconceptions that are policy rooted by staying constantly informed: read your graduate handbook, ask questions of recent graduates, and consult with your mentor as well as the administrators and specialists in charge of student affairs. Note that some candidates either do not know that they must maintain continuous enrollment once in candidacy or forget to register for dissertation hours. Penalties can range from being fined to official dismissal.

Graduating master's and doctoral students obtain a signature from their advisor for the thesis procedure. This gives students who have the approval the green light for proceeding with the format check and final submission of the thesis or dissertation. Carefully follow the thesis and dissertation manuscript processing steps that your institution provides. For example, students anticipating graduation might need to enroll in the minimum thesis or dissertation hours and will no doubt have to complete paperwork, usually posted online, such as the application for degree form. Policy or custom can call for students to forward e-copies (in the past, bound copies) of their theses or dissertations to their committees.

Learn about **electronic dissertations/theses (ETD)** and the wide variety of options for customizing your document from university websites. Electronic copies of dissertations and theses are posted at university libraries' digital websites, in addition to dissertation databases (e.g., NC Docks at libres.uncg.edu/ir).

As you browse websites, read theses and dissertations of interest. Do not wait until you are finalizing your document. Instead, early on become familiar with digital collections of knowledge and scholarship that make manuscripts available online as full-text files, in addition to their abstracts and other features, such as advisors' names and completion dates. Students will also want to investigate the special e-features that the electronic copy can accommodate, such as real-time hyperlinks, layered graphics, animations, images for movable gifs, and videos, including those on YouTube. Be sure to have any e-content adjustments cleared.

SUMMARY

We know that it is not enough just to form groups, dyads, and committees—it is essential that these relationships be developed, maintained, and nurtured through positive interactions and honest communication. In order to do so, mechanisms must be established for resolving conflicts and empowering students (and faculty members) to help identify them. As one education professor concluded about the "prized" mentoring dyads in her own department, "I believe that through strong mentoring relationships, peer support, and exposure to diverse genres of scholarship, our students receive an excellent education and applied research perspective."

However, the "excellent education" is not uniformly extended to or perceived by all. This is evident from the concerns that some doctoral students express and the "flight" reactions of noncompleters. On behalf of students who do not complete their programs, an assertive mindset is needed for better understanding the complex issues and dynamics involved, and mentoring interventions that can best assist entering and persisting students. Mentor awareness and institutional sensitivity are necessary for supporting the thesis/dissertation progress of all persevering, talented students. Doctoral candidates who move as anticipated through their programs require not just good modeling but also mentoring scaffolds. These are foundational to what Dewey (1938) describes as "opportunities for continuing growth in new directions" (36).

Navigational Prompts

- *Keep a doctoral committee communications log.* Monitor your correspondence, interactions, and activities. Document any problems and solutions, chances for engagement and advancement, progress and major breakthroughs, emotional connections, and anything else. Maintain this log throughout your program's duration. Periodically search for patterns. Does this exercise yield new insight into your mentoring relationships? How about the types of opportunities you are requesting or being extended? (See appendix C for an illustration of doctoral students' documented communications with their committees.)
- *Study the implicit behaviors outlined in course syllabi* to get a clearer picture of the expected norms. Another idea is to look over the agreement that some cohort members are expected to develop or sign. What did you learn or find?
- *See if you can be a guest of a cohort in your area of interest* and, if possible, prepare for the session by doing the assigned readings. What did you observe? Experience? Learn?
- *Talk with noncompleter candidates* to find out why they withdrew from their programs. Generate a list of constructive ideas or topics. Apply what you have learned to your own doctorate or mentoring dyad (such as the need for regular communications and timely follow-through).
- *Investigate whether the dissertation chair you might be interested in working with forms doctoral committees based on student input and interest.* By looking over the committee signature forms that have been filed for students, you will quickly be able to tell whether the committees are custom designed or cookie cutter.
- *Look up your institution's guide on the preparation of theses and dissertations.* Seek clarification from your advisor on areas of ambiguity. Act on this as early as possible so your planned production conforms to the official guidelines. Become familiar with any electronic theses/dissertations requirements. In addition, list special e-features that your institution will accommodate. Consider the content of your work from the perspective of technology-based elements (e.g., table set-up) that will enhance the quality and accessibility of your ideas or results. Also, ease the work for readers through user-friendly hyperlinks that facilitate automated movement among the parts of your work (e.g., table of contents, tables, references).

GLOSSARY

doctoral candidacy. Graduate-degree-seeking students who have completed their coursework and, if required, comprehensive qualifying exams to become eligible to register for dissertation hours.

electronic dissertations/theses (ETD). Theses/dissertations are submitted electronically as a portable document format (PDF) file to the home institution. ETD offers latitude for customizing manuscripts, such as use of hypermedia and audiovisual media (e.g., pictures, music, video, audio). Templates from the home university's graduate school specify parameters; for example, citing/creating links to websites or objects in the "outside world" that might change is discouraged. The final version of the entire work is the purview of advisors.

hidden curriculum. Implicit messages communicated to students about their place in school and society, and their perceived worth and value.

noncompleter candidates. Individuals experiencing program attrition; ABD students who did not complete their programs within their college's stipulated period of time (usually seven years from entry into the doctoral program in education) and for whom reinstatement would need to be officially sought (Stripling 2004).

peer/cohort group. Study, peer, or support groups; can be peer or faculty–student driven, and formal as well as informal (Mullen et al. 2007).

time to degree. The total years taken to complete a doctorate, which varies by discipline (Heiberger and Vick 2003, chronicle.com/jobs/2003/07/2003070301c.htm, para. 37). Also called time to doctorate.

Chapter Five

Joining Mentoring Networks and Programs

Against all odds, while Ryan was a doctoral candidate, he overcame a major hurdle, making it conceivable that we can all "Climb every mountain / Ford every stream / Follow every rainbow / Till you find your dream" (Andrews 1965).

Yes, I certainly had a "mountain" to climb for my PhD. Since having graduated one year ago, I got a job as an assistant professor at a very reputable university. The "mountain" I will discuss occurred between my proposal defense and the dissertation—in fact, it seemed to suddenly arise out of nowhere. In accordance with what I had thought was an all-around agreement with my committee and myself, I proposed to conduct a standardized statistical analysis of data on my subject population—high-school students from single-parent, low-income homes. You see, I am quantitatively trained so was stunned when, at my proposal defense, it was somehow decided that the proposed statistical treatment and analysis failed to make sense. I thought this was the bomb being dropped on me, only to realize it had merely been the test explosive. In fact, the committee had also decided to fail my defense, meaning that I should *not* have been permitted to continue in my program.

However, the committee agreed that I could proceed as long as I changed my methodology to a qualitative study. My committee, together with the administration, had decided that one and only one person was right to guide this new journey. So, of course, everything hinged on whether the expert who had been the outside chair would agree to be my new major professor. Almost overnight, "Dr. Caller" got on board in this unanticipated capacity. The nature of our relationship would determine my progress and fate. Thankfully, we hit it off right away. He seemed determined to get me through. He had carefully read my dissertation proposal, made comments on it, and said, to my relief, that I was "brilliant, just caught on a methodological snag." Tucked inside his notes was a list of qualitative texts I was to read, along with areas to study (e.g., philosophical outlook, study design, case study, action research, data collection, reliability issues). His pointers ended up being markers on my new roadmap. An experienced chair and a strong student advocate, he was from outside not only my college but also my discipline! I was glad that I did not have to change my rationale, context, or subject population for my study.

For fifteen months, I worked intensively, retooling my thinking, reading new books, and discoursing about qualitative research. This very exciting approach to studying human problems is something I am still trying to understand in some basic ways. I moved successfully through my proposal defense—and the committee, by the way, had a few replacements on it, folks I knew and liked. Once over this hurdle, I worked on my dissertation for days at a time, learning new frameworks. I interacted with my new chair and his study group, getting detailed feedback on my chapters. I felt totally accepted, even though I'd been trained to approach research problems statistically.

Despite my nervousness, I managed to feel more confident before the repeat of the proposal defense occurred—it took hard work to bring my self-esteem back up, and my chair maintained faith in me. As a presenter, I was very well prepared and obtained through my chair detailed feedback (and approval) on both the oral and written aspects.

For the dissertation defense, I followed this work pattern with my mentor. I even managed to enjoy myself during the defense—indulging in the things that I wanted to talk about, even alluding at one point to "the cobweb" in the corner of my mind. I'm at peace now, though indebted to my committee and study group for all they did to help me along. However, I simply could *never* have gotten the doctorate without my new chair's all-out investment in me.

CASE ANALYSIS

This powerful story came my way after I contacted graduate-program coordinators from different universities in the United States. Seeking a diverse sample, I asked if they could invite doctoral candidates and recent graduates in their college "to submit a story revealing the greatest mountain you have had to climb thus far or overall in your doctoral process." In all, fifteen stories from nine universities were forwarded, seven of which were roughly the length of Ryan's account.

Although Ryan's was the most dramatic account I received, others (amounting to about 40 percent of the sample) also addressed academic struggles. Within the group of potential noncompleters, several of the candidates were grappling with the proposal defense (after having been denied committee signatures), and several others hinted at attrition based on such overwhelming problems as unsatisfactory (or lack of) progress, multiple responsibilities, recent promotions at work, and new family obligations. The rest of the respondents also identified "mountains" (e.g., defenses, personal insecurities, conflicts), but these were all being resolved.

Habits of mind and attitudes toward learning, as well as conflict resolutions, were revealed in my analysis of the data, in particular where the same type of problem was viewed differently. For example, while some doctoral candidates identified conflicts with committee members as insurmountable problems, others viewed these as workable. Interestingly, the student responses offer a glimpse into what happens nationally with attrition, foreshadowing the graduation of about one half of those in doctoral candidacy (see preface).

Returning to Ryan's case, let us pause to explore the crises, personal and scholarly, that he explicitly and implicitly mentioned. In my view, the failure of the dissertation proposal defense is the salient event through which a domino effect of emotional and intellectual hurdles occurred: methodological refocusing, new dissertation chair, reformed committee, new study group, shattered nerves, and plummeted self-esteem.

Notably, this doctoral candidate accepted the difficult scholarly challenge before him even though he felt defeated. Nonetheless, with the support and faith of mentors, colleagues, and family, and, most importantly, the strength derived from his own inner resources, he managed to recreate himself within a relatively short time. Successful defenses followed, of both his revised proposal and dissertation—and within just fifteen months. (Obviously, the academic community as a whole can find ways to better guide students through the advanced stages of the doctorate; in this spirit, consult appendixes D and E for templates that are in actual use.)

Ryan's achievement was inextricably linked to mentors, which may be why he attributed much of his success to external sources. Consequently, the crucial role his **inner core** played, particularly the originating sources of personal strength, was just a sidebar. Wanting to learn more about Ryan's inner resources that enabled his success, I probed his thinking with this e-mail message:

Dear Ryan:

Thank you for your story. Can you reveal more about your "inner core"—what scaffolds you put in place or what you did that helped you to cope with the first proposal defense outcome and new committee? For example, did you practice meditation? Do yoga? Rely on friendship or familial support? Turn to prayer? I am curious to learn why you did not just pick up and leave your university program after the salient event of failure had occurred and also how you managed to survive the tremendous learning curve ahead. Put simply, where did your psychological resiliency come from?

C. M.

In response, I received fifteen paragraphs e-mailed to me at 5 a.m., the following of which is an excerpt focused on my questions and extending back in time:

Dear Dr. Mullen:

The PhD became a mountain for me to climb and proof of a theory I've always had that my given talents were unusual and that responding to my instincts with action was a personal strength. As a contemporary author has written, the universe works in mysterious ways, helping us live out our personal journeys and dreams. I gravitate toward this magical notion.

In my family, advanced education was presumed to be a standard, not a privilege. My older sisters graduated from Ivy League colleges on scholarships. My parents, grandparents, and uncles were also college graduates. However, my father had not completed his master's degree in politics, contributing to my pushing forward. It was not until my father passed away that I learned this family truth: his work had been rejected, characterized as an anti-American thesis on McCarthyism. Refusing to change his topic, he promptly left college. Unlike my mother, I found it inspiring that my father could not be arm wrestled against his will. As he lay dying, I vowed to finish and did, graduating with my doctorate just one year later.

When I started my PhD, I had the feeling of having the opportunity to live out my personal legend. One of my sisters died in the nineties. Had Sally been alive during my doctoral studies, I would have never been so unprepared at my first proposal defense. In retrospect, I believe she would have counseled me against defending my work on the basis of the statistical design being proposed. She thought my ideas were of the qualitative sort anyway and, though she was a statistician, attended to instinctual matters herself.

At the time my college assigned the outside chair for the proposal defense, I had no idea who the professor was. But I intuited that Dr. Caller had been put in my life for a special reason, to help me live out my personal legend. When my first proposal defense failed, I was devastated, but a dream returned to me. Several weeks earlier I had dreamed that while preparing a recipe for a big dinner party I found a live rat in a bag of flour. My friend and I stared at the rat, puzzling over whether to throw out the sack. Josie suggested that we use the best of the flour after delicately removing the rat—the flour, I suspect, represented my dissertation and the rat, well, at that time I was mystified. The next day the outside chair of my defense actually telephoned to introduce himself and, when I expressed my nervousness over the upcoming defense, replied, "Ryan, think of your proposal defense and committee as a warm dinner party among good friends to which you have invited me, a guest." I nearly fell out of my office chair!

Soon after the failed defense, I told a continuing committee member that I was going to quit the program. He said that I needed to "play the game" right and act on Dr. Caller's advice about reforming the committee. (Dr. Caller had been my outside chair at the defense and then, suddenly, became my new supervisor.) Others also exclaimed, "Get rid of the rat!" Dr. Caller and I delicately removed "the rat" and another naysayer. Dr. Caller was the inspiration behind my having kept "the flour" and discarding "the rat" so my dinner party could continue. I am indeed celebrating!

In addition to his new dissertation chair (a university accommodation and exception to that university's graduate school policy), committee members, colleagues, and family, Ryan's external resources included, importantly, the professor's support group: "I had the feeling of being an anomaly, someone with a strange gift that was too difficult to harness into any workable form." Within this context he was accepted on his own terms and, because he had to explain himself in layman's terms to peers outside his discipline, his cryptic scholarly style of writing vastly improved, becoming readable.

Ryan's internal resources included his philosophy of "personal legends," dream awareness, and intuitive understanding. He also identified, as other core-strengthening activities, yoga, meditation, prayer, and exercise. His especially trying dissertation journey had ended positively, strengthened by a sense of inner peace.

INFORMAL MENTORING: NETWORKS AND GROUPS

Mentoring Network Types

A major facet of Ryan's account is the mentoring network, which took forms ranging from his professor's study group to his family, his yoga class, and, finally, his new doctoral committee. To varying degrees, each played a vital role in his development and adjustment.

Different types of mentoring networks exist and, for this reason, graduate students should not rely on only a single source. These networks range from the traditional to the modern and from the formal to the informal. And they take multiple forms; for example, some manifestations are faculty led, whereas others are student led, and while some are strictly electronic, others are more personal or combined with e-forms. In this section I examine the informal expression of the mentoring network, equivalent to the faculty-led study group that Ryan joined. In the academy, the support group is a critical vehicle for aiding individual adjustment, survival, and success.

Learning communities and networks can be one of the most important doorways in the academy. Individuals who join or create discussion groups on the Internet are seeking a range of opportunities, such as the chance to share their social profile with others worldwide. Others connect more directly with like-minded individuals who express the same core values and commitment to causes. Identity-based websites are popular for bringing together individuals seeking to fulfill a mission, such as providing role modeling and resources for disadvantaged and underserved populations.

Peer/cohort groups (see chapters 1 and 4) address the particular interests and needs of graduate populations. Cohort mentoring (defined in chapter 1) is an expression of group learning built upon faculty–student membership, including in educational leadership programs like my own. This type of mentoring uses a team-based transformational model that makes group work the primary method of support, performance, and achievement (Michaelsen, Knight, and Fink 2002). Academic networks exhibit social acts of interdependence through discourse, critique, and demonstration.

Networks, such as the support group that Ryan alluded to, are typically informal mentoring vehicles that promote intellectual and professional development, belonging, and acceptance, including for those who feel somehow different. **Informal mentoring** can involve greater commitment by individual faculty supervisors than **formal mentoring**, yet it also necessitates higher risk, as the assistance promised may or may not happen, and it often does not. However, informal mentoring can be more beneficial for protégés in many cases. Informality provides the conditions for interpersonal bonding and comentoring to occur more naturally. Unfortunately, few descriptive studies of informal group mentoring in education have been published (see, e.g., Mullen 2005, 2011a), so this premise remains largely untested.

Mentoring groups are suitable not only for advanced students writing theses/dissertations. At the master's level, collaborative faculty–student support groups unite students and their instructor for a short but intense and synergistic period of learning. At the doctoral level, the group functions as a cohort that joins doctoral students and their academic mentor(s) for a specified number of years and presumes a deeply relational, lifelong model of learning and leading. As recognized in the adult-education literature, dissertation cohorts fulfill the expedient goal of allowing dissertation supervisors to manage a number of doctoral students as a group.

Comentoring Learning Structure

Whether in an informal or formal context, the comentoring or collaborative structure of learning enables individuals who relate well as colleagues to make significant progress (see chapter 3). A focus on mutuality stresses the value of interdependent, reciprocal learning that challenges assumptions about hierarchy, rank, status, and, consequently, who is doing the teaching and the learning.

The issue of belonging is also readily apparent, as nontraditional or nondominant groups and individuals are deliberately built into the mentoring process. Feminist critiques of group process generally focus on issues of authority, power, and oppression (e.g., Beyene et al. 2002). Mentoring in its reenvisioned forms ideally promotes social justice agendas and enhances diversity, affirming difference in relation to race, ethnicity, disability, sexual orientation, and more. Political activism identities include lesbian, gay, bisexual, transgender, queer, and questioning (LGBTQQ, also known as LGBT).

Applied to a support-group context, comentoring can help members transcend issues often attributed to one-to-one mentoring. For example, the important but unsettled issue of whether it is critical to construct mentor pairing with respect to similarities in gender, ethnicity, age, and discipline (e.g., Wilson, Pereira, and Valentine 2002) becomes greatly diminished when groups are put together because they are diverse.

Some students from traditionally disadvantaged groups might feel that mentors who are ethnic, for instance, would be more ideal but nonetheless draw strength from cohort peers to whom they can best relate. And women university students, who have been reported to generally prefer female mentors because of the perceived opening for personal contact and the value placed on interpersonal skills (Wilson et al. 2002), can derive satisfaction from mixed-gendered groups led by male mentors. (See chapter 4 for more about cultural affinity and diversity in mentor pairings.)

Formal Mentoring: Programs and Systems

Formal mentoring is a more familiar but not necessarily more frequent practice than informal mentoring. Note that research on cohorts deals almost exclusively with formal mentoring because the institutionalized option is both visible and customary. Horn (2001) and Mullen (2005) add that the advantages of the formal structure (e.g., developing critical skills in writing and research) can outweigh the drawbacks (e.g., new faculty mentors must adjust to premade, unfamiliar cohorts).

Elements of Formal Mentoring

Assuming you are a student seeking strategies and options for promoting your survival and success in graduate school, how might you get started? For one thing, you will need to know what elements make formal mentoring programs as effective as possible. Brown, Davis, and McClendon (1999) stated that these ten activities (in random order) are part of outstanding mentoring programs:

1. Assignment of a faculty mentor
2. Assignment of a student or peer advisor
3. Formally established student or peer networks
4. Academic assistance workshops
5. Computer skills workshops and assistance
6. Research, writing, and professional publication guidance
7. Social activities and programming
8. Provision of financial assistance
9. Orientation or welcome programs
10. Career decision-making and planning workshops (3–4)

Guidelines for Groups

Guidelines are common in formal support groups and, though worth doing, they are less characteristic of informal groups. Graduate program cohorts have formal agreements, even contracts. These are either created within the group itself or established as a preformed document that the members discuss and possibly sign. General guidelines include the critical components of learning environment (the conditions established for learning, the physical setup of the room, and the schedule), psychological safety (encouragement of sharing and trust between students and teachers, constructive criticism, and playfulness), ground rules (the need for agreement on the direction/focus of the group, space for all to speak and be heard, embracing of emotions, and prevention of abusive and abrasive conduct).

The Cohort Structure

Support, satisfaction, progress, and completion are among the benefits reaped by cohort participants (Horn 2001; Mullen 2011a). Specifically, faculty–student mentoring cohorts can support numerous, salient outcomes. Benefits include:

- Efficiency of program delivery (Laing and Bradshaw 2003)
- A professional development emphasis within twenty-first-century graduate programs (Tareilo and Bizzell 2012)
- Shift away from the traditional, top-down style of discourse toward a collegial style within the group setting (Laing and Bradshaw 2003)
- Persistence and retention, reflected by a higher completion rate than traditional doctoral programs (Dorn and Papalewis 1997; Horn 2001)
- Team-building practices that maintain focus and direction and improve task completion (Dorn and Papalewis 1997)
- Focus on interpersonal relations and dynamics, providing fertile ground for promoting a critical review of social-justice issues in schools (Horn 2001)
- Scholarly writing for guiding professional practice, collaborative identity development, and informed decision making (Mullen 2001; 2005, 26)

- Technology-based learning in online cohorts (Tareilo and Bizzell 2012)

For students in cohort-mentoring situations, they can practice the very skills, thinking, and capacities expected of adult learners in school and at work. In the educational leadership and counseling psychology fields, among others where school projects, programs, and processes depend upon cooperative teamwork, it makes sense to practice such skills within small graduate groups. The support-group context, whether formal or informal, is an excellent vehicle for graduate students to develop the thinking and personal skills required of exemplary inquirers, cooperative team players, and proficient leaders.

Graduate students especially value cohorts with a dissertation or thesis focus. These confront the perennial problem of student disillusionment and academic failure, as well as writing and inquiry challenges. A doctoral student who e-mailed me reinforced this message: "Everyone knows that many students finish classes but do not earn a doctorate. Our cohort helps me stay true to completing the dissertation."

Cohorts that foster student-centered inquiry report such outcomes as research and writing progress, real-world application, professional development, and collegial sharing and friendship (Horn 2001). Benefit also accrues from experiencing coherence in what one is learning, as a Writers in Training (WIT) member shared:

> Traditional courses are all about work for others and nothing connects, and then you're supposed to spend years writing a dissertation alone. I had resigned myself to this vision until the WITs helped me to see this is old-school philosophy.

Drawbacks must not be overlooked and should be carefully monitored, including structural and organizational problems and penalties for students unable to follow a prescribed program (Laing and Bradshaw 2003). Browne-Ferrigno, Barnett, and Muth (2003) cautioned that while many university faculty members (including me) strongly favor the cohort model in their own programs, "little empirical evidence exists about the long-term effects of the cohort experience on [for example] aspiring principals' future professional practices" (277). In the research, there is also lopsided focus on the learning and transformation that occur within the cohort structure, without much attention on the impact on students' leadership practices and workplace behaviors.

Higher-education support groups that function formally operate within the university's schedules and calendars, or, at best, on alternative calendars (such as Saturday meetings). New territory concerns informal doctoral cohorts that have incorporated such formal structural elements as management, expectation, and scheduling.

However, the educational and corporate literature seems to overly differentiate formal from informal mentoring rather than seeing their blended possibilities. One such notion presents a view of the modified informal cohort as thriving in part because of its structured components—bimonthly meetings, turn taking, and guidelines for producing work. (For an extended case study of my seven-year cohort called the WIT, see Mullen [2005].) Conversely, formal cohorts that promote qualities of the informal arrangement—such as student input on all decision-making matters, including scheduling, direction, and assessment—are more familiar (Horn 2001).

A STUDY-GROUP TEMPLATE

Readers interested in forming a cohort or group, whether formal or informal, or who want to make changes to their own study groups might find these suggestions useful.

1. *Identity and belonging.* Students struggle with acceptable writing style and quality in educational research (e.g., humanistic and social science models of inquiry) and likely encounter a learning curve in achieving satisfactory results. Various approaches can be used to address these challenges (e.g., the creation of a student-driven agenda that includes questions for discussion).
2. *Interdependence and goals.* Group cohesion and a can-do attitude appear to academically and socially motivate many individuals. With one another's support, meeting deadlines and following guidelines become easier. In fact, the simple accountability of knowing that their work will be peer reviewed can encourage doctoral students to focus and excel. Many desire to be associated with productive learning communities that model quality work.
3. Interdependence also means that students will sometimes comprehend one another more clearly than their mentors; they learn how to decode academic language and unravel complex messages. Also, cohorts can work toward empowerment through heterogeneous forms that reach across programmatic levels and differences, primarily gender, race, class, disability, and political identification. Momentary discomforts—some attributed to ego conflicts—are all part of the interdependence at play within almost any group and mentoring relationship (see chapter 4 for an elaboration on these themes).
4. *Faculty–student support and synergy.* Creating a socially vibrant mentoring model is critical for building positive synergy. More than either force acting alone, assistance from both peers and professors enables students to better develop scholastically. Indeed, a cohort's synergy can illuminate difficulties in socialization: The dissertation or thesis is a daunting task, unnatural to most. Cohorts facilitate adjustment for students because the use of peers as a "sounding board" breeds security, confidence, and risk taking.

In a subsection titled "Participate in Collegial Groups" of chapter 6, you will find more specifics for mentors and students prepared to act on the previous suggestions.

POINTS TO REMEMBER

Ryan's case provides powerful lessons to graduate students keen to learn the dynamics behind a peer's resiliency and success in which not just external influences but also resources play a key role (see chapter 3 for more information about resources). Students who are deeply in touch with their inner self, a process resulting from either a painful or peaked experience, can certainly make proactive protégés, as well as perceptive guides, confidants, or mentors. Most mentors have had to overcome various hardships in graduate school, including coping with a significant learning curve and surpassing difficulties, which only strengthens who they are today. Search for those who are survivors and trailblazers, with a profound story of identity transformation, to inspire your own journey.

Learning during a crisis in our lives means facing the situation and deriving insight or value from it when it is the toughest to do so. Ryan did just this. The plight of a crisis is such that we often do not see it coming or have time to prepare for it. Ryan's experience and growth suggest that someone of his caliber could make an outstanding mentor. His identity and doctorate were stripped away, but through this personal change process, were reclaimed.

People who know firsthand what it feels like, metaphorically speaking, to have recovered from having fallen not only develop resiliency but can also become an indomitable force of protection for others. Someone with the depth and intuitive capacity of this magnitude should be able to transfer what has been learned, creating empowering conditions of learning in which people can meet high expectations.

Overcoming crisis and trauma, Ryan found peace within. Once he resolved the turmoil associated with his degree, he consequently became much more competent as a researcher, more flexible intellectually, and perhaps best of all, more emotionally adept. Ryan has appreciation for the work of his committee, study group, and especially dissertation chair in helping his writing become intellectually rigorous and his inner core stronger. However, he might have overlooked two critical parties—the university administrators who facilitated his retention and "life-saving" mentoring relationship and, as controversial as this might sound, his former committee. The members who failed his defense did not insist that their vote be registered with the authorities and, moreover, they recommended a research methodology that better suited his study and lifelong sensibilities; several of the original members even stayed on, supporting him and the new chair.

Self-directed learning is critical for the development of self-knowledge (Merriam 2001), as well as reciprocity (see chapter 6). Ryan proved to be increasingly capable as a self-directed learner for the biographical and academic reasons explained. A primary role of the mentor, then, is to assist learners in enhancing their capability as self-directed learners, not to "save" them.

SUMMARY

Mentoring is an essential part of graduate education for all, no longer to be viewed as compensation for at-risk and struggling student populations (Gross 2002). Mentoring networks and programs offer students invaluable resources for the purposes of adjustment, socialization, liberation, belonging, support, acceptance, transformation, and promotion. Adopt the best guides possible as you encounter new doors, some of which are hard to open, others seemingly closed: Look inward, maintain your stride, and keep your chin up, no matter what.

Navigational Prompts

- *Write your story revealing the hardest or heaviest door (e.g., person, committee, group, tradition, process, procedure) you have confronted* so far or overall in graduate school. Instead of writing, try another medium such as drawing, sculpting, dancing, video making, or role playing.
- *Ask mentors about their own graduate stories of transformation* as a way of discovering who they are and what they value.
- *Generate a list of all of the formal and informal mentoring supports you can possibly identify* in your graduate-school context. What is being provided and by whom? Did you locate guidelines for students to follow? If so, what elements are stressed in them?

- *With a study group, analyze a member's transcription of an interview* for recurring words, phrases, and themes. Also, discuss areas of individual interest vis-à-vis the document that might aid in the inquiry of the topic at hand. Sample transcriptions can be used for this qualitative research activity so members can practice the related skills of analysis, discourse, and negotiation. For a book that describes steps of systematically coding verbal data, see Geisler's (2004) *Analyzing Streams of Language*. The helpful strategies presented for pursuing an in-depth analysis of verbal data—mainly, determining units of analysis such as paragraphs and exchanges, as well as coding schemes that can be comprehensive or selective in nature—will have to be adapted for particular groups.
- *Use "Documenting Changes on a Graduate Defense Form"* (appendix D) as an advanced organizer for any graduate defenses you give, visit, or oversee, or simply share it with colleagues. On it, faculty members' changes are listed and specified relative to the student's document, along with an overview and positive statements. Defending students will find it invaluable as a tool for managing all of the feedback and for making the necessary modifications to their work; such templates should be included in departmental and graduate handbooks. (Professors and students can scan this form and alter it as desired, bringing it with them to defenses so that the changes recommended can be more easily tracked at the time.)
- *Apply the "Listing Amendments on a Dissertation Review Form"* (appendix E) to your own study in progress as a doctoral candidate or as a supervisor of dissertation writers. This template can be used before or after the proposal and dissertation defenses. (Adopt the relevant ideas previously listed for appendix D.)
- *Identify all of the changes made in your proposals, chapters, and coauthored writings using, for example, the automatic tracking feature in Microsoft Word or a specialized software program of your choice.* Text changes are visually marked, typically in colors. Readers of your file can more readily see what you have changed in the original and help you with deciding what revisions to keep or further change. (Use this approach for highlighting revisions in your text *and* for specifying these on the "Listing Amendments on a Dissertation Review Form" [appendix E].)

GLOSSARY

formal mentoring. A one-on-one relationship between a mentor and protégé that has been assigned by another party; an institutionalized cohort led by a qualified mentor for a limited time and according to a predetermined schedule.

informal mentoring. Spontaneous (or naturally occurring) teaching and learning relationships that are not managed, structured, or officially recognized (Mullen 2007a).

inner core. "The heart of who we are" that goes deeper than personal beliefs and values (Apps 1996, 65); heart, or soul, is not a static thing "but a quality or dimension of experiencing life and ourselves," extending to "depth, value, relatedness, and personal substance" (Apps 1996, 65; relates to "selfhood," see preface).

self-directed learning. Taking personal responsibility for one's own progress, engaging in critical thought and introspection, and taking risks that lead to emancipation and support social action are all critical for the development of self-knowledge (Merriam 2001).

Chapter Six

Practicing Mutuality and Reciprocity

Kris, a new doctoral student hitting the ground running with a publication in hand, responds to two questions asked of fifty graduate students studying in different universities: "Have you had any authoring or publishing experiences with a professor, student, or another colleague? If so, who contributed what skills or portions to the work itself, and how do you feel about the overall experience?"

I am the proud author of a journal article with two professors. I contributed my pilot study from a master's course with one of them. Instead of just thanking me in the publication, they actually included me as third author. At the time they asked me to contribute, I had a lot on my plate—adjusting to my new school as a beginning teacher while looking into a doctoral program in a different state. I was getting psyched up to move, so I just e-mailed my pilot study without improving it. This article might have given me the edge in getting accepted into a really good university for my doctoral program because when I referred to this project during my interview, it sparked interest.

My pilot study features the research I did in secondary schools on the role of administrators and teachers communicating with technology inside the building and outside with communities. The professors added to my pilot study, putting it in the third person and analyzing it at great length. They included the technology user survey I developed (with my instructor's input) for teachers, administrators, students, and parents, and the early results. After talking directly with me and understanding more about my study, they included my reaction in their description of the results. For example, they thought it was important to build on the gulf I had identified in expectations between students/families who assumed that school personnel would regularly use the Internet and e-mail them and school personnel (teachers and administrators) who actually did.

The professors followed through, spending a few months writing the paper and improving my contribution. They addressed these major points:

- Concepts and frameworks related to communications technology and public relations (e.g., unresolved problems in public relations resulting from national technology standards; issues of equity and access to technology in schools)
- Key terms supported by the literature (e.g., communications technology and public relations)
- Relevant educational policies and standards for school leaders
- Know-how for school teachers and leaders, such as facilitating school–home partnerships through communications technology (e.g., e-newsletters) and closing the digital divide by giving people the skills and resources to use digital technologies
- The vital role of technology in public relations for school communities, drawing on stakeholder feedback, best practices, policies, and standards

I was asked for my input before the paper was sent off for review. I really liked the manuscript they wrote, so just one correction (to further conceal my identity). Then I got the proofs for final approval (after the professors had fixed them) and, finally, months later, the publication arrived. I am amazed by just how good the article really is. I appreciate all the work that went into it. I share the article with everyone who can bear to see it.

CASE ANALYSIS

As Kris suggests, the learning exchange that a student experiences in an academic relationship can be extremely beneficial. This can enhance motivation, model good practice, improve scholarly capacity, and foster success. Collaborative writing and coauthoring, while very challenging, can be stimulating learning experiences and when successful, these are academic and career gateways.

Beyond academic progress, these can contribute to a body of knowledge and make a difference for targeted readers and populations. Combined with learning new skills, students who have healthy mentoring relationships feel empowered and more scholastically capable. Kris's case provides a window into relational dynamics—specifically mutuality and reciprocity—that foster self-directed learning and interdependence between students and professors. Metaphorically, this student, who was raised to "stand on mountains" and "walk on stormy seas," felt "strong" on others' "shoulders." By demonstrating real-world writing for scholar-practitioners, Kris became "more than [she] can be" (Groban 2004).

Given what this doctoral student has communicated, how impressive do you find her contribution to the publishing experience? Before moving ahead, we need to clarify some concepts. Building on chapters 3 and 4, **mutuality** and *comentoring* refer to collaboration as student-centered learning and activism that forces antiquated systems to change. Mutuality and reciprocity, synergy, **connectivity**, and **interdependence** are at a premium in dynamic learning situations and environments.

Work relationships benefit from establishing clarification around mutuality and reciprocity and expectations for these learning dynamics. For this purpose, collaborators and potential coauthors can use the Mullen Mentoring-Based Reciprocity Gauge, a tool for reflectively gauging the extent to which a relationship, group, or network is mutual and reciprocal. This five-part schema arose out of my extensive experience with adult learners of coauthoring collaborations, along with statements from students and professors.

The Mullen Gauge is a framework denoting levels of **mentoring-based reciprocity**, ranging from the highest (5) to the lowest quality (1):

- *Exemplary* (5). The novice collaborator (e.g., graduate student) functions as a fully supportive partner, making necessary sacrifices; contributes equally to the text through shared or divided tasks, such as data collection, analysis, and writing, possibly identifying relevant journals or publishers, even preparing the manuscript for publication review; is available for revising the text if accepted with changes and for any follow-up work; expresses deepened curiosity over time; and will likely help prepare the work for presentation at a conference or for dissemination through the Internet (e.g., wiki, blog).
- *High* (4). The novice collaborator contributes in important ways, although not as extensively. Areas of contribution are impressive and can include data collection, analysis, writing, graphics, and materials production, as well as improving the work and possibly preparing it for dissemination.

- *Middle* (3). The novice collaborator provides valuable information or research data or writing (e.g., a pilot study or data set with preliminary analysis) for the larger work (manuscript).
- *Low* (2). The novice collaborator is engaged only superficially in the joint work and production; instead, s/he makes a minor contribution (e.g., creates a research schedule and surveys or interviews participants; verifies the professor's analysis of the data collected; supplies a portion of previously written, unpublished work).
- *Lowest* (1). The novice collaborator provides minimal support, typically not requiring sophisticated skills. S/he may, for example, do a preliminary search of digital databases, resources, and references using agreed-upon descriptors and prepare an annotated bibliography.

This broad, flexible framework can be applied to any scholarly situation involving writing, researching, creating, publishing, and disseminating. It can also be used in different collaborative relationships between faculty and students, students and their peers, and beginning faculty and seasoned faculty. Furthermore, it is relevant for distributing workloads in preferred formats, either in person or online.

After mulling over the schema, consider Kris's contribution to the coauthored work. What level of support and overall coauthoring effort did she bring to the writing project? Before concluding, consider her engagement in the work throughout the project—how intensive or complete was her involvement? Given these criteria, her contribution would likely be in the middle range (perhaps a score of 3). As a novice collaborator, she made quality contributions with respect to both her pilot study and personal reactions to the results that the professors had prepared. She removed herself from the intensive writing work that followed. Her contribution exclusively benefited the inception of the project.

Responding to my query, Kris explained her coauthors' contributions to the article. Their extensive efforts included the rewriting of her pilot study and the writing of the entire manuscript, as well as securing publication. As implied, Kris was neither expected to perform any of these activities nor was she prepared to. Although there is only one vantage point from which to view this coauthoring relationship—the student author's—from Kris's perspective it was undergirded by mutual understanding and benefited from the involvement of experienced scholars. No misconceptions or conflicts were mentioned. She was positive about her scholarly debut—she reported that the article had academic capital.

Overall, then, Kris benefited from the publishing experience in these ways:

- Pride in and excitement about her own accomplishment
- A competitive edge in the doctoral-admissions process
- Seeing a seed study's development into a larger scholarly work
- Opportunity to debrief about personal responses to the data
- Exposure to/inclusion in the review and proofreading stages

Regardless of whether this particular coauthoring relationship was forged into a full-fledged partnership, the student acquired valuable knowledge and academic capital, in addition to interpersonal and disseminating skills. Beyond learning about teamwork and negotiating her contribution to a larger, multiauthored work, Kris witnessed the results of a seed study being developed into a rigorous work that passed muster with a journal's peer reviewers.

PRINCIPLES OF COMENTORING-BASED RECIPROCITY

Desirable Strengths and Qualities

Participants engaged in comentoring-based reciprocity exhibit commitment and willingness, in addition to numerous other strengths. Anyone interested in developing, improving, or enriching relationships with short- and long-term goals will want to foster mutuality in learning and two-way gains.

Consider this expanded list of strengths, also human qualities, developed by Kealy (2000), for fostering mutuality:

- *Interpersonal skills*. The need for teamwork and team building in a culturally diverse world. Given the complexity of current research questions and the methodologies for addressing them, the days of the lone researcher are fading fast. A key word in academia is *collaboration*, and graduates are expected to work effectively as partners in interdisciplinary teams and are assessed as such for jobs and promotions.
- *Versatility*. The capability of using alternative methodologies and knowledge bases. Along with the ability to work with scholars from other disciplines, future professionals in academe need to know how to study problems from multiple perspectives. Inherent strengths of both the orthodox and unconventional approaches to research are being brought to bear on today's problems. Valiantly defending one's knowledge niche or method (without knowledge of or sensitivity to others) is an anachronism that probably comes across as a defense mechanism.
- *Resourcefulness*. Advisors have a role in ensuring that students can use the available and expected university resources for achieving program goals. Technological mastery, including computer literacy, for analyzing, publishing, and presenting research, is an indispensable skill for academic careers. Advisors foster technological competency through leading by example and learning from students and specialists.
- *Integrity*. Before students graduate and begin a career or change direction, professional moral standards should be evident in their character, work, and dealings with others. Advisors are among those who need to communicate what these expectations are and for whom they should be modeled. Integrity (e.g., academic honesty) is perhaps the most highly regarded quality in this list.
- *Knowledge*. An essential part of successful mentoring is knowing one's discipline, which requires staying abreast of current research in the field. Similarly, mentors should urge their students to avidly read professional journals and books to build on ideas. As Krathwohl (1994) advises, if mentors encourage *active* reading, students can get into the habit of mindfully and critically processing what they read and their natural inquisitiveness will follow, along with a flow of connected ideas.
- *Humility*. Not to be confused with timidity or meekness, it is, instead, the quality that holds arrogance in check. Humility is a source of strength and compassion. Egotistical and self-serving behaviors can lead to alienation. In academia, intellectual humility is a catalyst for knowledge. (185–86)

Ethics in Adult Learning

Ethical issues and dilemmas are common in the work of scholars and these permeate and influence your own decision making. Based on Shapiro and Stefkovich's (2010) prominent work in ethics in adult learning and leadership (that builds on the foundational work of many researchers), the following framework delineates broad descriptions of four types, the fourth one of which is an original contribution. All of these types of ethics interweave and combine across in real-life situations:

1. *Ethic of justice.* This ethic focuses on the abstract principles of rights, laws, and privileges as the overarching principle of justice and in accordance with societal understandings that teach individuals how to behave in their communities, regardless of a situation's particular circumstances.
2. *Ethic of critique.* The ethic of critique focuses on issues of social justice that emerge out of a critical theory lens and that focus attention on issues of power, authority, hierarchy, culture, language, race, gender, and social class.
3. *Ethic of care.* This paradigm emphasizes context and relationship, spotlighting connections, collaboration, cooperation, interpersonal value, learning, and a sense of belonging in one's daily work and as part of decision making.
4. *Ethic of the profession.* This ethic refers to issues that leaders must be aware of with respect to personal and professional codes of behavior and ethical standards of competence; the codes translate into leading and developing an ethical work environment, in addition to setting examples by such means as articulating statements of morality by members of the profession.

Ethic of duty (see Pratt 1998) can be viewed as a component of the more comprehensive ethic of the profession. The duty ethic rechannels the endless issue of right and wrong, rooting moral questions and decisions in the essential duties expected of all professionals in education (and other domains of work) for guiding ethical conduct and competent behavior.

Ethics refers to people's sense of justice, critique, caring, and profession, and to high professional moral standards and intellectual honesty (see also chapter 2). Ethical conduct is an expression of respect and responsible, fair behavior, which shows up in how people govern themselves in real-life and online environments. Trustworthiness and reliability go hand in hand, as in when a professor or student promises the other work for which there is an agreement but no follow-through. A different kind of example of the ethic of the profession in action involves a violation of professional codes, as in the use of materials passed off as one's own and not properly acknowledged. Handy digital access to open-access resources, proliferating worldwide, necessitates professional behavior, as well as widespread reeducation.

Even in how she presents her story, Kris's vignette suggests ethics that influence her thinking and professional behavior. Ethics of the profession and of duty seem evident, since even her research expresses her concern about high-school leaders' fulfillment of their duties as public relations communicators. She thinks they should communicate regularly using technology not as a means unto itself but as a practice for fostering communications and, likely, connections with families. Issues of justice and caring are not explicit in her opening case, but they are suggestive where teachers and administrators are said to have the responsibility of communicating digitally with students and families.

Beyond e-mail, extended use of communications technology includes updated websites and bulletins, blogs that invite comments, online modules for students, and adaptive software for students with disabilities and other populations, including gifted students. An accommodation that is not new is storing homework assignments so students and guardians can access them. School practitioners are expected, in Kris's mind and in accordance with national technology standards, to create conditions for maximizing student learning.

Changing Power Hierarchies

An ethic of justice, caring, critique, the profession, and duty, or a mixture of these might knowingly or unknowingly drive mentors and students in their work. Critical thinkers are *not* accommodating of the status quo in the academy (schools and elsewhere) that shows up in the privileges of rank and role separation.

Educators who are in earnest about manifesting an ethic of care honor the gifts that the novice possesses, as well the promise of what the adult learner—*and* themselves—can become through collaboration and helpful critique. Through "being in-relation with the other" (Pratt 1998, 119), professors and students for whom care is a moral guide can forge meaningful connections that inspire others. When these energies are geared toward creating equitable conditions for access to and success within all schools, systems of power are challenged and sometimes even transformed.

Kris's story illustrates the possibilities of empowerment, even while the faculty–student relationship itself remains asymmetrical (i.e., the professors did the leading). Even the most exemplary collaborative relationships between coauthoring teachers and learners tend to be asymmetrical. Issues of status, power, and authority are all engrained in our very being. Also, there remain differences in what each individual can give to the relationship. Predictions about quality of contribution are not dependent on who the teacher is and the learner, although background knowledge, skill, tenacity, and motivation are key determinants.

Marriage is "a good framework from which to consider a comentoring relationship" (Miller 1999, xiii). Miller, a former education dean, explained:

> While many believe in marriage as an "equal" partnership in its totality, certainly what each member has to contribute to the other is not equal, situation by situation. In some instances one partner has far more knowledge and background and can contribute greatly to the advancement of the other, while in other instances those roles will be reversed. This takes both individuals who are willing to teach and learn and a recognition that these roles can change, based on the type of learning to occur. (xiii)

Miller's outlook on education suggests new possibilities for mutuality and reciprocity between teacher and learner, leader and follower, and mentor and mentee. In contrast, power differences and hierarchies fan the flames of competition, isolation, and selfishness, forcing students and professors to act in ways that they might not otherwise. The comentoring vision does not accommodate student withdrawal from sources of support or treatment of students as interruptions, "blank slates," or "lesser than." Examples of not only faculty but also institutional and organizational support include targeted skills development, assistantships and scholarships, coteaching, payment, recognition or credit, opportunities and recommendations, and career advice and preparation. Comentoring relationships, networks, and especially whole-community efforts, unify people's commitment to ethics of justice, critique, caring, and duty from all walks of life. Humane treatment and meaningful work inspire people to work together to make a difference.

Beyond One-Way Mentoring

One-way mentoring is a traditional, even limited, approach to learning in higher-education institutions. For example, in traditional apprenticeships, only one party (the learner) has something to learn, and the other party (the mentor) has knowledge. Yet many mentors and students learn from one another in such enriching relationships as comentoring, team-based mentoring, or networked mentoring (see section in this chapter, "Participate in Collegial Groups," and chapters 2, 5, and 10).

It is not unusual to see graduate students relying heavily on one-way systems of mentoring exclusively with their advisors or doctoral advisory/dissertation committees. They turn only to their advisors or committees for intensive feedback, including brainstorming and preliminary writing. To do otherwise means having ownership over their ideas, writing, and learning. Students will want to avoid being overdemanding or dependent, and mentors will want to prove responsive and reassuring without being a human crutch (Barkham 2005).

Inescapably, it is an illusion to think that it only takes the student and advisor to produce a high-quality thesis or dissertation. A "village" of interacting professors, students, and staff members contribute to move students through programs to the point of completion, in addition to invisible workers. These "busy bees" are from different parts of the university (and outside world), fulfilling support functions in such areas as student affairs, instructional technology, and digital cataloging. Increasingly, students are learning skills that support themselves—take, for example, the fact that many writers function as a digital librarian, locating hard-to-find materials using the Internet and other technology tools.

While the thesis and dissertation require self-directed learning, the process necessitates that students have reciprocal exchanges within a highly functional support system. Reciprocity is integral to self-directed learning and a student's success (e.g., Mullen 2005).

Affirming this point, Wisker and Braun (2004) assembled a group of newly minted PhDs to discuss areas of support for student researchers. One of their questions was about personal and institutional strategies. Repeatedly, the participants disclosed that their greatest support systems were external ("sharing ideas with colleagues") and internal ("constant inner self-dialogues on questions") (4). One PhD said that while "researchers are individualists who often work alone, if their ideas are to take root and grow, they need regular contact with others and feedback on their creations" (5).

The PhDs in the Wisker and Braun study said that developmental programs (e.g., teams, workshops, and projects) beyond supervisory relationships (i.e., faculty mentors) were major systems of support. Reciprocity was tagged as "working with supervisors" across multiple platforms, such as in person, by e-mail, and through Internet conferencing. The mentoring process yielded, for one PhD, "high scaffolding and new points of view," "guidance" that supported "creative and constant dialogue," and help finding "the right ideas" (5).

One-way mentoring can work effectively for students, as just seen, but not always, and certainly not always for professors. Case in point, when doing the research for this book, I invited impromptu examples of reciprocity in faculty–student writing relationships. None of the fifteen professors provided a "glowing" representation. Many were stumped, describing solid one-way mentoring relationships at best.

When further prompted, most of the professors revealed they had not collaborated on writing with a student. But a few did describe coauthorships (usually on conference papers and a few on articles) where doctoral students had made competent contributions or just half-hearted ones. A few professors described single-authored chapters they had received from students for their own edited books and monographs that were underdeveloped, requiring extensive rewriting. The mentors put in extra time for publication to happen. At most, they characterized coauthoring relationships within the lower to middle ranges of the reciprocity schema (presented earlier in this chapter), implying modest assistance from students.

Why might some student collaborators exhibit capacity within the lower to middle ranges of mutuality?

- Students will need months and years to develop the necessary scholarly skills to cultivate sophistication in research and writing.
- Students need to learn to take ownership of writing in all of its complexity in order to collaborate more effectively.
- Students need to overcome socialization geared at knowing their place and assimilating role identities that do not fit them.

In the publishing experiences of my faculty colleagues with student coauthors (and coeditors), their overall contributions range from levels 1 through 4, with exceptional work at level 5. While I personally derive value from all types of coauthoring relationships, I appreciate collaborations marked by passion for the topic and a strong commitment to the project throughout, including revisions.

Collaboration fueled by mentoring-based reciprocity can become the purview of many more academicians. Students who are new to the habits and skills that foster mutually beneficial, synergistic partnerships can best develop these with models. Strive to develop balanced partnerships with committed, willing professors and peers. Take the time to build trust and use your talent, and in turn elicit theirs.

Strategies for Developing Reciprocity

Write Your Life Philosophy

You are not alone with the question, "who am I?" Your identity matters to your personal and professional growth—it is the hinge on which future development depends (Chickering and Reisser 1993). Theory and practice are very much informed by one another. Beliefs, attitudes, and values, aspects of personal **life philosophy**, are real-life influences in the work we do and life we lead (Zinn 1998).

My life philosophy has evolved through multiple influences and collaborations with professors and students in mentoring, leadership, and social justice. I make relationships my foothold for scholarship because I believe we live more completely *in* the experience of "making" with others. For me, "making" is not only about creative production but also about creativity in relationship, community, and interaction.

Dewey's (1938) principle of interaction supports mentoring-based reciprocity. Interaction "includes what is done by the educator and the way in which it is done, not only words spoken but [also] the tone of voice in which they are spoken" (45). This sensibility extends to the "total social set-up of the situations in which the person is engaged" (45), so that the "objective conditions" of learning are influenced by the quality of interaction.

While there are abundant opportunities for being responsive and interactive using mobile and digital technologies, the high-volume demands have "put on trial" our very life philosophies. **Cyber-wellness** is the new frontier where wellness of professors and students is challenged. Student-centered, highly responsive advisors struggle to care for their psychological and emotional well-being in the digital environment. Graduate students who work full time in high-demand positions especially seek adaptations to the higher education environment that include "live" electronic access to professors during off-hours.

Strategies for developing reciprocity in comentoring relationships benefit from mutual understandings of not only the work to be done and how but also of how people express themselves online, as well as respect for private time, including restorative needs.

Writing your life philosophy can translate into meaningful connections and relationships for which mutuality is the glue. Knowing who you are and what you are becoming can enhance your ability to develop a critical capacity, problem solve at complex levels, and deepen self-awareness (Zinn 1998). Knowing who the others are around you and what they are becoming takes awareness to the next level.

In my digital notebook (an evolving collection of digital tablet, laptop, desktop, thumb drive, and regular paper) reside journals—jottings and recordings of my spontaneous ideas for writing alone and with others. This natural repository enables the development of mutuality in my academic relationships and comentoring.

User-friendly tools are conducive to journaling and dialoging in cyberspace in ways that simultaneously foster productivity and reciprocity. Examples include free blogging in either private or public spaces, with attention on personalizing your messages and eliciting commentaries from coauthors and/or intended readers. Collaborating using software designed for text upload, response, and response tracking (such as Google Docs, docs.google.com, and Crocodoc, crocodoc.com) offers real-time spaces in which to write, create, and respond while accessing documents online.

Tech-savvy individuals using different software platforms can foster **dialogue journaling**. Digital tools spawned by Web 2.0, the second generation of the Internet, allow for comentoring worldwide through document access and live interchanges. Reciprocity is spawned with a digital presence and commitment. Students and professors are teaching one another how to personalize collaborative online writing tools for study, interaction, and progress toward goals. Writers/readers can highlight their own responses (e.g., by using different colors) to a selected text (e.g., thesis/dissertation proposal), which can increase interest and motivation and enhance interdependence for teams.

A "Crocodoc team" tested just such an experiment. Members were seasoned and beginning scholar-practitioners from educational-leadership programs across the United States. Part of this group, we "kept each other's feet to the fire" even though we were mostly new colleagues. We got to know each other as online collaborators by responding to *Educational Leadership at 2050* by English et al. (2012) on the future for mid-century leaders and leadership in public and higher education. After we finished, I did a preliminary textual analysis of the "bubbled" comments made in the margins of the e-book. This revealed that the Crocodoc team showed higher intellectual activity/interest around particular ideas.

It turns out that the Crocodoc team had commented with greater frequency on predictive trends involving such themes as management and efficiency. Historically, professors who espouse management and efficiency ideologies in the same way that industrialists promote bureaucratic efficiency, top-down leadership, and economy of scale have taught educational administration curriculum.

The team wrote sidebar statements about the *2050* book and we commented on each other's comments. As we engaged in dialogue journaling, we expressed that, in many ways, the managerial mindset and approach is still prevalent, and that "the influence of market-based reforms (re)turns us towards the technical work of a manager-leader." We discerned that practicing leaders who are recent graduates may either need more training/focus on these topics or perceive this need for themselves.

About how administration has evolved out of an industrial management lens on schools as "factories," we rallied around such concerns for the future as "high-stakes testing" that could "push us backwards to this again." The narrowing of the curriculum for schools, and how governmental entities are increasingly controlling it, was a persistent refrain in our commentaries.

The Crocodoc team decided to further develop our enriching dialogue using Wimba (which functions much like Skype). We converted our audio streams and chat box commentaries into a single text, integrating our Crocodoc responses. These interactive response elements fed our digital dialogue, which served as the basis of a multi-authored manuscript (Mullen et al. 2012). This reciprocal writing functions as not only a textual response to and development of some key perspectives in the English et al. (2012) book but also as our "take" on the future for mid-century leaders. We found these strategies useful for engaging differently and more expansively our own learning-oriented leadership communities.

Engage in Visioning Exercises

Visioning exercises—meditation, yoga, walking, sketching, journaling, and more—can be channeled to promote reflection and foster connections among ideas and activities with others. Casual or informal conversation is another strong contender for stimulating the mind. When we walk, breathe deeply, and let our unconscious roam freely, our synapses connect in new ways. Spontaneous connections occur naturally; these invisible influences give fluidity and depth to our ideas.

We can surprise ourselves almost effortlessly and endlessly, and we can intentionally channel the new ideas into our relationships, work, and writing. Exercises are personal vehicles for releasing stress, removing rigidity, and branching outward while centering ourselves in lives otherwise consumed by high-volume digital trafficking. Visioning exercises paradoxically promote focus while redirecting otherwise-wasted energy.

Students in collegial support groups, led by professors or not, have shared that when peer-based mentoring works well, they learn and write more. Mentoring-based reciprocity has great potential when *peers* intentionally support peers and develop rituals (i.e., habits). These can be individual or collective visioning exercises. The following excerpt from a doctoral student response captures these peer dynamics:

> One of the most consistent and sustained ways in which I am supported in my professor's writing group occurs at 4:50 a.m. three days a week—during which time another student and I walk and talk for forty minutes. While this is certainly an informal support, I am able to talk through brain freezes, frustrations, and brainstorms. This casual conversation—about each of our topics—allows ideas to flow and become unstuck. We also remind each other of resources we had read, utilized, or heard about. Even when things get busy elsewhere and we can't communicate via phone or e-mail, I know that I am able to bring something to the walk with me—in fact, we often text each other on our cell phones and remind the other that we have something to address. In addition to these informal conversations, I share my drafts before and after feedback in order to get an objective perspective on that feedback. My friend does the same with me.

Notice how this graduate student, who, like many writers suffers from writing blocks ("brain freezes"), uses visioning exercises to regulate her writing flow and productivity. She incorporates the feedback from her walks, talks, and texting. She also shares her drafts to elicit feedback. In turn, she provides these supports to her walking pal. The scholarly life is one in which an ongoing stream of contact and communication deepens academic work rooted in mutuality. The exercises benefit her relationship with a selected peer and both of their writing productivity. This snapshot of real-life reciprocity between peers within a higher-education environment shows students taking ownership of their writing and program success.

Participate in Collegial Groups

In comentoring relationships fostered within collegial groups, mentors and students are teaching each other knowledge and skills. Peers may exclusively constitute collegial groups, so these can be made up of students only or professors only. The members offer specialization in particular areas, such as technology and editing, and they compensate for areas of weakness. All writers benefit from brainstorming with trusted others, and from constructive feedback. The routines established are mutually rewarding and motivating, with no one person overly used.

Relating the topic of mentoring-based reciprocity to peer/cohort groups, as mentioned elsewhere in this book, various techniques facilitate interdependence and mutuality within groups:

1. Generate guidelines (written expectations, commitments, or even promises).
2. Create student-driven agendas where applicable, along with questions for discussion.
3. Establish protocols for satisfying performance standards and meeting deadlines.
4. Model heterogeneous membership that bridges boundaries (e.g., race, gender, disability, discipline).
5. Model and reinforce desirable qualities and strengths (e.g., empathy, safety, deep listening, responsiveness, reliability, caring, camaraderie, humor).
6. Take intellectual risks in writing and research, and encourage others to do the same.
7. Promote **reflection** as a collaborative means for focusing interaction and generating feedback on documents, as well as improvements.
8. Engage in constructive critique one-to-one and as an entire group.
9. Foster a scholarly identity, perhaps rooted in a social cause, that honors give-and-take in relationships (mutuality).

Item 7 on this list refers to Dewey's notion of reflection as taking thinking to the next level: "In so far as we are partners in common undertakings, the things which others communicate to us as the consequences of their particular share in the enterprise blend at once into the experience resulting from our own special doing" (as cited in Rodgers [2002, 857]). Kowalski (2005) says that because reflection is modeled and elicited, students and professionals cultivate this practice; an especially viable way of accomplishing this is in graduate groups whereby research concepts and dilemmas, decision making, and problem solving can all be tackled from multiple perspectives.

At least three benefits of "collaborative reflection" are afforded to those who engage in this process: "affirmation of the value of one's experience," "seeing things 'newly': others offer alternative meanings, broadening the field of understanding," and "support to engage in the process of inquiry"—here the discipline one needs for reflecting intensively and over time is supported by the responsibility we feel toward others. A group, such as a "reflective community," provides a forum for channeling and expressing inner thoughts and feelings (Rodgers 2002, 857).

Item 8 also warrants expansion. Scholarly critique within my long-term cohort, the WIT, was a conscious part of our shared identity as well as a steadfast commitment (Mullen 2011a). Although "no one likes criticism," one student commented, "the WITs need to learn how to write more reflectively and how to accept criticism." A few WITs initially felt "wounded" by my "probing purple writing" on their papers.

An admirer of Crockett Johnson's adventures of Harold and his purple crayon, I imagine using my own remarkable purple crayon for "drawing" new possibilities for all of my advisees. So when they feel overwhelmed by the feedback, for example, or get stuck in other ways, they can be magically helped around the problem to feel better, just like when Harold "found his ladybug friend . . . stuck in a spiderweb [he] jumped into the web. It was sticky! Harold drew a pair of scissors. Snip, Snip! The ladybug was free! (HarperCollins Publishers 2003, 16–19). However, becoming a scholar means committing to the very practical work of honing a writing habit that includes learning how to accept and offer feedback. Criticism is a learned skill.

The growth of the WITs around learning how to engage constructive criticism on draft writing after initially feeling wounded supports scholarly benefits. Nonetheless, graduate mentors would be wise to remember that novice writers can feel overwhelmed or even hurt when their work seems defaced. The authentic expression of the text has been undermined in the mind of the struggling writer, especially when a line-by-line critique does not have explanations or reasons, or include any positive reactions. Writers appreciate critique that has balance. Sometimes peers are better poised to ensure that these subtleties are covered.

One solution, albeit general, is for mentors to sensitively manage the writing process and critique in particular (Styles and Radloff 2001). I find that this works best when the writer receives feedback from me and his or her peers simultaneously *and* when ample opportunity is given for dialogue regarding the writer's intention and the reader's reaction. My support groups talk at great length about every draft, a process of appreciative critique followed by collective problem solving. Power is also monitored by having student peers produce critiques and the agenda for writing (or research tools and results) to be reviewed by the group. Ironically, this strategy of peer-group response enables students to work more comfortably with me.

The issue of critique within graduate groups is getting attention. Many students respond more positively to an interactive critique of their writing by peers over a more traditional approach involving an isolated reading by professors (Caffarella and Barnett 2000). The critiquing process within groups is essential for helping members produce scholarship that their academic peers, including dissertation/thesis committees, find acceptable—it is a safe rehearsal or test run. Overall, students value critique that occurs more informally and is personalized and ongoing.

Item 9 on my list also requires further development. In the WIT cohort, scholarly identity was described as a developmental learning process, aided by academic socialization within the doctoral group. Participants spoke about how an identity was revealed to them through the cohort: "Switching from another chair gave me an immediate identity and ways of working with a support group that were not previously available." The identity that individuals brought to the WIT group and developed was collectively owned and renewed by each new member: "My goal is to become a highly effective school principal, which became more real after I joined and saw that we share a commitment to improve schools."

Comments about group identity highlighted shared values and the benefits of feedback from peers, in addition to dissertation chairs: "Having that sense of identity as a group is beneficial, unlike in the case of someone who struggles along, doing whatever the chair says, and not having anybody else to work with." Support for scholarly writing from a higher education group of trusted colleagues was underscored: "I now have a network available to me: people I e-mail for procedural information and reactions to my scholarly work. Ours is a hidden cohort that works in ways unappreciated by outsiders."

Synergy is released from informal mentoring networks that share core values and make progress on writing tasks toward individual and collective goals. Scholarly identity has at least two meanings within a group—one made available by the collective and one developed in relation to others but also reflecting personal ownership.

Finally, studies of the WIT group (using interviews, surveys, and reflective activities) underscore dynamics of synergy, connectivity, and interdependence. Study outcomes demonstrate comentoring-based reciprocity. The quotations are from the participating student members who expressed the value of the group:

1. *Opportunity to connect with others.* "You get support from others going through the same process, facing the same challenges, who are ahead or behind you in their studies."
2. *Increased confidence.* "I feel more confident knowing I'm not doing my dissertation alone."
3. *Familial support system.* "I'm now able to commit to the long haul as part of an academic family, which I was needing, with interactions beyond my mentor."
4. *Discovery of reciprocal learning.* "I thrive on how we bring out the best in each other, review each other's work, and give suggestions."
5. *Holistic development as a scholar-practitioner.* "I'm experiencing mentoring of my whole person." (Mullen 2011a)

POINTS TO REMEMBER

The value of the Mullen Mentoring-Based Reciprocity Gauge is to spotlight an individual's contribution to a collective work. Moreover, individuals, pairs, or teams can use this tool to spark introspection for making transparent their coauthoring realities (who contributed what?) and possibilities for further growth (who can grow and how?). Furthermore, the schema can be applied for different purposes, such as weighing the mentoring and comentoring aspects of a relationship in terms of one-way teaching and shared learning.

Regarding Kris's story, the coauthoring student does not need to make a stellar contribution (i.e., a 4 or a 5) in order to grow intellectually and contribute to a collective work. Students and professors collaborating together can make terrific progress, demonstrating becoming more than they would otherwise be.

Finally, experiences of reciprocity and comentoring within mentoring dyads, triads, and groups all start with the self. This chapter's message is that understanding one's self and life philosophy, and practicing visioning exercises alone and with others, promotes mutuality and fosters connectedness. Progress and success follow.

SUMMARY

In short, desirable qualities and strengths that build comentoring reciprocity are interpersonal skills, versatility, resourcefulness, integrity, knowledge, and humility. Furthermore, principles of comentoring-based reciprocity include ethics in adult learning, improved working conditions, critical awareness of socialization for which alternatives such as collegial groups provide leverage, and mutuality with others. Writing a life philosophy, practicing visioning exercises, and participating in networks are proven strategies for developing resiliency, renewing energies, cultivating intellectual capacities, fostering bonds, and moving along projects.

Navigational Prompts

- *Build reciprocity by sharing your research ideas* with peers and faculty members to find points of convergence, overlaps, and new combinations in each other's work.
- *Journal with a person or group*; decide on a context of reflection (e.g., article, book, blog, wiki, video) read or viewed by all and then share impressions and reactions.
- *Assess the success of your own support group* in terms of comentoring (reciprocal learning). To do this, you can use the results of the WIT study reported here and in Mullen (2011a). Create an interview guide or survey (Likert scale) with these (or other) items:

> opportunity to connect with others
> increased confidence
> familial support system
> discovery of reciprocal learning
> holistic development as a scholar-practitioner

GLOSSARY

connectivity. When people are linked by core values or beliefs and conduct themselves from a premise of connection (Mullen 2005).

cyber-wellness. The need for wellness has been tagged a serious concern in digital environments relative to safety and security online and people's psychological and emotional well-being; although the focus is on children and youth, this issue is not limited to them but also pertains to adult learners (Cyberspace Research Unit 2006, www.fkbko.co.uk/root/Parents/cyberwellness/Cyber_Wellness.htm).

dialogue journaling (my term). Allows writers to comment on each other's texts or another text, such as a blog, article, dissertation, or book.

interdependence. Fosters cooperative relationships since it takes cooperation for people's needs to be met; on a global scale it is "a conflict-prevention strategy" for promoting mutual reliance and peace building (Conflict Research Consortium 2004, magnet.undp.org/Docs/crisis/mapexercise.htm).

life philosophy. A structure that underlies people's "interpretation of the world and their actions within it"; "provide[s] a framework by which to live and act" (Zinn 1998, 38).

mentoring-based reciprocity. Interdependent people, groups, or nations that actively teach and learn from one another; constructive mutual dependence can transform self-sufficiency into a strength within academic contexts.

mutuality. Also comentoring, mutuality is an act of collaborative learning; uniting individuals in a collegial relationship, its glue can be any professional context, including teaching, networking, creating, and writing.

reflection. "Consideration of some subject matter, idea, or purpose; a thought, idea, or opinion formed or a remark made as a result of meditation" (*Merriam-Webster* 2012).

III

Emerging Prepared

Networks and Markets

Chapter Seven

Gaining Disseminating and Publishing Skills

Neal's captivating story features his disseminating and publishing experiences as a doctoral student. Students who are authors of journal articles and books were the basis of interest for this chapter. Potential respondents were located through Internet searches that identified their graduate status at the time of their **publication**.

After selecting possible candidates for this question, I e-mailed the targeted population this prompt: "I see that you have published a work. Please describe how this article or work came about, specifically how you approached the writing process, about the origins and crafting of your ideas, and about any mentoring or help you might have received; also speak to the end points involving the publishing and revising processes. Any advice for students seeking to publish is welcome."

In response, Neal wrote:

> When I met my mentor-to-be in a campus restaurant, I showed her digital snapshots of the various artwork—sculptures, paintings, and crafts—that I had been developing since adolescence. I introduced myself through my art: she had suggested we bring artifacts to the visit as a way of "personalizing ourselves."
>
> "Dr. Byron" reciprocated with her artwork, after I awkwardly stumbled through mine. Her poetry, fiction, and graphics were impressive and scholarly in the connections she made with certain concepts. Unlike me, Dr. Byron was forthright about her passion, plunging excitedly into talk about the value of the arts to research, highlighting ideas from the arts-based works of prominent teacher educators, mostly Maxine Green and Elliot Eisner. I fell silent, not having heard of these methods or scholars. Then she shifted my thinking, encouraging me to see my work as "data" and myself as an arts researcher. Because this was all a natural fit for me, under her tutelage I approached the adult education field from this unique perspective.
>
> Since then I have published two articles, the first one with Dr. Byron and the second on my own. I have also been an assistant on different grants, in addition to presenting nationally five times at two different conferences, the first three once again with my mentor. I don't expect to be productive, with presenting and publishing, that is, while writing my dissertation, so I'm trying to get as much "extracurricular" activity under my belt now before I enter into candidacy and look for a job as a professor. Also, because I work very slowly while struggling against stress and health problems, I am trying to accomplish all that I can before graduation.
>
> You asked about my solo publication—well, I had done these other professional development things before returning to my "artifacts." In the meantime, though, I discussed the arts-based research method with my mentor. She provided sources to read and a few of her own publications. She drew attention to journals that welcome this offbeat research and opportunities for doctoral students. She even contacted the editor of a journal, someone she knows, and mentioned my piece

and how it would be submitted for review. This really got me going, now on the hook and feeling I had a better chance of being published under her wing. So I drafted my first article, using the journal issue that had my jottings from talks with Dr. Byron and thoughts about the articles and artwork. In my own article that I produced for this journal, I brought together key concepts from this scholarly method, reimagining it in a new way through the lens of my own autobiographical journey and artwork. I included a few of my artifacts and wrote about their relevance.

For the writing and crafting, I did not involve my mentor other than for consultation around smart strategies. She asked me to select an advanced peer from among her mentees as my sounding board and copy editor, so I did. At first I felt abandoned, but it made sense in hindsight. My mentor is neither my personal copy editor nor my codependent friend—and I did have her as my sounding board during the warming up and publishing stages. After contacting "Bob," a keen reader, I got more help. (I have given him attention he is due on his dissertation, which is in turn helping me with that nerve-wracking phase.)

Feeling alternatively stressed out and absorbed, it took me three months (the summer) to write the journal article. After submitting my manuscript to the editor, I received acknowledgment stating that it had gone out for review. This got my hopes up. It was four months before I heard anything; when I did, I was given only three weeks to make a bunch of changes. I couldn't believe the time crunch, so I contacted my mentor to see what this meant. She said that I should feel lucky—it looked like my work was being seriously considered for the next issue of the journal, hence "the squeeze." So I got busy, panicky at first. I made all the changes, showed them to my bud, then did a letter outlining the changes. My mentor gave me one of her own to follow. It wasn't until then that I realized I was expected to notate the changes I had made in response to the reviewers. In all, it took me three weeks to make the manuscript changes and four hours to write the overview letter. [See author's summary of changes subsequent to manuscript review, appendix G.]

My changes were accepted "as is." Six months later, I had the publication copy. This national press did an amazing job, producing a high-quality issue.

CASE ANALYSIS

Even though Neal was not yet writing his dissertation, he had already activated a mentor/peer/publishing network. This gave him a foothold for producing quality work leading to presentation in national conference venues and peer-reviewed publishing. The other nine students who wrote about their authoring experiences also underscored challenges and rewards, advancing clarification about the novice writer's steep **learning curve.**

Neal obviously made the most of mentoring and self-directed learning, leading to productivity and success in dissemination and publication. What elements of his story communicate this growth and accomplishment to you? The following mentoring elements played an essential role:

- *Working closely with a faculty mentor.* Neal utilized Dr. Byron as a sounding board in his doctoral program and on the topic of his manuscript. His mentor was the catalyst introducing him to the arts-based method and facilitating his networking, providing the foundation for his ideas and the editorial connection. Many interrelated elements led to a published article. Persisting, he acted on his mentor's advice to submit a paper for review to a particular journal, and he consulted her about subsequent steps.
- *Developing relationships with peer readers.* After consulting with his mentor, Neal learned about being self-reliant and having peer critics. A peer relationship shifted from a sounding board into a reciprocal one.

About self-directed learning, these elements lent integrity to Neal's publishing experience:

- *Writing the article.* Neal wrote the article and used existing data (journaling and artwork) as its foundation, incorporating ideas from the literature.
- *Preparing the manuscript.* To prepare the work for publication, Neal would have precisely followed the journal's submission guidelines, which can vary from one publisher to another.
- *Revising the work.* After clarifying the meaning of the compressed timeframe with his mentor, Neal tackled the recommended changes, showing them to his "buddy" reader (for an example of an accomplished academic's actual review of a manuscript submitted to a journal, see appendix H). Another key resource, he adapted his mentor's model of an overview letter (also known as "summary of changes"; see appendix G) so the reviewers' changes could be addressed in the revised manuscript.

As a new navigator of the publishing/disseminating roadmap, Neal was learning to stand on his own. But he had mentoring scaffolds in place. Paradoxically, self-reliance is also a necessary part of healthy mentoring relationships and robust networks. This student was making progress toward his goals, and if he was going to go anywhere, he needed to produce high-quality work.

Some discomfort naturally comes with the terrain of such steep learning. In his case, at least four challenging dynamics converged:

1. Mysterious codes of academic publishing needed translation and it became clear that various communications were to accompany the work.
2. The panic of a striving writer encountering a complex task depended on his ability to integrate bits of information from different sources.
3. The mentor's role had to be interpreted, centering around the types of supports deemed acceptable and the types to be handled independently.
4. The peer's role needed serious attention, revolving around focused academic intervention and, with deliberation, two-way giving.

As is the case, only some students beat the odds and graduate, realizing their dreams with a doctorate of philosophy (PhD) or education (EdD). But Neal's is not out of the ordinary for someone who is motivated, resourceful, and self-directed, and who is being guided to benefit from and contribute to high-quality mentoring.

WRITING AND PUBLISHING ADVICE

Writing and publishing advice comes from different corners of academia. Some writers and researchers will resonate with your needs and style, while others will not, so experiment to discover what works. But stay open and be adaptive to the situations you encounter, which will aid your communication and success. For example, if a manuscript is rejected, use the reviews to improve the work; then after you have done this, submit the revised manuscript to another publication. This is common, expected practice in academia, although submitting the same work as the original without improvement is to be discouraged. Success is the flip side of failure. Persevere: be highly intentional and strategic; almost any failure can yield success.

In contrast, some writers' goals do not seem realistic. To illustrate, one evening on *The Charlie Rose Show* (aired on Public Broadcasting Service), fiction writers—finalists for a national award—shared glimpses into their creative writing process (www.charlierose.com, December 23, 2004). After discussing dynamics of prose writing and sentence construction, the writers each disclosed that they only write a new sentence after the one being worked on feels (or is) exactly right.

This "take" on writing in academia sets off alarm bells even for accomplished scholars. Advisors and mentors rarely receive first-time submissions of writing from their students that are ready for review by thesis committee members, for example. Academic writing is all about improved writing and rewriting. This cultural norm for high-quality communication in graduate programs is rarely spoken, even though it characterizes our work with students and other academics. Major changes are to be expected, so plan on this. Rewriting original documents is a very time-consuming endeavor that necessitates planned review time by writers for mentors and readers.

Thesis and dissertation writers must account for this reality when they plan to write, when they write, and when they calculate their time to graduation. A responsive and receptive attitude toward feedback and revision transfers as students and graduates work with publishers, editors, and reviewers.

With the dissertation/thesis proposal as a reference point, Pajares' (2007) psychological perspective is that scholarly writing is all about rewriting and revision. Addressing students in his field, he offered these tips, which I fully endorse (and have given names to and paraphrased):

- *Write*. Write and keep writing at all costs. Write poorly if necessary, but get the prose on the page/screen. Trust your editing and revising. There are no good writers; there are only good rewriters.
- *Incubate*. Put aside your drafts and reread them after a delay. Work the manuscript in your mind during periods of relaxation. Remember that time and reflection are synthetic. This requires that you make good use of time and do not leave manuscripts until the last minute.
- *Proofread carefully*. Few things irritate committee members more than sloppy submissions. Have peers or editors proofread your work as well.
- *Read aloud*. Read your paper to someone or a digital recorder. Get a colleague to read your proposal to you. Listen to your prose and take notes.
- *Critique*. Ask a colleague to dissect the draft. Ready your mind to accept the criticism. Become your own best critic.
- *Form collegial groups*. Devote time to discussing manuscripts in depth and reciprocate by reading others' works in progress.
- *View articles as models*. Consider how authors you admire handle the problems you are confronting, such as abstracts and summaries.
- *Practice precision and clarity*. Select members of your intended audience (e.g., school leaders) so your work will have value. Properly attribute all sources; helpful readers can be acknowledged or credited too.

Graduate students greatly benefit from seeking assistance on their academic writing from a mosaic of people, not only mentors but also peers, readers, networks, writing centers, and more. While striving to improve your writing and disseminate work, use resources from inside and outside your program or institution early on (see chapter 3). Don't wait until the last minute! Highly focused peer-writing groups are essential for year-round support: Summer is an especially important time for many graduate students; they can make more progress then but may not be able to tap the fruits of faculty labor to the same extent. Professors are typically on nine-month contracts that do not cover summer, so their availability at off-times is widely variable. Many are traveling, researching, and writing. Find about their personal policies for productivity and wellness, and plan your work and readers accordingly.

Writing centers can offer expert help and during off-hours, especially online services. In the 1980s, as an undergraduate student, I volunteered as a tutor at York University, Canada. The center was founded on Scardamalia and Bereiter's (1986) breakthrough research. It was a privilege to be selected. Tutors were trained to use a cognitive approach for feedback on drafts. It was the practice of giving feedback that helped us support struggling writers. While learning tools for supportive critique, I also progressed on my own writing. I benefited from reading widely and closely papers from different disciplines and from demonstrating strategies with students who asked good questions.

As a tutor-in-the-making, I started to become aware of my own mental processes as a reader and writer. I would think about the strategies I was accessing and applying to different papers. Later, as a dissertation supervision and journal editor, I would give detailed feedback with the goal of helping novice academic writers develop awareness of metacognitive strategies without becoming overly self-conscious. The idea for writers is to be generative *and* self-critical, a fine balance that varies from one individual to another. Writers who prematurely edit themselves (or are edited) block writing flow and creativity. Prolific academics have an ingrained sense of when to write, edit, and elicit critical feedback, and not usually as a linear progression (see chapter 4; also consult Johnson and Mullen 2007).

Writing centers and networks can offer legitimate support to students pursuing advanced degrees. No one is above benefiting from feedback. For this book, I researched writing centers online and e-mailed counselors who offer student-friendly services (such as tutoring during off-hours). Quality services are those where tutors or counselors, often students themselves, are ahead of the tutee. Thesis/dissertation writers may need to be vigilant about securing feedback from tutors capable of providing criticism on work at a level they expect. Feedback on drafts can be life changing when the strategies learned leave an imprint.

Writing tutors approach drafts as eagles, seeing the work as a whole from afar. They offer cognitive strategies and pinpoint difficulties in hard-to-detect areas, such as planning and execution. Second-language learners' learning curve is especially challenging, involving writing both in another language *and* in the specialized, academic language of their discipline. Tutees can sound out their written words. Others are shown how to attribute sources according to the expected standards of their field.

Tutees are sometimes counseled on writing deductively, not inductively, particularly in the social and behavioral sciences. But rules and norms vary, as some academic writing begins anecdotally. Novices are often shown how to reorganize/rearrange their work. They also are cautioned against having major points (e.g., topic sentences) buried or popping up at the end of paragraphs and sections, causing readers to rethink the work just to follow it. Many writers think as they write; this is good, but an early draft is different from the version produced for distribution.

Such writing sessions are nonevaluative and geared toward the individual writer's planning, drafting, or revising. Tutors have boundaries, saying that they do not "correct" or "fix" students' papers or work on a rush deadline. Not all writing centers are free, but many are; they can be in person or online or have electronic components, such as sign-up sheets/screens. Some sessions are for groups of students, as in the case of a special topics seminar on specific writing issues. Take courses and workshops on academic writing and create your own peer groups.

Some professional associations match students and/or junior faculty with experienced scholars, seasoned faculty who are editors and publishers, directors and executive leaders (Mullen 2008). As noted in the "Nonprint Resources" of the references section, professional associations annually sponsor mentoring programs geared to novice scholars' professional development in the areas of writing publication and/or career development. Sessions and ongoing work require excellent planning on the part of novices. Notably, for the workshop programs I have designed and facilitated for several national professional associations over two decades, doctoral students and junior faculty work personally with leading scholars on their academic goals. Students learn how to produce high-quality works for dissemination, decode the codes of scholarly communities, navigate the politics of academia, and land a job they want. They also develop influential contacts.

Mentoring interventions are designed for emerging scholars around their goals, while others attract diverse populations for which mentoring is highly targeted. Some programs work with less structure, and others with more. Find creative and varied ways of accessing editors/mentors and for brainstorming writing challenges.

In structured programs, novices are stepped through the process of forming and developing the relationship. They may be prompted to select a journal editor from a prevetted list and then contact that individual(s) with a description of their paper and research interests. Development of the academic relationship and meeting deadline for paper review are both standards to be met. An insider's tip is that these all potentially serve as excellent opportunities for highly personalized professional development that yield the extra help and buy-in of busy editors and publishers.

Opportunities abound through conferences for emerging scholars to obtain targeted feedback on their writing through coaching on how to prepare and disseminate their work. Whether in one-on-one sessions with journal editors and experienced scholars, in the audience of editors sharing knowledge and tips or at fireside chats, or in webinars with published scholars about the writing process, interested novices can access insiders and certainly their most cherished ideas.

At an invited address I recently gave at the American Education Research Association, I talked about making the most of mentoring in doctoral education and academic careers. During the discussion, dissertation writers and graduates from various disciplines expressed concern about guidance relative to writing feedback and publication coaching from their advisors, and only a few mentioned working with productive writing and support groups. More could have benefitted from pursuing academic and career enhancement beyond one-to-one mentoring through peer networks, mentoring programs, online collaborations, and targeted supports.

In case you're wondering about metastrategies I'm using in this book, for one thing I am addressing a specific audience, that is, graduate students worldwide, who have various cultural and disciplinary backgrounds. Additionally, I am using different strategies for expressing my ideas and for being understood, notably graphics, metaphors, and conventional language (as figure 0.1 and all the chapters demonstrate). Furthermore, I am securing my ideas in data-based studies that extend to my originating study. I am using a blended narrative style and empirical sensibility that link stories and results, hoping to broaden my reach and impact. I weigh writing approaches. These include when to present my ideas deductively (e.g., by introducing a topic at the outset) and inductively (e.g., by starting anecdotally with a case from a student or professor). I plan when to step out from my construction of others' thoughts by communicating directly in a mentor's voice and when to pay tribute to others' ideas, allowing messages to reverberate subtly.

When people ask how I've managed to write so many books and articles, I recall this formative tutoring (writing and reviewing) experience, in addition to my English literature courses that laid the foundation. Most of all, I think about time in the seat spent writing, alone and interactively, and of honing metastrategies to shape my scholarly craft and improve my techniques. I appreciate supporters and strive for reciprocity in our work; for the sake of wellness and growth, I mentally befriend critics, usually virtual reviewers unknown to me, who review my work. It is amazing all of the services that global publishing community provides.

Dissemination-Specific Tips

Increasingly, students and others are publishing in open-source venues, hopefully honing their work before electronic distribution. Online resources (like Merlot.com) function as a repository of articles, lessons, and more generated by members, with select peer review for some categories of materials only.

In contrast, more traditional peer review with scholarly journals and prestigious publishers function very differently. The academic level, quality, and skills involved for becoming a published author take years to develop and the disseminated work takes a long time before it materializes online or in print—just ask any professor.

But while developing the necessary intellectual and strategic skills, you can accelerate. Realize results sooner—you are living and working in the digital age. Publication is not only of articles in prestigious journals but also self-authored dissemination of smaller works, such as lesson plans, for which originality or copyright will not be compromised. Test the waters. Post an idea, probe a question, or demo some aspect of professional development in a blog, wiki, video, or applet (i.e., short live simulation). Large class projects, such as books done with youth, are available for consultation in open book websites (e.g., Merlot.com). These same works are not typically produced for peer review with traditional publishing outlets.

More ways to get your publishing feet wet: try submitting your fuller work to a journal that has a high(er) acceptance rate or less-demanding **peer review** process. Or, still yet, publish your better piece in a journal or outlet with a call for papers on a theme that you can address.

What associations and networks do the people you know belong to and participate in as members, leaders, and consultants? What worldwide associations and organizations in your area of interest sponsor **conference proceedings**, online journals, and other publishing and professional development opportunities, especially for emerging scholars? If you're interested in publishing, editing, and/or networking, participate in tech labs to learn about the best resources and the most strategic ways to research them, as well as to present or record your work.

Finding outlets within your topic range takes patience, multiple searches of digital databases and the Internet, and interchanges with knowledgeable academics. For example, searches of the topic *community-engaged scholarship* in higher education yields many useful leads. Searching the Internet with this term, I located international and national associations, networks-conference proceedings, journals, articles, and promotion-and-tenure guidelines. Some topics, like this one, are more conducive to mentoring graduate students and including them in scholarly work; another such term that yields opportunities is *social justice*. Students can volunteer for roles and responsibilities, such as reviewer, communicator, organizer, and assistant, with journals, publishers, and organizations. Being nominated by a more senior person, such as a mentor or insider, can help forge desirable connections.

Regarding the traditional route of publication that academies have long expected, did you know, for starters, that a paper submitted for review to a peer-reviewed journal might not actually undergo review? This is a privilege not automatically granted to prospective authors. Journal guidelines use the jargon "review consideration," meaning that editors are not obligated to forward a paper for review after it has been "screened" by them or a designated other, such as an editorial board member. It is the editor's prerogative whether to have a paper reviewed in-house or externally; if the decision is not to, reasons do not have to be given.

A generic reason typically accompanies rejection, such as "the paper does not fit the scope of the journal" or "many high-quality manuscripts were received." This is only code for a long list of possibilities: examples are that the writing may be considered weak or unsubstantiated or the data analysis may be incomplete or lack rigor. Learn from colleagues what other outlets to try. Know that dissertation material submitted for review purposes must be up to date and meet scholarly standards.

This list outlines more insider information and pointers for writing success (note that it is neither exhaustive nor presented in any particular order):

- *Decide where you will submit your paper for review during its preparation, not when it is done.* Search for potential journals using electronic venues that publish student papers, special themes, or whatever interests you. Explore online digital libraries using key words or descriptors. Universities have free full text and searchable databases. Some databases charge fees for articles after you've been routed through an electronic loop to the document retrieval screen. The Educational Resources Information Center (ERIC) Clearinghouse, www.eric.ed.gov, is one such database.
- *Research the journals for which you have potential interest.* Identify research journals in your subject (e.g., curriculum, psychology) using a more systematic approach. Cabell's Directories, subscription only, helps with deciding which journal(s) will most likely accept the manuscript (www.cabells.com/using.aspx#x2). To help you decide, compare the characteristics of your manuscript and the needs of selected journals. Facts related to the journals are cataloged for easy navigation; these include the topics of articles published in them, manuscript guidelines, acceptance rates, and review processes. And the journals are characterized relative to their overall theme, method, and prestige.
- *Learn about the quality of e-journals in which you have interest by searching directories.* The Directory of Open Access Journals is a globally accessible catalog of journals with quality assurances of scientific rigor (www.doaj.org). Explore directories and catalogs that provide manuscript guidelines and full text; monitor publication costs (for some journals) and find out from your colleagues about any opportunities for editorial board memberships, which are by invitation only. Search the websites of scholarly and other reputable publishers (e.g., Springer). Find out about state, national, and international journals in your field that have the stamp of approval of quality associations, organizations, and networks. Where do your colleagues and advisors publish, and what relative value do they place on e-journals, self-authorship, and non-peer-review outlets?
- *Find out the acceptance rates of journals in which you have interest.* The lower the acceptance rate (the fewer manuscripts published that are received), the higher the prestige. Glatthorn (1998) recommends submitting the first manuscript or few to less selective journals that publish a high number of those received. Open-access e-journals tend to have higher acceptance rates, which involve trade-offs in scholarly rigor and reputation, although not consistently. E-journals afford the benefits of speed, visibility, ease, and distribution, as well as publication of novel ideas and presentation of nontextual features, such as video and artwork.

- *When possible, target special issues of journals (i.e., calls for papers).* The acceptance rate is generally higher for these than nonthematic journal issues (Henson 1999). Special issues can present excellent opportunities for authors seeking access to high-quality, rigorous journals with wide distribution. Locate calls for papers on forthcoming themes at journal and publisher websites. Authors can contact other authors appearing in the same issue once the publication appears. Presumably, works on similar or related topics will have been featured. This kind of collection provides an opportunity to broaden one's network in an area of study.

- *Contact the editor, more likely the editorial assistant or manager, ahead of time to communicate your intention of submitting a manuscript for review.* Ask probing questions, such as whether this is the best outlet for your work, by succinctly describing your paper. If this is not the best outlet, perhaps the editor or designee can suggest where your work might be a better fit—reach out and inquire. As a new scholar, you can inquire about whether there are any special provisions for beginners, such as writing support on initial manuscripts (e.g., from editorial board members). Also, ask whether you'll be promptly informed if your submission is incomplete.

- *Include on the first page of the paper the manuscript title, address, and contact information.* A functioning e-mail address is essential. A second page ideally provides the title only, to aid with the blind-review process. Authors should not count on extra work being done on their behalf and should thus take the necessary steps to be precise with their submissions.

- *If required, include an abstract that adheres to the stipulated word length, arranged as a single paragraph.* For research articles, the abstract usually covers the essential elements of the paper—often highlighted in the main headings—such as topic, purpose and scope, methods and data analysis, and insights or findings and significance.

- *Even though journal guidelines in education typically require American Psychological Association (APA) documentation, this is not always closely followed.* If a house style deviates from the norm, adjustments should be made accordingly. Such journals will specify the variations to be addressed, especially for citation and referencing purposes—this request, typical of international journals, is often outlined on websites (e.g., Routledge).

- *Manuscripts submitted for review sometimes exceed the specified length and require extensive editing.* Related problems include a lack of focus, redundancy, and extended references (beyond the works cited). Proofreading errors are not uncommon. In some cases, it appears that an abbreviated form of one's dissertation has been submitted without the necessary crystallization of ideas, tight editing, and reorganization required for a journal article (Glatthorn 1998).

- *Although manuscripts might be well written and address important topics, they can be conversationally oriented, insufficiently substantiated, or based on opinion with little data or literature to support them.* Depending on the type of journal, some even require a larger subject pool, more extensive analyses of the data, and profound or original insights.

- *During the revision process, be patient with any requests for improving your work.* Take these seriously, and distance yourself from any feelings of personal insult. In my own experience as a writer, I say that I must have grown "a new brain" from the time of submission to revision, as the changes to be made come much more easily and seem more obvious then. (See appendix H for an academic review of a manuscript.)

- *Bring on board knowledgeable colleagues to read your work.* Some journal editors (like me) ask that all writers have their work proofread before and subsequent to submission. Also, acknowledge others' efforts in writing when appropriate. Seek illumination from informed mentors and peers, guides, mentoring interventions, workshops, and quality Internet outlets.

Publishing Timeline and Vital Documents

Publishing Timeline

Speaking from all sides of the publishing picture as an author, journal editor, book editor, and publisher, manuscripts submitted for publication review in traditional peer-review outlets can take months before a decision is communicated. A typical period of review with a national- or international-level journal is five to eight months; the wait time is usually shorter for electronic and state-level journals.

Similarly, chapter writing undergoes review stages before one's contribution to an edited book is ready. Chapters are typically solicited by professors (through publishing companies, on the Internet, or in person) who serve as book editors; one's outline or preliminary writing is reviewed, and if accepted, the draft text is critiqued, complete with changes on the next version. Writing chapters for books by scholars is a preferred mentoring and publishing process for many emerging scholars. Many seasoned authors also gravitate toward the relative liberation (e.g., of speech, style, ownership) this provides over traditional article-review processes.

Vital Documents

What journal editorial teams expect from authors regarding writing and publishing conventions and procedures follows a similar pattern but can be idiosyncratic. Documents that typify article publishing in education include:

- *Manuscript-preparation guidelines.* While your work is being written or prepared for submission, it is considered **in preparation**. Just like Neal (we are assuming) in the opening case, prepare your work responsibly for publication using the journal's instructions to authors. This information can be found on any journal's website or in a printed issue; or, contact the assistant directly for the guidelines. You might even find it necessary to contact the editor's designee to get answers to your questions, such as whether an abstract is required, what the maximum length is for a manuscript submission, or what formatting style should be used.
- *Cover letter accompanying manuscript submission* (see appendix F for template). Carefully attend to the special instructions to authors and address these in your cover letter to show that they have been followed. If you are uncertain about any of the instructions, ask an informed professor or contact the editorial assistant or publisher. You will likely be submitting your work using the popular web-based central manuscript system that has been set up for the journal of your choice. These commonly share such features as a tracking tool for knowing where your manuscript is in the review process, including online peer review intended to speed up the process. Provide a cover letter or statement that briefly describes the fit between the work and the journal. Once you have uploaded the relevant documents,

such as the paper and cover letter (or e-mail message), your work is deemed **under submission**. When you receive notice that the paper has been moved to the next stage, your work is **in review**. This notification comes as good news indeed.

- *Summary of changes subsequent to manuscript review* (see appendix G for a model). In order to help the manuscript reach its potential (you might be only a revision away from publication acceptance—or multiple rigorous rewritings), incorporate the suggested changes. Ask yourself what the editor wants. Because few manuscripts are accepted outright, expect to fall within the respected range of acceptance, which includes "conditional acceptance" and "accept with changes." Editors who provide specifics governing recommended changes might, for example, provide questions around which the next (perhaps final) version will be centered. For example, they might request a sharpening of the work's focus, improved organization, or statement of international significance. Hopefully the editor will say that the revised manuscript is significantly improved over the earlier version. As frequently happens when substantial revisions are undertaken, new weaknesses are revealed, which are opportunities for improving the work. It takes time and experience to grow in the craft of addressing critiques. Stay focused on the product and its quality, and don't get sidetracked by distractions or negative self-talk.
- After you've revised the paper, address any concerns of the editor or reviewers. The expectation may be that a detailed letter describing all of the changes made will accompany your revised work. Use the sample letter provided in appendix G. There may be a way for you to communicate with the editor or representative during this revision process to state whether the reviews are useful and whether you plan to address them and resubmit, and you might even provide a timeframe. Sometimes authors want to discuss the feedback with editorial insiders. If granted this somewhat rare opportunity, be very well prepared: pinpoint concerns and brainstorm solutions (i.e., a workable plan). A good place to find editors and designees is at the journal roundtable sessions scheduled by some major conferences.

Once you have revised your manuscript, the scenario that unfolds typically corresponds to one of the following: (1) the revised paper is accepted as is, for which the terms **forthcoming** and *in press* are used; (2) additional changes are required that might have been introduced during the revision or skirted altogether; or (3) the paper is rejected on the basis that the changes did not meet the journal's standards. Avoid the last one, a severe rejection, by taking very seriously the requested amendments and by making additional changes yourself. An outlier situation involves unprofessional ethical behavior of editorial teams, ranging from months-long, delayed responses to ignoring the author altogether. Authors can be neglected when the editor is in transition or when a journal no longer exists.

Know that the publishing steps and documents outlined in this section are broad stages only. Your own academic research and context will introduce a wild card, meaning that the provided templates cannot be adopted literally, as they were generated out of my own circumstances. Refer to the templates in the appendixes to see the publishing process from a bird's-eye view. Use them as you see fit and generate correspondence that suits you.

Publishing Trends Involving Student Writers

Unsurprisingly, research on the publishing productivity of doctoral students that involves sole authorships (e.g., Dinham and Scott 2001) and collaborations with faculty (Rendina-Gobioff and Watson 2004) indicates that too few students are afforded the advantages of this growth experience. Consistent with this picture, Neal's disseminating record was among the exceptional profiles I received from respondents, although more opportunities exist with web-based communications and worldwide access to people. While doctoral students might privately long for just such an opportunity, many are in a sink-or-swim mode, having not thought seriously along these lines or benefited from mentorship.

Education graduate students have confessed that their greatest challenge in academia is to acquire the necessary mindset and skills for publishable research (Mullen 2005a). While this is attributable to the high demands placed on their lives, it is also due to shortcomings in their academic programs. Students need guidance in the scholarly writing process and exposure to educational interventions—mentoring—to write for academe (Dinham and Scott 2001; Johnson and Mullen 2007). A study of doctoral graduates from thirteen institutions also revealed that writing for publication was not part of their training (Engstrom 1999). Writing itself and for a research audience is also mostly overlooked as a fundamental area of practice. Compounding this, many graduate students fear writing and have a greater fear of failure. Some enter professional fields without having developed the mindset and skill set that are essential for a flourishing self and career.

Opportunities are more apparent for graduate students to publish with professors and on their own in peer-reviewed outlets through national organizations and publishing presses. Student-friendly publishing opportunities are perhaps less explicitly of a mentoring nature than when professors reach out to students, or reach back, to coauthor and share resources.

Professors who are influential within their organizations are changing their environments just by recognizing that "coauthoring with graduate students is unique and shows that our programs care about mentoring our students" (anonymous faculty respondent). As a result, articles, journals, and books are vetted, supported, and published with professors and the organizations they lead. Their mission is the preparation of the next generation of professionals in a particular field. The National Council of Professors of Educational Administration (NCPEA) has created opportunities for graduate students preparing for educational leadership positions in the field and academia to express themselves by publishing peer-reviewed works with NCPEA Press.

Developing as Published Writers

Publication by graduate students has been tackled only sporadically in the literature. Books and articles published over the last forty years mainly address writing the dissertation, often taking the form of personal and professional narratives (Mullen et al. 2000), including descriptions of shared teacher–student writing relationships (Johnson-Bailey and Cervero 2004) and especially advice giving or how-to retrospectives (Phillips and Pugh 1994). Such works shed light on the process by which this difficult transformation can take place.

What is still needed, however, is an exhaustive account that shows how learning to write for dissemination can be shaped in different environments spanning the classroom, supervisory context, mentoring programs, and self-directed learning. Scholarly spaces in the academy are slowly being dedicated to the writing process itself (see, e.g., Bolton 1994; Connelly and Clandinin 1988; Mullen 2011a; Richardson 1994). I have developed publication-based writing models for this purpose (e.g., Mullen 2001, 2005a, 2011a).

Furthermore, literature is needed to affirm these crucial points:

1. All graduate students should be considered candidates for learning how to write and disseminate their original works.
2. Students should be exposed to a formal curriculum that moves them through the complex phases of developing studies of interest and publishable quality.

3. Professors who mentor students' publishing growth should be recognized for these crucial efforts as part of the scholarly profile of a research university.
4. Institutions should create mentoring-based policy initiatives that motivate faculty members to mentor emerging scholars and that reward excellence.

This enlarged ethic of responsibility would support the professional development of students and professors alike and increase their collaboration on important issues.

POINTS TO REMEMBER

The case that launched this chapter encourages graduate students to work strategically with supportive insiders. For instance, Neal's dissertation chair contacted the editor on his behalf. Neal's work was then reviewed, and his first publication experience was positive.

Careful not to press Dr. Byron when she advised him to turn to a peer for review purposes, Neal was astute. He initially felt off balance, even abandoned, which is only natural, but then he put words to action. He showed he was resourceful and reliable—the contact he established with Bob, his professor's mentee, led to an authentic working relationship. All graduate students benefit from relationships with peer readers from which they grow intellectually and reflectively. Through reciprocal exchanges with peers, students learn independence as well as interdependence, and they broaden their contacts and establish deeper collegiality.

Neal took his mentor's advice regarding the overview letter. Although the editor had not asked for the letter (because it may be assumed when not explicitly requested), Neal produced it to accompany his revised manuscript. (Some writers incorporate the summary of changes into a cover letter.) As a self-directed learner, Neal took on the publishing challenge, demonstrating his ability to see his work through from inception to production. Neal's case shares aspects of conscientious learning around student publication; it also provides tips for supporting comentoring development with faculty and peers and engagement with editors.

The overviews covering academic writing and publication in education, including Pajares' (2007) resonating truth—there are no good writers, only good rewriters—are helpful guides. These are a synthesis of my extensive work as an author and editor, in addition to the relevant literature and data collected for this book.

SUMMARY

Detailed writing and publishing advice is presented for assisting novice writers based on real-life situations intended for reflection and application. The chapter has examples, guidelines, templates, tips, and know-how for guiding motivated graduate students to develop a mindset for disseminating their works and collaborating with others. Insiders are encouraging students to take ownership of their writing before they graduate or seek jobs and promotion. Students can systematically study the journals and other publishing venues in their field and develop enriching connections with knowledgeable professors and peers, and with supportive organizations, publishers, and networks. Self-published students who form networks of their own and author their ideas by having a strong digital presence (e.g., via blogs, wikis, e-journals, e-books, videos) have opened new doors.

Navigational Prompts

- *Identify some other ways Neal could have acted* at these critical junctures (or choose your own) and the imagined consequences of doing so:

  deciding to write his second article solo
  opting for an arts-based research approach to adult education
  taking the mentor's advice to locate a peer reviewer
  working in a reciprocal fashion with the peer reviewer
  preparing an overview letter (or summary of changes)
  developing skills needed for article revision

- *Describe the specifics* regarding how Neal's actions demonstrated receiving and giving and how these supported his development and mentorship.
- *Select a mentor, peer, or group* to discuss the writing and publishing guidelines and templates. Swap resonating (or differing) stories of experience and your own goals related to academic dissemination, including publication.
- *Adapt the publishing templates* in appendixes F and G to your own purposes and begin developing a manuscript; select a journal consulting the advice provided in this chapter, then submit your work after carefully investigating the journal's potential fit and notes to authors.
- *Locate additional writing and publishing templates* through the Internet, your mentor, or another means, and make them work for you. Share with others.
- *Use the ideas* (e.g., metacognitive strategies, dictionaries) outlined herein to assist with your writing process and progress as a developing author.

GLOSSARY

   conference proceedings. The collection of academic papers that are published after delivery at a conference, with distribution as e-books or printed books. Usually peer reviewed, these reflect a selection of the works presented (a vita entry).

   forthcoming. Indicates that "an article has been completed and accepted for publication"—note this on your vita (Heiberger and Vick 2003, para. 13). Also referred to as "in press."

   in preparation. Shows that although your manuscript has been neither completed nor accepted, it is in progress (Heiberger and Vick 2003, para. 13).

   in review. Refers to a paper that has moved past the "under submission" phase and prescreening stage (assuming there is one) and is currently being peer reviewed.

   learning curve. An unavoidable and inevitable period of disequilibrium (Mendis 2001) in which an individual is developing a new mindset and set of skills.

   peer review. A scholarly process involving experts typically not disclosed to the author used in the review and publication of manuscripts and proposals: "Publishers and funding agencies use peer review to select and to screen submissions. The process also assists authors in meeting the standards of their discipline. Publications and awards that have not undergone peer review are liable to be regarded with suspicion by scholars and professionals in many fields" (*Wikipedia* 2012). Also, publishers and journal editors decide the precise form of peer review; manuscripts are sent out to two to three reviewers (up to five) in the topic area of the paper.

publication. In the simplest sense, means to make content available to the public. What is being published is text, images, audiovisual content, or something else; in electronic publishing, what is being publically disseminated are websites, e-books, wikis, blogs, videos, or other things.

under submission. When a manuscript has been completed and submitted but not accepted (Heiberger and Vick 2003, para. 13).

Chapter Eight

Overcoming Job-Marketing Barriers

A group of beginning professors was invited to share recent job-search experiences: "What insights do you have about marketing, networking, and job hunting that can benefit other job seekers?" Belicia, a Hispanic female in her forties, responded with this caveat: "I'm fine with telling my marketing story, but I don't know whether it might be useful for up-and-coming graduates." She continued,

> While doing my PhD it never crossed my mind that I would become a college professor one day. It wasn't until my dissertation chair put this idea in my head (when I was admitted to doctoral candidacy) that I started to even consider it. Until then, I had been viewing the doctorate in very simple terms—as an extension of the master's degree, just with more courses added. Because of this mistaken notion, I naturally assumed that my postgraduate career would follow the same path and that I would end up with a more senior position than I currently had as an educational trainer. I learned at this time, however, that just about anyone with a doctorate in the corporate world is "overqualified" and ends up working for managers with less education. In a manner of speaking, I was being retooled for the academy without knowing it.
>
> As I became engrossed in my dissertation, the light bulb came on—I started putting energy toward the academy as a career move. Before I even defended, I discovered thirty-nine positions in my field through *The Chronicle of Higher Education* and the websites of professional associations. Over six months, I submitted all thirty-nine job applications. I got only one bite. Because the university that expressed interest in me was just advertising for a **visiting assistant professor** on an **annually renewable** contract, and because it was located in a place that has freezing winters, I was disinterested. But "Dr. Beatty," my chair, persuaded me, saying that I could benefit from the interview experience and that I could always plan to move on to a prestigious university afterward. So I put my best foot forward and got the job.
>
> Two years later, while doing extremely well in my discipline, I moved into a **tenure-track** position at a research institution. While at the first college, I had tried hard to obtain just such a line, but my applications were turned down. I became a candidate for one highly desirable position after agreeing to a **convention interview**. My **job talk** served up a buffet of the best of my ideas to the exclusively male department. However, I got this job only in view of the fact that the other finalist (a male) turned down the offer. I understand that my competition had found the salary offer too low, but it was definitely higher than my current one. What I knew at the time was that the prestigious institution was an excellent fit with my professional aspirations.
>
> Some hidden stuff has since crept to the surface. This last year, my publishing accomplishments outran my departmental colleagues' annual records, yet we all received the same merit raise. To fit in, I've had to pull back on my public enthusiasm for scholarship and teaching, downplay my project involvement and publication successes, and tame my seemingly flighty ways. This doesn't mean that I can get away with being less than competent as a teacher and scholar. I work

doubly hard! I don't know how much of this has to do with gender issues or an atmosphere of repression in the academy. I'm fortunate that my former advisor helps me distinguish what's important and what's not in my hornets' nest of worries. We have witty names for things—a stress release! I do worry about getting tenure. My department's vote counts, so I do put in the time with a leisurely tenured lunch crowd.

CASE ANALYSIS

Productive career strategies include conventional job-marketing approaches and highly focused, targeted professional networking. In fact, in a marketplace interview that aired in 2012 on *American Public Media* (for the complete transcript, go to www.marketplace.org/topics/your-money/dream-job-reality), the market specialist emphasized networking for the job you want. He saw less value in preparing and distributing résumés and cover letters and more in making use of support networks. He also expressed less value in generic networks like job fairs and more in intentional networking strategies that too few applicants adopt.

Spend time researching the places you might want to work and getting to know insiders by connecting with them. Other take-aways are that the job market is tight and flooded with applications, so your letters and packages must be tailored and contacts already made with professors (and others). Networking with those who are where you want to be is the strong message here. You can accomplish this through a variety of means, such as introductions with search-committee faculty members and administrators at conferences and events, professional linking on social media websites, active participation in webinars and seminars, and social time over coffee.

Job applicants who reach out to confidants, such as successful peers and other keen insiders, will likely experience more progress. With this, brainstorm about career-related areas of the job search for which you have questions, such as the application package, interview, and hiring process, in addition to psychological areas involving fit and comfort. Learn to strategically navigate the academy's politics not only as you market yourself but also after landing that first position.

More details on this topic are in the section "Marketing Yourself in or beyond Academe" (this chapter). Next, space is devoted to some of the cultural elements suggested in Belicia's case and their relevance to academic and professional careers.

The testimonies that were submitted in response to the initiating question about experiences of the job market overlap with Belicia's in these broad respects:

1. Most of the beginning faculty members (males and females) had made the shift from student to professor relatively late as adults.
2. PhD graduates and those with years of experience in the academy identified compression (and vulnerability) as prevalent, evidenced by temporary faculty appointments and the elusive (out-of-reach) tenure track position.
3. The female beginning professors were employed at universities in a male-dominated discipline and articulated dynamics of unfairness and inequity.
4. Influence networks were at play in shaping applicants' chances for success from the outset of the job search to its conclusion and on the job.

Gender and race imbalances have been known to characterize academic job pools and finalist selections. Another issue is that faculty promotions to desirable ranks are not accompanied by job searches or peer review. Studies and personal testimonies from the academic world (e.g.,

Wilson 2004) and practitioner world (e.g., Banks 2000) alike reveal such problems as inequities in how candidates are handled and how executive decision making occurs. Entry-level positions and those offering advancement need to follow comprehensive search protocols and diversity policies.

Belicia became motivated to land that academic dream job. In the meantime, she had to compromise by accepting a temporary contract at a college that did not have the prestige she was seeking. She had no alternatives, so she and her advisor agreed this move would at least get her academic career under way.

Some doctoral candidates search for academic jobs before **degree in hand**, while others have successfully defended their dissertation. PhD graduates are considered a success by their home institutions and, paradoxically, on the job circuit as a beginner who may not stand out, perhaps due to the sheer volume of competition or because search processes *are*, to some extent, political. Regardless, this gives heightened importance to influence networks and targeting networking for candidates.

Belicia's initial job was temporary. The role of visiting assistant professor holds greater promise for an academic career than the **adjunct** role, which carries a lesser status, albeit a legitimate record of accomplishment and solid experience. But the adjunct role does not as readily translate into viability for a tenure-earning position as an **assistant professor**. **Postdoctoral fellow** positions have cachet when sponsored by top-notch research universities or esteemed professors.

Securing a tenure-track position at a research university requires ongoing persistence and targeted networking, just as earning tenure does. In actuality, higher education appears to be a women's domain these days. For the first time, in 2001–2002, women earned more doctorates than men in the United States (as cited in Wilson [2004]). However, when looking across all disciplines and beyond professions like English and psychology, it becomes clear that "at the country's big research universities, the vast majority of professors [70 percent] are men" (Wilson 2004, A8). Even at the entry level of assistant professor and postdoctoral fellow, males tend to occupy more of the positions at top-notch research universities. Exceptions include networked females who have been tapped, sponsored, and mentored into these positions; the same goes for coveted leadership roles in premier organizations.

With record speed, temporary faculty constitute much more of the academy than do full-time faculty and tenure-earning faculty. **Contingent faculty appointments** are more the norm, as the American Association of University Professors (AAUP) has reported: "46 percent of all faculty are part-time, and non–tenure-track positions of all types account for 65 percent of all faculty appointments in American higher education" (2012, www.aaup.org/ AAUP/issues/contingent).

When one considers the odds—that an early-career female scholar managed to secure a tenure-track position at a "powerhouse" institution (one of the top fifty US universities)—luck seems to have been on Belicia's side. However, negative gender bias was a dynamic. Tenure-earning females (like Belicia) at doctorate-granting institutions must deal with multiple inequities (Wilson 2004). As examples, they may be paid less than their male counterparts (Belicia's male competitor was offered a higher salary), they may work harder than their colleagues, and they may advance more slowly or receive fewer privileges. For such reasons, it appears that female faculty members are more prone to be dissatisfied with their work environments.

Certainly, female faculty have been making inroads in higher education, statistically speaking, rising by 28 percent over an eleven-year period (from 1989–1990 to 2001–2002), but "the more prestigious the institution, the fewer women it has" (Wilson 2004, A8). "Despite these significant gains," according to the American Association of University Women (AAUW), females struggle for equal and fair representation in higher education and especially in that coveted echelon: the rank of tenured professor (2012, www.aauw.org).

The AAUW's publication *Tenure Denied: Cases of Sex Discrimination in Academia* (2004) covers nineteen legal court cases. It explains that gender discrimination is a factor in why female faculty members are denied tenure at four-year degree-granting colleges and universities where women make up only 27 percent of tenured faculty. Moreover, female faculty and faculty of color are less likely than white male faculty to have tenure; in fact, "academe remains substantially white" (Schneider 1998, 3). More women are decision makers now, and more females and males have women as senior leaders, so the demographics of the academy are changing.

Belicia also cited fairness (or the lack thereof) involving productivity and recognition. The reported gender difference in work being accomplished did not result in proportional pay. As the only female in her department, her annual productivity (for the one year she was employed there) apparently outshone her male colleagues, yet they received the same merit pay as she. Virginia Valian (as cited in Wilson [2004]), distinguished professor of psychology and linguistics, points out that most women do not perceive themselves as being subjects of prejudice because the dynamics of discrimination occur under the radar.

One tenure-earning female respondent disclosed that although she had received differentiated merit pay at her institution one time, she had not gotten a raise for years. Neither had any of her productive colleagues, all of whom had been given far too many courses to teach, students to advise, and services to perform. Faculty morale has taken a nosedive. Legislative assemblies "freeze" faculty and administrative salaries. In many universities nationwide, both genders struggle in a fallen economy. Faculty members cannot get the basic help they need. Due to extreme budget deficits, fewer support staff members are available to assist; they are overwhelmed and terribly compressed. Many vital support staff positions are simply left unfilled.

In "dreaming the impossible dream," how does one "right the unrightable wrong" (Darion 1972)? Not only was Belicia unrecognized for her achievements, in effect neutralizing the weaker accomplishments of her male counterparts, but also her salary was lowballed at the hiring stage. Her gratitude for being offered the position aside, the scope of fair and equitable decisions is the purview of academe.

Belicia felt ill at ease being told the circumstances of her hiring. That is, she had gotten the job—the same one she had legitimately competed for and been offered—because a male finalist did not take it. Granted, it is tricky for a newcomer to ask about a negotiation that happened behind closed doors. "Back room deals" and other nontransparent decision making are the work of covert cliques and alliances, which in turn reduce accountability. Executive leaders, including search committees, must ensure that hiring and promotional practices are fair and above board.

Belicia can apply what she has learned as an academic insider to benefit herself in the future, as well as other graduates who are seeking jobs. She is more astute now and can educate others about career preparation and equity in decision making, volunteer for service on search committees, and uphold her beliefs in her workplace and networks. The compounded issues of salary and merit pay, and coercive power dynamics such as the voting lunch crowd, point to deep concerns. A chilly climate "suffocate[s] women's enthusiasm for their work and steer[s] them away from research careers" (Wilson 2004, A8). Male academics also find themselves on the receiving end of a toxic atmosphere; females are not automatically exempt from being negative influences or being negatively influenced.

As another spin on in-group favoritism, Valian (as cited in Wilson [2004]) mentions an underground gender dynamic. Female protégés may be promoted less by their advisors than male protégés; advisors commonly believe more in the potential of their male PhD graduates and hence actively network to get them into the most prestigious universities and coveted positions. With respect to Belicia's situation, there is an absence of information regarding this deep-seated marketing dynamic—she distributed numerous applications for both positions, perhaps not targeted enough in her approach, and little reference was made to any assistance received.

A director of a faculty-mentoring program at a prestigious research university confirms that a possible discriminatory nature confronts newly hired women and minorities:

> Eleven years ago, the impetus for our faculty-mentoring program came out of a study conducted by the Women's Caucus that examined the climate for women and minority faculty members. Finding that these groups did not feel as welcome on campus as their male and majority counterparts, the Women's Caucus suggested the development of a mentoring program, which was wisely made open to all new faculty members.

Peg Boyle Single was also in charge of a comprehensive structured mentoring intervention that informs campus-wide, research-based practices, such as training, coaching, group mentoring, and community building (see Mullen [2008] for a full description by Single). A program goal is to practice institutional vigilance and equality in the treatment of all faculty members. Single advocated for including faculty members on temporary contracts and in nontenure positions in mentoring programs; on her campus, like most campuses, they have a growing presence and are vital to the health of the academic community.

The first thing she did as a mentoring director was open up the program to all new faculty members, including instructors. After finalizing the initial logistics, she enlisted campus leaders and asked, "What is your vision for the faculty mentoring program? What should be the measures of success for the program? What would you like to see occur through the faculty program that is not currently happening?" The buy-in of leaders is a crucial support for newcomers.

Educators have encouraged formalized mentoring to meet the special academic needs of females and members of underserved groups. Mentoring programs help ensure that females, persons of color, individuals with disabilities, and LGBTQQ individuals will not be excluded from mentoring. (Chapter 5 has more examples of mentoring networks and programs; consult Mullen [2008] for an extensive treatment of practice-based research on formal mentoring and democratic processes.)

WALKING THE BALANCE BEAM OF THE ACADEMY

What follows is more specific advice and encouragement, along with areas of consideration and caution articulated by junior faculty members, tenured professors, writers about the job search process, and education researchers. Each subsection reflects a dilemma to be weighed by the job candidate and academic newcomer.

Staying at or Leaving Your Home Institution

As mentioned earlier in this book, one rule of thumb in the academy is *not* to do your undergraduate and graduate degrees at the same university. When applying for jobs, carefully weigh the benefits and drawbacks of each institution before and after you interview. Of note, public and private institutions place different demands on faculty. Public research institutions (e.g., doctoral-degree-granting institutions) place much more emphasis on scholarly research productivity than other types of institutions (e.g., liberal arts and comprehensive colleges) in which teaching and advising are more valued. Demands are dramatically different for academic faculty positions and clinical faculty positions. Also variable are expectations for teaching, scholarship, and advising, in addition to civic duty, an unquantifiable area of purposeful collegiality. Ask yourself, "What are my professional goals and where do *I* belong?"

Securing and Building on Temp Positions

Working contractually or part-time as a lecturer or adjunct can get you in the door and started in the academy. Use this time to gain valuable experience and skills and develop your networks. Also take advantage of the flex time for other work activity (McClain 2003). Research the positions you desire—what knowledge and skills do these require? Closely study the job advertisements that reflect your goals and interests, and create a plan for gaining experience and credentials in the listed domains of work.

Examples cited in academic job ads increasingly cite experience with online teaching using current technologies. Assistant professor positions advertised in education (teaching, learning, and leadership) also typically require teaching and advising graduate and undergraduate students. There is also an expectation for sustaining an active/visible program of scholarly activity, as well as participating in departmental, college, and university governance, in addition to partnerships that connect colleges to communities.

As you learn about career profiles in the desired area of work, be thinking about how to show correspondences between the expected qualifications and your own, as well as how to address gaps (e.g., skills, credentials). Can you work toward filling the gaps you are identifying? If so, what is your plan for academic development?

Be sure to have current and relevant teaching experience during your doctoral program: "Whatever academic job a student seeks is likely to require teaching, and mentors should be seeing to it that their advisees get experience" (Jenkins 2011, A39). Conversely, advisees need to get the essential teaching experience within their doctoral programs or go elsewhere (e.g., community colleges). With mentors or administrators, negotiate research duties to incorporate useful teaching experience, in addition to professional development that supports teaching adults. Teaching involves many vital skills, such as knowing how to organize experiential learning in student groups and how to assess student work. Foster your own professional development online using web-based tools. Technology-enabled active learning is one such source (sponsor, Massachusetts Institute of Technology [MIT], web.mit.edu/edtech/casestudies/teal.html).

While working in temp positions, don't get stuck—be future-minded and develop your niche expertise while shoring up the additional experiences you need to stand out as an academic. An example of a scholarly niche might be educational policy that focuses on equity and achievement in public schools. Learn about how networks function while participating in them, as you will be developing them for others. Opportunities for professional development and academic job seeking abound; these range from conferences to executive leadership academies to webinars to online courses.

Temporary positions as a lecturer or an adjunct in higher education allow for gains in critical areas of teaching experience. Many academics can benefit from learning and experimenting without the tenure clock ticking and then can hit the ground running once they are in a permanent position. McClain (2003), a professor reflecting on when she was an adjunct, counsels those interested in going this route to stay put at their current institution; write and get published to increase their worth; know their value and channel their talents; seek payment for their work (e.g., multimedia design); and sell others on their assets using the Internet.

This advice applies to graduate students who aspire to earn tenure. Many new graduates must accept a temp or nontenure position at their alma mater or elsewhere for a limited period. Perhaps they are searching for a full-time job and need relevant teaching experience to be competitive in a crowded job market. Or maybe they have family or other obligations that restrict travel, delaying their career trajectory. Underemployment and inadequate pay are setbacks but also opportunities for gaining clarity and credentials that help with landing a dream job.

But the dread is that part-time teaching is "the limbo in which the unsuccessful might be stuck" (Smallwood 2005, A11). (Note: Language like "the unsuccessful" is not helpful—it is stigmatizing.) Across university campuses, large undergraduate courses are taught by adjuncts and graduate courses requiring off-campus travel to poorly equipped sites, yielding a modest stipend.

Most of the female graduates who responded to my marketing question had decided to work in a temp capacity for the reasons cited earlier. Some wanted greater flexibility for their families, whereas others had found themselves compressed over time. In one case, a female professor had been slated for a visiting assistant professorship at a top-notch research university for more than ten years, while "publishing up a storm," as she put it—her partner, a distinguished professor, was not prepared to move from their institution or his home state. Although stressed, she was persistent and was eventually hired onto a tenure-track line. While extreme, this situation resonates for many academics and for some it is deeply disconcerting.

Of course, male junior faculty members also face job stresses, as adjuncts testify. Rohrer (2004) wrote a memorable graduate story of job seeking—he used a pseudonym for self-protection, so we do not know who he is. He says it took him four years to land "the elusive" tenure-track position in political science, first having been an adjunct from where he graduated, a postdoc at a prestigious university for another year, and a visiting professor at other colleges. He moved his family twice within two years and commuted 450 miles each direction the third time, just to avoid relocating again. The pay he got was so low that his family qualified for the Women, Infants, and Children food program. Even with an outstanding publication record, he was interviewed only a few times; furthermore, the university for which he was doing part-time teaching did not keep its word of advertising a tenure-track job.

After enduring constant stress and uncertainty, Rohrer got a tenure position at a liberal-arts college, but the salary was low. However, despite his trials and tribulations, he says that he refuses to complain about having been exploited and to see the system as immoral and abusive toward new PhD graduates. Instead, he ventures that "belief" and "worth" are misguided notions, arguing that faculty members do a disservice to themselves when they become emotionally tied to a sense of their self-worth and any entitlements owed them.

"The tough reality," Rohrer pushes, is that "in the market, academics are a dime a dozen. So that's about what we get paid. Some of us seem to believe we have some kind of intrinsic value that others must recognize and reward" (4). He feels fortunate, enjoying his work and the job security that gives him time for his interests and family. He says that academics are foolish to believe we are pawns of the system or that we are somehow irreplaceable, adding our situations could be worse—what if we were forced to bid for our jobs the way some companies have to?

About the hardship of a fluctuating job market, temporary work, and low pay, I can relate. After graduating with a PhD in Canada, I moved to the United States in 1995, where I was a visiting assistant professor for one year at a research university making what some graduate assistants make. Contracts were not up for renewal, so my partner and I moved to another state where, for two years, I held an unstable, nontenure position for which I only made a stipend for *one* summer course.

But I took advantage of the flex time and got really busy developing my career by writing for publication and joining academic networks. I set a schedule for myself every day, as though I had a full-time job, and studiously worked on the necessary skills. At a virtual distance, I created a formal mentoring program for a national organization that remains active to this day. Also, a collaborative self-study group of mine became the basis of my book with Falmer Press, a leading publisher.

To obtain a tenure-earning post in education that matched my credentials, I actually had to move away to yet a third state. For two long, lonely years I focused on amassing publications (my health suffered). I then landed a tenure-earning position at a research institution with my partner. Although the struggle for realizing my dream of being awarded tenure and for work that had a political dimension to it (mentoring as a venue for changing higher education relationships and systems), the sacrifices were worth it. We ended up with dual tenured positions, as well as early promotions (and my good health returned). After being tenured, I was awarded full professor status, and in my mid-forties I was hired as a department chair at yet another research university. I found myself in a situation where my peers were of my choosing; together we work hard to make mentoring systems vibrant and to turn temp positions into permanent positions while treating lecturers as core faculty.

Returning to Rohrer's appraisal of the academy, while complaining and feeling entitled to rewards may be endemic, part-time faculty and tenured faculty members are also increasingly overworked *and* underpaid. National advocacy groups (e.g., AAUW) disclose egregious violations of fair practices and the unfair treatment of people and groups, especially traditionally disenfranchised populations in vulnerable circumstances. Advocacy, diversity, inclusion, and other professional practices must be the gold standard if higher education institutions are to thrive.

It *is* an issue when PhD graduates are exploited and when they are left to their own devices to figure out how to navigate the academy. Beginning professors often shoulder more of the workload, despite the harsh reality that they need the time for development in such areas as writing, researching, publishing, networking, and teaching. A former dean of a prominent US research university observed that some senior faculty are largely absent from their units and the core work (Bell 2010).

Applicants may want to monitor the workloads of the places to which they are applying, as well as implicit gender- and race-based expectations. Communicate with trusted associates about where to apply and interview, and especially where to accept jobs. Documented imbalances in workload distribution generally occur in mentoring and advising for female faculty, and the same for black faculty who carry heavier service loads than other faculty (Griffin and Reddick 2011). Workplace inequities extend to course loads, new course preparations, teaching placements, start-up and budget allocations, study leaves, and spousal issues.

Belicia's story (that introduced this chapter) hints at some of these realities. Job applicants can seek association with organizations that are shepherds of fair practice.

Taking or Leaving Joint/Split Appointments

Tenure-earning faculty members shared views on joint appointments, unfavorably known by some as "split" appointments. One defined the joint faculty appointment as "100 percent of **full-time equivalent** divided between two different organizations, such as English literature and childhood education, or between two different colleges, such as education and business." Two cautioned against accepting such positions. One individual had accepted a position with 100 percent of the appointment split evenly between two different colleges. The problem was that the tenure line was held in her home academic unit, yet most of the time she was seen only at meetings. The majority of her time was spent in the nonacademic unit, where she was responsible for carrying out service grants that did not count. Tenure was denied in this case.

In another example of a "high-alert" situation, the new faculty member accepted a faculty–administrative position within two different units of the same college. She received tenure, but only after spending an inordinate amount of time writing for publication—the director's position did not count as a plus for tenure either.

Contrasting with these scenarios, a faculty member established a joint appointment after being hired and thinking the arrangement could be beneficial. He negotiated the terms with his department chair and the center director, ensuring that they were all on the same page. He saw this cross-affiliated role as a platform for solidifying his academic identity and reputation. He flourished in it, providing enrichment and access to underserved students from across the campus.

When I asked the respondents about value-added aspects of the joint/split appointment, one said, "Nothing at all—tell your readers to avoid this situation because you end up sacrificing being sponsored by a group of colleagues—out of sight, out of mind." The second one contrarily replied with this glimmer of hope: "You learn a great deal of skills, become adept at time management, and develop a deep network that becomes invaluable once you get tenure." The third person for whom the situation was working attributed this to being an insider entrusted to create the terms of his work. He saw it as an opportunity for advocacy outreach.

The cautionary message is for anyone who may have interest in joint appointments to know how this aligns with the expectations for tenure and/or promotion at your institution and to have agreements put in writing.

Weighing Spousal Arrangements

Spousal hiring is the deal-breaker when it comes to the bigger picture of faculty recruitment, that is, over any other variable—salary, start up packages, work assignments, research leaves, and so forth (Bell 2010). There is national advocacy for universities to get on board with the reality that many faculty applicants have spouses who are also working or striving academics. However, spousal accommodation is treated differently among universities—as well as across disciplines—and remains a controversial matter.

While many universities support spousal hires, the practice is not always favorable at the unit level, partly due to an old stigma that reflects faculty concern over the governance issues and the quality of individuals unknown to them. The advocacy and decision-making power of deans plays a significant role in this hiring issue. The relationship between deans and departments influences the resulting work environment experienced by the person who is the "spousal hire" ("trailing spouse").

Proactive policies for attracting and retaining high-performing faculty members and their spouses are the gold standard among forward-looking universities. This policy outlook extends to the inclusion of same-sex, dual-career couples.

Given the importance of this matter, respondents to this book advise readers to find out the policy (assuming there is one) on spousal hiring at the universities to which they are applying, if relevant to their situation. Know in advance before you even apply what your needs are and what the best-match employment situations are possible for you. Be prepared to negotiate.

Marketing Yourself in or beyond Academe

The Scope of Career Preparation

Getting ready for professional life requires laser-like focus. Bring this to your career preparation, professional development, and job search process. Many websites post current job openings for academic positions. Additionally, members of professional associations typically receive automated notices. For more information, read the free appendix titled "Finding News about the Academy and the Academic Job Market and Locating Jobs across the Disciplines" (www.styluspub.com/resrcs/user/jsappendix.pdf), also available in Formo and Reed's (2011) guidebook.

Essential websites for job applicants include:

- LinkedIn (www.linkedin.com) is a global platform for professional networking that subscribers configure to their needs. Job seekers use it to link with others through a pyramid of associates. It communicates to select networks that you are searching for work, and it spotlights the profile you want to create, allowing for full-text uploads (e.g., articles, vita, letters of reference). Some employers consult it even when they use more traditional hiring practices. Other career websites are available as well. Social media websites used for more personal networking, such as Facebook and Twitter, can rouse career interest and even serendipitously help you navigate desirable jobs.
- *The Chronicle of Higher Education* (chronicle.com) is a widely established academic career resource. Avidly read the section "Chronicle Careers" (chronicle.com/jobs). Do targeted searches for jobs in such categories as academic field (e.g., humanities, social and behavioral sciences), personnel type (e.g., faculty, administrator), and institutional type (e.g., college, university). Surf the website using your own descriptors. Have job notices within targeted areas delivered directly to your personal inbox so deadlines are not missed. At the website, find related information, such as job-related advice, career stories, and more.
- The New York Times Company (gradschool.about.com/lr/curriculum) provides specific guidance on how to write an academic vita, complete with samples. Learn how to address research and teaching experience, dissemination of works, grants and fellowships, professional associations and licenses, and awards and other information in your job applications. Consider advice for customizing your vita and cover letter. Make your submission stand out but keep it very professional.
- Contact leaders in your field for potential job openings by consulting the research directories in your field. Some of these are produced by professional associations and are useful for identifying names, contact information, and areas of expertise. For one such document, see *The NCPEA Member Research Directory* by the National Council of Professors of Educational Administration (www.emich.edu/ncpeaprofessors).
- Academic Careers Online (www.academiccareers.com) is a global marketplace of activity where job applicants search for jobs and submit materials and where employers search jobs and post materials. The website offers a broad spectrum of academic jobs. Online job fairs that foster diversity and other goals for job applicants and employers are also available via the website.

- *Education Week* (www.edweek.org/ew/index.html), sponsored by the Editorial Projects in Education, focuses on the top school and district jobs in public education for teachers, leaders, directors, and others. Career resources are provided, along with professional-development events and opportunities, such as webinars. Users can access resources and post materials. Read the current news in education and post comments.
- HigherEdJobs (www.higheredjobs.com) is an online company that offers a suite of tools ranging from job notices in higher education to the contact information for people the user is seeking to reach. The career resources vary from posting job-search materials to tips for producing cover letters and vitae to locating the median salaries for faculty and administrators. This information helps with identifying salary ranges.
- H-Net: Humanities and Social Sciences Online (www.h-net.org; sponsor, Michigan State University) is an open community of people in the humanities and social sciences that fosters discussion networks, provides access to databases that include peer-reviewed materials, and gives users access to job notices. Projects, partners, and events are highlighted.

The Job Application–Hiring Cycle

The job application–hiring cycle involves identifying competitive jobs in the academy and preparing an effective vita, a job-specific cover letter—also known as the statement of purpose (see appendix I for a sample relevant to the assistant professorial rank)—and materials. Applicants go through a screening process and interview that takes place on a campus (or another physical site) or as an Internet-activated conference; they also complete postinterview negotiations that include salary as well as other terms and agreements, such as workload and expectations.

Seek guidance with these major steps. Ask peers who recently got jobs to review your presentation (e.g., slides, video, notes). Tailor it for each targeted position. Rehearse your presentation and responses to anticipated interview questions.

Design your presentation to incorporate the context in which you are seeking to work. "Hooks" include the mission or vision of the place and how your work, goals, and plans support it. Another example is the curriculum taught in the program to which you are applying and how your background and expertise provide support and address gaps. Perhaps students would benefit from an immersive experience you could lead. The "fit" as you see it between your profile and the unit's is yet another potentially important "hook." Presentations do not need to focus exclusively on your research projects, even for interviews at doctoral-degree-granting institutions, and thus can be extended to incorporate the workplace to which you aspire.

For a handy overview, consult Murray's (1998) postulates for psychology students that are helpful to anyone seeking a job. For a more in-depth read, consult Formo and Reed's (2011) *Job Search in Academe*. This engaging research-based narrative includes useful notes in chart form. Rhetorical strategies for getting the position you want are covered, and the job cycle is explained, with specifics about advertisements, academic lingo, and salary (contract) negotiations.

Also check out *The Academic Job Search Handbook*. Heiberger and Vick (2001) take readers from planning the job search to preparing written materials, and from conducting the interview to anticipating life after the job. Once you have the position, expand your marketability and extend your global reach. They describe crucial structural and cultural issues of higher education that help clarify different types of positions (e.g., tenure track, nontenure contracts). They also discuss the prospect of administrative posts and reasons for moving to new positions.

Diversifying the Work Portfolio

Diversifying your academic or work portfolio—settings, skills, and activities—means venturing outside the standard realms of academe or practice. You will be dividing your time between, say, teaching, writing, fieldwork, and consultation: "While some may find freedom in the decline of the straight and narrow career path, others see it as unsettling. Without clear direction, how do you build a career that's custom-made for you?" (Murray 1998, para. 2).

Hearing feedback from successful academicians and clinicians, Murray says that adaptability and flexibility are crucial. One can use the research skills gleaned from training or practice (e.g., psychology) to pursue work in another field (e.g., demographics and policy making). After completing his clinical internship in psychology, someone accepted a position as a senior research associate doing research that guides psychology-related policy. Murray encourages job seekers to "be willing to promote and apply your skills in new settings. Also be open to part-time consulting or contractual jobs" (para. 8). The economic analogy of stocks is used—people should avoid putting all of their money in one stock—for explaining the logic behind why some serious careerists prefer to diversify.

Preparing before Graduation

Well-organized graduate students squeeze career preparation into a busy schedule. Use your vita to communicate your identity as a professional; patterns should be clear throughout your areas of accomplishment, education, and foci (see chapter 2). Update your vita regularly; adapt it for different types of applications, such as jobs, scholarships, grants, internships, and networks. Explore what you find appealing.

An esteemed nationwide network is the AACTE Holmes Scholars Program (part of the American Association of Colleges for Teacher Education). This program is a diversity advocacy group made up of partnerships with seasoned scholars that prepare talented students for higher education and leadership positions. Participants are "doctoral students from underrepresented backgrounds" who experience "mentorship, peer support, and rich professional development opportunities." The program also helps AACTE member institutions to diversify their faculty (2012, aacte.org/pdf/Programs/Holmes-Scholars/holmes-scholars-brochure.pdf).

As you do career planning, consider Murray's (1998) generic tips that follow, as they arose from consultation with academics with expertise in career preparation:

- *Seek practical work experience.* This is especially important if practicum experience is not a required part of your educational or training program; internships are key to landing some jobs.
- *Equip yourself with "vogue skills."* Computer proficiency is essential in most jobs. Attend informative workshops, webinars, or seminars. Also, if you think you might want your own business or to run your own agency one day (and hence diversify), get exposed early on and plan over time.
- *Gear yourself for booming areas.* What are the emerging routes in your own discipline? In psychology, these include demographic research, human factors, and technology; in educational leadership, statistical analyses of standardized test results, school-district technology infusion, staff development training, teacher competency, mentorship, vocational programming, student achievement, desegregation of school districts, and more. The field of special education is a boom area in higher education where vacancies are going unfilled (Miller, Pearl, and Wienke 2004).

- *Connect with people in the field.* Make contact with those whose careers interest you, ask them how they got to where they are, and shadow role models for a short time; also consult your mentors (e.g., academic adviser) about your professional goals.

Targeting Unusual Jobs

Use these strategies for finding unusual jobs that might interest you:

- *Articulate your professional identity.* Who are you, what are your core values, and what do you have to offer? Avoid generic descriptions of your job profile. If you have an unconventional job in mind, tailor your title to the type of job you will pursue, instead of automatically falling back on familiar titles (e.g., educational leader, clinical psychologist.) Alternatively, describe your preparation for a particular or unspecified position. Popular ones like "executive coach" and "personnel trainer" are clichés. Reflect on your professional identity, try it out, and market it.
- *Educate potential employers about what you offer.* Emphasize that your education and skills are not just in one particular area, such as administration. Perhaps your academic background would make you a good statistician, data analyst, or digital media specialist. When seeking an unconventional job, be strategic and savvy about the people you select as references and periodically check in for feedback (see chapter 2).
- *Be open to working contractually or part time.* Across the marketplace, part-time and contract-based positions have increased. Contract work is a way to build experience and juggle appealing projects (Murray 1998).

Negotiating Job Salary

A very popular job-seeking guide is Bolles's (2011) *What Color Is Your Parachute?* Generic negotiation strategies can be adopted for just about any purpose. The tips provided in Bolles's yearly compendium are universal in the sense that they are supported by other texts. He says that the very word *negotiate* makes people cringe, but the process itself is not that difficult; however, there are some basic conventions to observe. As always, context matters, so note any cues that might alter or even contradict the rules.

To summarize, tips for negotiating salaries are:

1. Wait to discuss salary until the end of the interviewing process.
2. Use the salary negotiation to find out how much the employer is willing to pay you and what other perks or benefits are available.
3. Let the employer mention the salary first.
4. Research what salary you will need if you are given a job offer.
5. Learn what the typical salaries are for your field and for that organization.
6. Come up with a salary range for the employer and an interrelated range for yourself.
7. Know how and when to end the salary negotiation. (Bolles 2011)

POINTS TO REMEMBER

Returning to the opening job-search account, obstacles were identified and overcome that remain significant challenges for the academy. Belicia won her dream job as an assistant professor while learning that she had been offered a lower salary than her male competitor.

One explanation, provided by Joan Williams (as cited in Wilson [2004]), law professor and director of a work program, is that institutional rules are more rigidly applied to women candidates. Close attention is paid to their accomplishments, whereas for a male candidate it is his "promise" that matters—a covert gender bias that insiders, professors, and leaders all need to closely monitor.

The relevance of Belicia's case to marketing and job searching is not whether men and women are both lowballed but is whether females receive lower job offers for the same work and status. In-group favoritism that benefits male faculty is pervasive beyond salary and merit pay, as working conditions are also generally inferior for new female faculty. A significant study of 983 assistant professors at six major research institutions (conducted in 2002 by Harvard's Graduate School of Education) found that, on nineteen out of twenty-eight measures, female scholars were less satisfied as employees than males. Areas of dissatisfaction included lack of clarity about tenure expectations, insufficient time and funds for research, and poor support from department leaders (as cited in Wilson [2004]).

Another concern is the extent to which graduate students are proactively preparing for their professional life. How many are aware of the opportunities offered in today's job market, especially in their own fields, and the networking they must do to become a known quantity and an appealing candidate? Because graduate school rarely prepares students for the job-search process, let alone unique job niches, be especially proactive. As a developing leader, you are expected to be resourceful and self-reliant. Eisner (2004) says, "It's what students do with what they learn when they can do what they want to that is the real measure of educational achievement" (302). In other words, many graduate students get As in their courses and write good dissertations. But the real "test" comes from being able to transfer learning from one's degree to unknown work domains of job markets and workforces, building networks beyond the advisor, and successfully competing and standing out as a job candidate. Another learning curve comes from turning unsatisfying work environments into vibrant professional learning communities.

SUMMARY

Herein you have been provided with information relative to the job application–hiring cycle with respect to career preparation, professional development, and job search. Three major themes were also addressed: the covert practices of discrimination in hiring and evaluation, temp positions and other balance beams in the academy, and self-marketing in or beyond academe.

Navigational Prompts

- *Go to the website Preparing Future Faculty* (www.preparing-faculty.org). After searching it, read *The Preparing Future Faculty Program* (www.preparing-faculty.org/Brochure.pdf). Research ways for engaging in academic and professional development at the department level, campus level, and partner campus level. Examples include participating in forums for doctoral alumni and shadowing role models.
- *Find out what the booming areas* or emerging routes are in your discipline. Consult the venues of career news that have been outlined; also explore new websites and talk with advisors and market experts.

- *Visit career centers* online and physically at professional conferences and scrutinize job postings of interest. Subscribe to magazines and websites that assist job seekers. What specifications are required in your own field?
- *Search the reference (or job-hunting) section* of a bookstore, library, or digital database for marketing subjects. Choose texts on the topics of job hunting and career directories and in more specific areas such cover letters, résumés, and interviewing. Enelow and Kursmark's (2010) *Cover Letter Magic* has examples of cover letters and vitae. Adapt the focus on the corporate world—it is rarely inclusive of education as a market.
- *Go to talks by professors and recently employed graduates* and seek insight where possible into job interviews, work expectations, and climate issues. Ask questions of those who write reference letters and those who hire employees, as these are informative vantage points. Also ask questions of those who have gone through a complete job application –hiring cycle.

GLOSSARY

adjunct. A temporary position that is not on the tenure track; a person who teaches part time and is paid less than people in full-time positions.

annually renewable. These temp positions are filled by non–tenure-track instructors, lecturers, adjuncts, and visiting professors; these may offer good opportunities but can to lead to more short-term contracts and compression.

assistant professor. Rank on the track to potential tenure. Faculty members with tenure achieve the rank of associate professor. Assistant professors are referred to as junior faculty members, while associate and full professors are senior professors.

campus interview. The candidate is brought to campus to do a presentation and visit with key individuals so the department, search committee, or dean can assess the fit.

contingent faculty appointments. Part-time positions and non–tenure-track positions held by adjuncts, lecturers, postdocs, clinical, and other temporary faculty members in teaching and service roles.

convention interview. At conferences, interested candidates who are interviewed may be invited for campus visits as an outcome of this screening process.

degree in hand. All work for the degree has been completed and the candidate will be defending the dissertation or graduating by the time s/he takes the job or soon afterward.

full-time equivalent (FTE). The percentage of time a staff member works.

job talk. The presentation that the candidate gives on campus or virtually about his or her research or ideas as part of the hiring process.

postdoctoral fellow (postdoc). A PhD is paid for work in a university, research center, or other venue with the purpose of doing research or advanced training.

standing faculty. All the professors who have tenure or who are on the tenure track—professor, associate professor, and assistant professor.

tenure track. "Track" is a modifier of "tenure," indicating that the position (as an assistant professor) can lead to promotion with tenure in contrast with temporary and some permanent appointments.

visiting assistant professor. Faculty membership that is not part of the standing faculty; visiting assistant professors are on contract as temporary staff.

Note: All glossary terms (except for "visiting assistant professor," which is my addition and definition) are from Heiberger and Vick (2002).

Chapter Nine

Planning a Two-Way Mentorship Agenda

The case you are about to read is my personal academic story of planning a two-way, win-win mentoring agenda. Mutual, reciprocal mentoring renews relationship and systems, and can transform them from the inside out:

As a new visiting assistant professor from Canada at a doctoral-degree-granting university in the United States, I was not aware of planning a mentoring agenda, only of receiving and offering help as needed. Because no formal mentoring programs existed for new faculty in the education college, certainly not for non–tenure-track employees, I actively reached out to faculty members and administrators as situations arose. Not paired with an experienced professor or go-to administrator during my nine-month stint at the institution, I was immersed in a sink-or-swim mode. I did notice, though, that tenure-earning folks were assigned sponsors who actually spoke on behalf of their tenure dossiers to the college faculty committee, a potentially stellar mentoring practice.

I did receive notable mentoring assistance, however—through a center of collaborative learning communities in response to a grant application I submitted as the principal investigator of a study titled "The Voice of Hispanic At-Risk Preservice Student Teachers." I experienced two-way mentoring from group members who knew the culture of this particular institution and state, both of which were foreign to me. Through this center I was awarded sponsorship and competitive funding from the Sid Richardson Foundation/Southwestern Bell, a catalytic gesture that set in motion a foundational research project that culminated in an article and a prospectus for a special issue of a journal. Both works were published, and the former paid for a master's student fluent in Spanish to translate the audiotapes I produced through interviews with undergraduate education bilingual students. Also, through this center I was introduced to the social-support structure for national grant awardees; along with about eight other faculty members, I was invited to formal meetings and lunches with the director, where our research ideas were shared, both in preliminary and final form. For such occasions, reports were produced and circulated by all of us, and accountability was rewarded through group membership and a certificate of research achievement. All of these mentoring scaffolds proved invaluable in shaping my research and social capacity at the time, although I was really only aware of this in hindsight.

Needless to say, we, the grant awardees, came to develop our own social structure that influenced our interactions and work in many other ways. Among these spin-offs, I was one of the forces behind establishing a mentoring network that brought together a small group of faculty members and doctoral students interested in exploring political issues in education and empowering forms of teaching and learning. We spent months meeting, reflecting, writing, reading, and critiquing one another's works. As authors, we each produced our own chapter dealing with K–12 public-school or higher-education topics for a book. We were joyous to receive a contract for our collection based on a prospectus that I prepared for the group. The book, which was published by a scholarly press, uses the metaphor of "breaking the circle of one," that is, creating community to find a shared purpose.

In my current role as a tenured faculty member, I have been able to learn from my experiences at three additional universities. For the last six years, doctoral students' academic progress and dissertation writing have benefited from careful planning and constant vigilance. This has resulted in my doctoral students graduating every year, regularity in my relations with mentees, and shared work. Mentorship extends to opportunities for coauthorship on articles and participation in grant projects, in addition to assistantships on my editorial projects. The sheer amount of work that goes into working closely with just one student on his or her text is phenomenal. It is difficult to articulate how one models all of the complex thinking and complicated steps involved because there is no set formula, and the picture changes depending on the situation and those involved.

In my master's and doctoral courses, I provide workshops on literature searches, academic writing, conference presentation, scholarly publication, and multifaceted dissemination. And I receive mentoring from faculty members, administrators, and students in many different ways, often unknown to them. For example, the firsthand, school-based experiences that my students collectively possess are very impressive and inform my current insider's knowledge. My own continually changing mentoring mosaic enriches me as a teacher, learner, and leader. Although I do not have any formally assigned mentors, certain astute individuals have risen to the occasion as my reciprocal teachers and they are selfless, knowing beings from whom I derive great support and deep insight. We are a constantly evolving network of scholars that adds new scholars, and we are productive and edgy, as well as forward-thinking. I strive to be a strategic mentor who is highly collaborative and responsive, as well as direct in my communications style, elements of my own selfhood that are crucial to refining the art of mentorship.

CASE ANALYSIS

This case captures the raw feelings associated with the vibrancy of my academic life as it unfolded in the earlier stages of my career, in 2006. Since 1995, I have taught in various capacities at different research universities in the United States. The value I place on a two-way mentoring agenda has evolved. I believe that not just seasoned professors but also early-career faculty members should deliberate on the mentoring they wish to receive *and* give. I have come to see how important it is for senior faculty to derive strength and renewal from their mentoring relationships and not be a human crutch, somehow cast for perpetuity as a lifelong mentor. I also believe more than ever how vital networked learning is for emerging scholars, not as a compensation for unsatisfactory mentoring with faculty so much as a necessity.

Partnerships and agencies can become highly synergistic if two-way benefits are being realized. Renowned educator Goodlad (1994) gave us the groundbreaking vision of simultaneous renewal in the context of institutional bodies. In this picture, universities and schools work closely together toward shared goals that are mutually established and outcomes that strengthen all parties. Goodlad's vision of **simultaneous renewal** can be awakened at the relationship level whereby academic mentoring is occurring, with the idea being that *all* parties develop and benefit.

My adaptation is what I refer to as **relational renewal** by the mentoring parties for which giving and taking is intentional, planned, and executed, benefitting all committed individuals. When relationships have mutuality of goals and outcomes, work environments can flourish, and academies can benefit from networked learning, collaboration, and community. Also, mutuality helps to renew mentors and avoid overtaxing them and their resources and services to the point of exhaustion, disillusionment, and burnout.

Planning and enabling a two-way mentoring agenda may seem like a high standard to reach. To graduate students and new professors alike, the focus is on surviving and seeking assistance. Thus, the comentoring vision might seem like an unimaginable stretch. However, even senior faculty mentors must experience renewal in order to perform consistently well over time. They are also seeking to learn and benefit from growth opportunities. Some commitments by faculty members and graduate students do speak to this vision of two-way mentoring. Articulating the vision as I am here is the first step in recognizing its value.

Relational mentoring includes such crucial behaviors as teaching, learning, helping, reflecting on practice, and improving (Roberts 2000). With regard to relationship efficacy, protégés and mentors who model reciprocal mentoring achieve a higher standard of professionalism. In such mentorships, the parties are attuned to developing the relationship, not just themselves or their own careers.

If you think of mentoring as including the relational elements Roberts described, then it becomes clear why one-way mentoring is of limited value. Significant mentoring relationships rooted in one-way support drain people and systems—they can have a detrimental effect on mentor or mentee energy and attitude, as well as advancement and promotion. Examples of mutuality are coteaching courses, cocoordinating events, coauthoring manuscripts, and copresenting at conferences. One-way mentorships may involve single-authored works borne of the concerted labor of mentors or mentees, years-long career support dependent on letters and phone calls, and an absence of communication or recognition of the other's toil.

In the initiating case for this chapter, the situations and dynamics I narrated match the elements Roberts (2000) identified. Helping is an area that goes beyond the strictly personal; it includes organizational (e.g., the academic center's sponsorship and national grant that it coordinated), group (e.g., scholarly networks and mentoring communities), and interpersonal (e.g., academic professional work shared by faculty members and students) domains. Teaching–learning is communicated through these contexts, which stress reciprocity in study groups (consisting of faculty members and students), in addition to the educational philosophy of teacher as learner. Reflective practice involves improving one's mentoring practice, deepening one's capacity to teach and learn, and being oriented to networked learning and mutual mentoring.

ORGANIZATIONAL AND SYSTEMIC

Limitations of Mentorship

Mentoring is, unfortunately, a taken-for-granted resource within the academic culture, even though universities would suffer without it. Advisors and dissertation chairs are rarely provided support, including assessing the quality of their own assistance, as well as stipends, course release time, or recognition of any kind; the work of a committee member is even more invisible. As the National Academic Advising Association (NACADA 2012) aptly attested,

> Many institutions of higher education have few effective systems in place for the evaluation of academic advising, and little reward or recognition is attached to its successful delivery. Good advising, like good teaching, publication and research, needs to be recognized . . . a tangible reward system can be an enhancement to effective advising.

This national association's stand is that faculty and institutions demonstrating good advising (and, presumably, mentoring) should be recognized and therefore rewarded. This position needs action. The fact that this association continues to honor its public stance not only acknowledges the important work of mentoring but also of the fact that faculty members often feel disconnected in their work and from their workplaces. Furthermore, effective mentoring is a highly complex science and art of which advising is but *one* component. Other major elements of graduate mentoring include coaching, teaching, instructing, scaffolding, and counseling.

Another limitation is that many graduate faculty members either do not commit to mentoring at all or fail to undertake this commitment to their satisfaction. There are many reasons for this reality that include and extend beyond the organizational realm. One unresolved issue is how workloads are constituted and how some faculty members are classroom teachers, not doctoral mentors and published researchers (Mullen 2005). Annual assignment of faculty duties that stipulate the percentages to be allocated for teaching, research, and service can be a contractual protection for including and thus not "omitting" mentoring commitments and expectations.

Since many universities do not provide "credit" in the form of assigned time (percentages) for graduate mentoring, not much negotiation is required of faculty members—in fact, the pressure to mentor really comes from within the culture or oneself. Some faculty members have gained the credentials for graduate supervision, which is a privileged status, without doing the hard work of thesis/dissertation supervision. Some even offload the duties onto others, such as committee members and administrators, which is unfair to faculty in general and students in particular.

Faculty members who are supported through assigned duties of mentoring have more time for managing dissertation loads and, if rewarded, for designing and implementing orientations, cohorts, study groups, collaborations, and other student-friendly innovations. Such mentoring and advising practices assist with the multiple demands on the professoriate and, if genuinely carried out, should be recognized by institutions. In a downturned economy, this balancing act becomes a real struggle for professors who have more students, fewer supports, and increased workloads.

It is perplexing that the roles and responsibilities of "permanent advisor" and "dissertation chair," as well as "committee member" are rarely communicated with clarity and precision. Faculty and graduate-student handbooks are crucial documents, but they do not address many of the cultural specifics that permeate mentoring roles. Tenured faculty members might be the only ones receiving vital information. If authorized by the institution's graduate school and/or accreditation bodies, they will hold graduate status. This in turn designates them to direct a doctoral student's program and chair committees. Tenure-earning faculty members are typically granted a lower designation, such as committee membership only.

Clearly, this is a passing nod given to the time-consuming, complex work of mentoring that does little to support faculty work and load distribution. Clarification is also necessary for accountability on the part of the mentor and the mentee—which party is responsible for what when it comes to thesis/dissertation supervision and its many tasks, including research management and academic writing, critique, and editing. Sometimes students seek supports that professors think they should be handling on their own and with their own resources, such as fine-tune editing.

Furthermore, the vision of excellence in doctoral education—on which institutions are highly dependent but not inclined to officially recognize—forces faculty members to go above and beyond to mentor students. This level of support means that their own research will progress more slowly—they are expected to carry out this mission of their respective universities relying solely (or mostly) on the intrinsic rewards of doing so. Some even jeopardize their own job security—accomplishments, tenure, and promotion—in the process or become compressed, sacrificing career momentum. Such dynamics can be compounded for mentors when mentees are assigned to them, not personally selected (Clark, Harden, and Johnson 2000).

Positive outcomes can be yielded from doctoral networks, including cohorts, but a virtual lack of bureaucratic support is a serious offset. Since universities do not officially sanction informal cohorts and learning communities, they might be ignored as just a compulsive "hobby" of the professor. Thus the workload assigned to a faculty mentor will not diminish with the extra responsibility.

Students expect to be guided during the summer months on their dissertations, but North American faculty members typically have only nine-month contracts. Incentives (e.g., merit pay, mentoring achievement awards, and reassignment based on equivalency loads) that help compensate for the time invested should be built into faculty workloads (Mullen 2005). In many US research institutions, a handful of doctoral students constitutes a supervisory load for dissertation chairs, although that number is modest and it has increased. This workload should be weighted relative to assigned faculty duties so the mentoring is not just left to happen but is planned. Such ideas extend Dinham and Scott's (2001) policy recommendations for requiring institutions to support the work of scholarly mentorship and hence the future professoriate itself.

Another organizational pressure that many active supervisors face in the academy is that doctoral education has become a means to an end for students seeking promotions, credentials, and salary increases. The diploma-mill mentality of doctoral education has been expedited by low-quality online degrees. About the changing values of universities and colleges as consumer markets, Weinstein (2004) quips that "The capitalist model of human behavior has restructured academic choice, and our goal has become to satisfy our students, not to provide them with an education" (105). Although Weinstein's focus is on university courses and the devaluing of knowledge and learning due to "consumer satisfaction," his sentiment applies to doctoral education. Students approaching their dissertation sometimes press their mentors to help them expeditiously complete their study so they can get on with their lives. Those who do not immerse themselves in the work will be trading off substance and the time needed to grow as reflective scholars and skilled researchers. Ironically, these are some of the very areas expected by academic employers for entry-level positions and especially for academic agendas.

This attitude gets perpetuated by the "professionalization" or "modernization" of the degree, particularly within the applied knowledge disciplines (Mullen 2007b; Nyquist and Woodford 2000). Unfortunately, this cultural change, intended to make scholarship practical, has inadvertently led to a "dumbing down" of the curriculum, a mindset that affects not only the quality of courses but also doctoral dissertations. Otherwise-willing faculty members simply do not want to spend the time educating adults within changing systems they do not personally endorse. Faculty mentors complain that some doctoral students do not exhibit the expected dispositions of lifelong learners: a willingness to learn new knowledge and skills; resiliency in the face of constructive criticism; passion for meaningful scholarship; the ability to be independent, solve problems, and build networks, a work habit characterized by reliability and high-quality work; *and* the capacity to foster two-way mentorships.

Such scenarios hint at deep fractures within higher-education institutions and beyond. Market forces shape people's thinking and behaviors. We need to reclaim the academy and the relational synergy that perpetuates high-quality work and desirable changes in our workplaces and society.

Core Value of Mentorship

Thankfully, some professors see dissertation advising and mentoring as an intrinsic part of their job and selfhood. However, mentoring researchers make the important point that this very orientation as mentor ironically leads to and even feeds faculty exploitation. For professors who were mentored successfully through their doctoral programs, and perhaps their initial job placements and publications, the realization that faculty involvement in mentoring varies tremendously can come as a shock. Regardless, even those who were ineffectively mentored still seem to possess a core value of mentorship, built into the "bones" of new assistant professors. The dawning realization might be that only *some* qualified professors actually support the doctoral mentoring enterprise due to its "voluntary" nature. A deeper revelation comes from witnessing how graduate faculty members attest to the value they place on mentoring, yet far fewer carry major loads and handle the most difficult student cases, graduating their students and seeing them through to job placement.

The difference between rhetoric and practice is most evident at the ground level within departments and units. This is where decisions and activities involving doctoral advising workloads occur and sacrifices ensue. As one theory–practice tension, only some professors believe that mentoring is also *their* responsibility.

An undercurrent within the academic culture is that some willing faculty members, even those with doctoral experience from former institutions, might, ironically, feel closed out. Perhaps the new faculty member, eager to gain the invaluable experience as a committee member and dissertation supervisor, is finding the "revered" status of the latter out of reach. Individuals in this situation will struggle to become established as chairs (and cochairs), even though it is customary that they first gain the experience. Thus, you will want to observe and shadow the best faculty mentors on your campus. There is an art and science to excellence in doctoral mentoring, and every institution has its own customs, procedures, and policies. Learn how to handle the many intricacies of this role, beyond the paperwork and giving feedback on proposals and dissertations.

University leaders can show vision by guiding early-career faculty members into becoming doctoral supervisors by modeling the steps involved and demonstrating the most educational of practices possible. Without established protocols for advising and mentoring workloads, new faculty members struggle. They feel confused, even disillusioned. They might wonder why their services are being thwarted within the upper ranks, and why they are getting mixed messages about their perceived value.

The transition from committee member to doctoral supervisor reflects a steep learning curve. Unfortunately, these natural institutional processes can be undermined by unfair practices (e.g., cronyism, infantilization, ostracization), especially of anyone seen as a threat. In contrast, collaboration among senior faculty combined with thoughtful invitations to new faculty creates a positive climate.

CLARIFICATION OF ROLE FUNCTIONS

Modeling and Molding

Important functions for mentors and students are **role modeling** and **role molding**, with both functions linked to academic socialization processes, including behavioral reinforcement. The former function has more latitude for critical and progressive forms of education.

Many of us can summon different people—teachers, influential leaders, famous writers and scientists, and so forth—who have inspired the patterning our own growth and achievements. However, unlike mentors, models and molders work more at the general motivational level and through osmosis. For example, you will observe a professional behavior, such as punctuality or organization, and then internalize it, stick to it, and in effect be modeling it yourself.

As a student, you should find mentors who will help ensure your progress and individualize your program, career trajectory, or scholarship. The mentoring you experience will be rewarding when the best interests of both parties are honored, a focus is maintained on career goals and research proclivities, and the relationship has regularity and mutual benefits.

Conversely, when mentees are "molded" by mentors into their own self-image, used to assist in low-leverage activities, or even demoralized to advance the mentor's agendas, the mentor will not have aided the student "in carving out his or her own niche" (Brown, Davis, and McClendon 1999, 5; see also Freire 1997). Even for students who thrive as disciples under the tutelage of stellar scholars, "it can come as a rude shock to find that hiring committees might no longer be so interested in snapping up a younger model of an older approach" (Damrosch 2000, B24). This point was reinforced by a faculty member's story of a promising job candidate who was not deemed worthy of an interview after being introduced in his mentor's supporting letter as "my oedipal son" (see Damrosch 2000, B24).

Role modeling is not to be confused with mentoring (Lee 1999). In fact, role modeling does not have to involve a conscious or even personal connection. Role models, such as academics at conferences, may not know they are modeling attitudes and behaviors that you are observing. A "role model" is not necessarily your mentor but may be inspirational and motivating nonetheless. Role models do not even have to be people we know—for example, John Goodlad's framework of simultaneous renewal has been a major influencer in people's work in school–university partnerships, providing a mindset for development and direction in such areas as democratic leadership, extending outside teacher education programs.

It is important to understand this distinction between role modeling and mentoring. Mentorship "is intentional and longitudinal" and generally has "a recognizable structure" (Lee 1999, 3). Effective mentoring can be shorter term, though, with all goals satisfied. In peak form, lifelong learning, when relational, synergistic, and sustained, has the generative character of **lifelong mentoring**.

Create Your Own Mentoring Program

Some American universities do not have formal mentoring programs for graduate students, which can be a hardship for people who feel marginalized. Yet, ironically, "one point on which most educators agree is that a mentoring program should begin as soon as possible after a student [or faculty member] makes contact with a university" (Freeman 1999, 2). Many insiders might see this commitment as overwhelming. But students thrive on the goodwill and sound advice, and many can thrive *only* in this context, particularly if they are from opportunity-deprived, poverty-stricken backgrounds. Students can help institutions and organizations generate needs-based formal mentoring programs through e-networks, for example.

Consider creating your own mentoring program even as a new student or faculty member, and continue this practice as you gain practical experience. In fact, you do not even have to wait until you become employed to do so. One student explained how she successfully did just this: self-described as a "black female doctoral student attempting to adjust to a new environment" (Robinson 1999, 1), Robinson emphasized how thorny it is to put a university-based mentoring program in place, particularly one that is student initiated and minority focused. But it can be done, as her story illustrates. One important tip is to consult with and involve administration in your decision making about any formal mentoring initiative. Another is to stick with the process despite the ups and downs along the way, such as reduction in funding. Strategic ideas, explained previously in this book, are to include white male professors in the mentoring of culturally ethnic student groups and digital immigrants in comentoring relationships with digital natives.

As a facilitator of networks over the years, I have seen, firsthand, that well-structured, synergistic groups make all of the difference for most students and greatly assist those who would not otherwise make it through their academic programs. And while some members commit to the collective spirit, others do not, regardless of pedagogical interventions. For example, only synergists (givers and receivers) support the goals of the group by, say, constructively reviewing their peers' writing or research materials. In contrast, self-centered behaviors include when peers are only available when their own work is being discussed.

Students who perform as spirited guides either simply absorb their nonreciprocating colleagues or resent them. For example, Amanda, a doctoral student who cofacilitated a study group (with her dissertation chair) seemed to justifiably complain via e-mail about a certain member's performance:

> I believe that Mike attends our meetings only when he has something for us to read of his own. When we're busy talking about other people's writing, he either grades his own student papers or reads something else. He hardly says a word or blurts out something inappropriately. Again at our last meeting he did not come with printouts of anyone's papers or contribute to the discussion of them. While he was thumbing through his own stack of papers, I could once again see that he was present only because of the feedback scheduled on his literature review—this irks me. I've been thinking that those of us who attend regularly and who are prepared and contribute should be given special consideration (e.g., extra time on the agenda). However, my major professor doesn't see what is happening with Mike because of the seating distance the student chooses. I have talked with Dr. Riley about my concerns; we've decided to keep a close watch without making any assumptions, then later see if action is needed.

Amanda is admirable for the leadership and ethical qualities suggested in her narration. She sounds like the kind of person who knows how to give and receive within a group context and who expects the same from others. Of course, many skilled faculty facilitators also experience uncertainty in such situations. While group behavior, such as reciprocity, sharing, and caring, is natural for some members, it is a learned behavior for others and a source of resistance for still others. In study groups, members can exhibit competitiveness, self-centeredness, game playing, or aggression. Leaders do not always see unfair behaviors that are borderline issues similar to the one Amanda described, which argues for strong coleadership between faculty and students and open discussion of expectations.

The nurturing of successful mentee qualities is vital. Barkham (2005) shared this advice about the qualities that members (students and professors) should possess and actions they can take to help ensure growth and success:

- Be open and honest.
- Be prepared to listen and reflect.
- Be respectful of colleagues.
- Constantly question.
- Be prepared to ask for help.
- Be sympathetic to others' problems.
- Be prepared to offer fresh ideas.
- Be prepared to work hard.
- Make friends—network.
- Enjoy the new life.

About the freedom to gather and express opinions in mentoring groups, many of us in Westernized countries take this right for granted. Nafisi's (2003/2004) autobiography about teaching Western classics in her homeland, Tehran, in politically repressive circumstances makes me stop and think. The secret cohort that she led met in her living room; young Iranian women, dressed in black veils, discussed not political sabotage but banned literary works.

The premise for the creation of Nafisi's cohort was disclosed at the first session. The members had been selected from the professor's courses because of their love of literature. For inspiration on that day, Nafisi recounted the story of Nabokov, just nineteen years old, who wrote his way through the Russian Revolution, not allowing the sound of bullets and fighting outside the window to distract him. Foreshadowing what was to come, despite the very serious challenges to the group's careers, reputations, and well-being, the women continued gathering: "It had become a habit with us, a permanent aspect of our relationship, to exchange stories" (Nafisi 2003/2004, 241).

Notably, even though all were courageous, handpicked women, various dispositions surfaced: Some acted altruistic and connecting, a few were closed minded, and still others angry and confrontational, a disposition that demands and depletes the goodwill of others. Mentors who lead groups will sometimes find themselves or others feeling off balance by unexpected dynamics and personality clashes and will need to restabilize the situation.

Nafisi's group took grave risks just to gather, read, and discuss, with hope for societal change in their hearts. This behind-the-scenes view of the group makes self-centered behaviors seem all the more limited, even childish, raising the bar for what we *should* expect from each other and ourselves.

Study groups, graduate seminars, and doctoral programs have the great potential to model the value of peer mentorship in inquiry and development (e.g., Mullen 2005, 2011a; Piantanida and Garman 1999). Support groups that faculty members lead or participate in guide members' quality of thinking and writing, so standards can be met for sound scholarship and situational politics can be navigated.

As you seek guidance, investigate interdisciplinary and collaborative groups that reach beyond your immediate locale and known world. Mentoring programs (statewide, nationwide, and global) are enabling students and graduates "to broaden their horizons beyond the boundaries of their immediate program, giving them more opportunities to work together at all stages of their study, and helping them work with a wide range of faculty members" (Damrosch 2000, B24; see also Mullen [2008] and chapter 8 for a discussion of network mentoring across diverse institutions).

Individualizing the Journey for Students

Faculty mentors who work one on one with their doctoral advisees or in groups will find it necessary to individualize their students' journeys. From the documented musings of one dissertation committee chair who assessed what had served to support the mentoring of doctoral graduates, several key areas surfaced.

Zimmerman (2004) had tapped doctoral advisees to learn about specific support behaviors that had enabled their success. Building on the perspectives she elicited, some ideas and tips follow:

- *Evaluation of the student's psychological needs.* The mentor determines what unique support a student requires. Chairs are responsible for evaluating their "academic strengths and weaknesses while assessing the relative degree of intervention and assistance required for successful degree completion." One critical issue concerns whether a mentee is "intrinsically or extrinsically motivated." Depending on the situation, the chair creates different learning contexts that satisfy each student's needs; some students depend on regular contact and deadlines, as well as encouragement for staying on track and being focused. While some dissertation writers enjoy the relative freedom of doctoral candidacy, others need the explicit support of peers and faculty (26–27).
- *Support for dissertation topic.* The mentor must figure out what will aid the student in being "personally invested in their learning." Democratic practice seems to suggest that students should be supported in selecting their own dissertation topic, although some might find assignment preferable. Chairs will also need to exercise caution when it comes to amending the chosen subject matter beyond recognition, as "topic police" can cost students their enthusiasm and drive (26–27).
- *Deadlines.* While goal setting is the easiest strategy to implement, meeting deadlines can be very difficult for some students. A chair who understands how best to relate to a particular student, what motivates that individual, and his or her needs will probably be more successful—deadlines can be jointly set and aligned with the anticipated phases of research or writing. Intrinsically motivated students will establish their own timeline and not need prodding, but they may need encouragement to make contact and reach out for what they need (27–28).
- *Direction to start writing and advisement to stop writing.* Thesis/dissertation candidates can benefit from hearing when it is time to stop reviewing the literature and start writing their chapters. Some hesitate to move past the relative safety of reading others' work to the risky, uncertain terrain of producing their own. Also, for some candidates, there is a feeling of security in continuing to revise the writing beyond the point where wrapping up is advisable. In this situation, the chair and committee usefully serve as a "brake" (28).

POINTS TO REMEMBER

Remember that engaging in and planning a two-way mentoring agenda is key to making the most of mentoring. Just as others will be assisting you, you will want to respond accordingly and even proactively. In fact, develop a clear vision of helping others that you can test and refine. While feeling lost as a newcomer, you will be assisting in your own adjustment—teach your peers what you are learning—this is the giving part. The tips you absorb for staying the course and improving as a thinker, writer, researcher, collaborator, and critic will surely increase your value as a colleague, friend, and, over time, collaborator.

Another implication of this chapter is that it is wise to read extensively about group dynamics and talk to facilitators to glean helpful ideas. Learn from others' hard-earned experiences while also tuning into your own intuition. Follow your own dream. Network beyond your locale. Numerous strategies have been suggested throughout this book, including developing an agreement of the work to be done and the duties and responsibilities of members' roles, including for study groups.

Forming cohorts is only one significant way serious doctoral mentors rise to the occasion with each advisee. Individualized programs of study, committee meetings, scholarly and professional development, ongoing feedback on writing, and therapeutic consultations are other such means. Some faculty members opt for in-person mentoring, while others prefer electronic supports and programs (for systematic discussion of e-mentoring programs and review of relevant innovations and literature, see Tareilo and Bizzell [2012]). Also, mentoring programs and processes should model the give and take of students working cooperatively and in earnest, not assume automatic reciprocity.

Finally, protégés like Amanda are prized for opening the door on interpersonal issues that might require attention. Implicit in her story are the words of Andrew Jackson, twelfth US president: "Take time to deliberate; but when the time for action arrives, stop thinking and go in" (www.brainyquote.com/quotes). Such developing student leaders have figured out how to "manage upward"—that is, to facilitate the mentoring work of faculty members in ways sensitive to their overload, personality, and shortcomings. Early-career professors considering creating their own mentoring networks would be wise to select students with whom they can take turns in the leadership role, share the workload, and assess the group's progress.

Mentoring as a core value transcends personal, interpersonal, and organizational issues, for it reflects a philosophical, passionate stance toward community and life itself. The famous words of Irish playwright George Bernard Shaw (1903) are fitting in this context:

> I am of the opinion that my life belongs to the whole community and as I live it is my privilege—my "privilege" to do for it whatever I can. I want to be thoroughly used up when I die, for the harder I work the more I love. I rejoice in life for its own sake. Life is no brief candle to me; it is a sort of splendid torch which I've got a hold of for the moment and I want to make it burn as brightly as possible before handing it on to future generations.

SUMMARY

This chapter features my own case history of planning a two-way mentoring agenda as an early-career faculty member. Related topics include organizational and systemic limitations of mentorship; core value of mentorship; clarification of role functions (modeling and molding); creating a mentoring program of one's own; and individualizing the journey for students. Reciprocity and mutuality in mentoring relationships are core values and synergy generators for people and their workplaces.

Navigational Prompts

* *Interview a successful leader who has organized a mentoring program* that fosters networked learning. For insights, inquire about issues related to purpose, goals, direction, program preparation, formation, development, reciprocity, refinement, assessment, strategies for resolving problems and personality differences, honoring diversity, and recognizing significant contributions.

- *Ask a seasoned faculty mentor* about how s/he individualizes the writing/research program of thesis/dissertation students or ask students how this was being done for and by them. Apply the four specific support behaviors described in this chapter's section titled "Individualizing the Journey for Students." Find out how participants get chosen and how their needs and interests are being assessed, and what you can learn from this.
- *Read accounts of groups, cohorts, networks, and learning communities*, such as first-person scholarly renditions (e.g., Piantanida and Garman 1999), practice-based narratives (e.g., Robinson 1999), nonfiction novels (e.g., Nafisi 2003/2004), and faculty self-study guides (e.g., Tareilo and Bizzell 2012). These can provide stimulation and even inspiration for developing mentoring opportunities, such as programs or networks, that suit your needs, interests, and goals. Create or seek combinations of informal mentoring relationships and formal mentoring structures.

GLOSSARY

lifelong mentoring. "Continually seeking, finding, and reconstructing mentoring and co-mentoring relationships" with different people (Mullen 2005, 25).

relational renewal. Mentoring parties that commit to and engage in relationships in which giving and taking is planned and for which relationships are reciprocal and mutually rewarding.

role modeling. A pervasive, frequently occurring form of socialization whereby individuals model desirable qualities, habits, or skills, and where people emulate the thinking, behavior, or habits of others in their lives (Lee 1999).

role molding. A focus on the "practical, pragmatic, and applied" commitment to shape students' lives into the academic, professional, and social forms institutions or professions expect (Brown et al. 1999, 5).

simultaneous renewal. For the purpose of renewing, not reforming, public education and schooling, universities and colleges partner closely with school communities to work together as equal but different partners to forge vibrant networks of collaboration that cross boundaries (Goodlad 1994).

Chapter Ten

Digital Networking as an Academic Entrepreneur

Believe in yourself. Be an **influencer**. Exert influence—change mindsets and behaviors. As a change agent, learn what you desire, find ways to harness peer collaboration, and strive to surpass your limits. Renowned educator Darling-Hammond (2010) urged educators and students alike to create possibilities in their academic lives and systems that allow all students "to invest in themselves" (30).

Invest in yourself: "You are the entrepreneur of your own life." Reid Hoffman (as cited in Hoffman and Burnett [2012]), cofounder of LinkedIn, uttered these hopeful words after having successfully launched an entrepreneurial vision of professional networking. As the creator of your own life, always ask yourself, what *is* my dream and what is my professional identity? Your dreams, fueled by action, impact the future. Forward-looking, you are transitioning from student to professor. Think about what difference you can or will make: How will you exert influence? What difference can your work, commitment, and moral vision make?

For this chapter, graduate students and professors were invited to describe their adaptation to technology in changing learning contexts and, specifically, their struggles and breakthroughs. **Digital immigrants** like the generation of students, graduates, and professors depicted in this book contrast with many younger readers, who are more likely a **digital native**. As another significant generational difference, many graduate students and even professors belong to the greatest demographic shift since the Baby Boomers—that is, people choosing to live and thrive alone, the **networked soloist**.

Meet Ruth, a female digital immigrant in her fifties. She is a tenured, midcareer professor who coleads a national organization in education. Linked with her colleagues, she uses online technology to facilitate an entrepreneurial approach to governance. She intimately knows the aches and pains of steep learning associated with technology-dependent leadership, yet she is rising to the occasion. She is heeding the call to action by actively performing the virtual roles of mentor, learner, and leader:

> After being voted onto the board of executive leaders of a professional association committed to improving public education and schooling, I was surprised to learn that computer-supported technology would be used for all governance work. Two-hour monthly meetings of the executive board were slated to occur via Elluminate and Skype. Professors who were self-taught, enthusiastic users of technology ran these meetings. Their comfort level set them apart from everyone else. So the

executive leaders had to help the rest of us, their peer leaders, retool in light of the new digital standards of our work. We all wanted to competently perform our tasks at a distance and with greater regularity.

For years, I have been using my university's BlackBoard system as an online library repository of selected materials for my web-based lecture courses and discussion board. I have used computers and digital tools in my writing. Suddenly, I was faced with needing to use Elluminate in what was a high-stakes situation for me in that this was the direction I had hoped to go with a national leadership role. I had little wiggle room for blunders.

Frustrated, I found myself alone in my office one day without any technology or office staff to help me get onto Elluminate, let alone actually use it. So I Googled its definition—it is an interactive social networking tool—and wrote out what the terminology meant, learning only then that I was heading for live interaction in a synchronous/asynchronous platform. I followed the online instructions. Reliance on this live interface via technology ignited dread for me.

Earlier that week, after receiving the first meeting agenda of the executive board through our electronic accounts, we were directed to retrieve all appending files from a website. Having to read everything in advance, this compelled us, as we do our own students, to learn expeditiously in spite of our own discomfort. We had to follow the instructions for accessing Elluminate at a centralized university server. The executive director, whose vision for the organization was to transform it into a year-round, highly productive network, calmly but firmly led us through the steps. These included setting up the Elluminate interface, clicking on the microphone icon when speaking, commenting in the scroll bar, and voting. We had to be ready to present our ideas and reports in this virtual space. There was a hotline to ring when stuck, but it was available only during the actual meetings.

All the board members scrambled to get onto the shared learning space the first time and every time, either because of tight schedules or technology glitches, or both. We couldn't always get onto the university's designated server, hear each other when we did, use the various tools properly, or overcome background static.

Over a year has gone by. We're using Elluminate well, albeit within the limited scope of our governance needs. Despite setbacks, we're taking the organization to an entirely new level of vision, as well as productivity and camaraderie.

Looking back, I had to quickly get Elluminate and this group's rapidly transitioned leadership style if I hoped to survive, let alone make substantive contributions. I improved by practicing, seeking help, and keeping records. Because not all of us knew one another, there was some awkwardness when instructions were gently repeated. We would forget to hand over the "microphone" after talking, and we'd get frazzled when downloading files. But we knew how to speak to a virtual room of nonpresent persons. Listening, I decided to concentrate on pacing, projection, and inflection. I strove to get to the point quickly; reinforce crucial messages, often in writing within the scroll bar; and speak more slowly. I kept written notes to the side of my computer.

After several fly-by-our-seat sessions, we moved ahead in our virtual community. With the new electronic systems at our fingertips, we kept each other on target, meeting deadlines. We asked tough questions, debated key points, gave updates, voted, and agreed on how to proceed. These dynamics worked because of the persistence and collaboration of the executive leaders. I sensed these technology buds must have felt the iconic pull of dragging their peers into the current century of web-based learning. Like the other leaders adapting to new technologies, I had to be led until I got the hang of the digital platform.

Taking turns as leaders and learners, we handle complex tasks and manage new e-activities like organizational branding and blog posting. I'm amazed by the benefits reaped for the members! We've expanded our publishing press, reviewed and published works, developed a state-of-the-art communications interface, created a virtual mentoring program, and more. While writing this, I'm pausing to forward the research directory project I've overseen. The director will upload it and notify the membership. Clearly, we depend on one another to make progress.

CASE ANALYSIS

Just as Ruth's case suggests, academia is dramatically changing. The digitization of much of our core work as students and faculty has inspired new ways of connecting and doing business. We can all experience entrepreneurial breakthroughs and commit to activism. Technology is not just revolutionizing how we work but also our professional identity and career.

Moving from student to professor, you will face an inevitable hurdle: translating your graduate degree into an academic career. Behind you is a complete work, your Internet-posted dissertation, perhaps with hyperlinks to websites and artifacts (e.g., reports, videos, artworks). You may have already defended this work. Perhaps you used sophisticated software for teleconferencing with faculty members from remote sites. In the future, teleconferencing may morph and be replaced with, for example, faculty holograms "talking" around a conference table or even avatars interacting in an online chat room. PowerPoint presentations may be old news too, although some people make clever use of its tools. A professor I know is teaching himself piano; using the interactive functions of PowerPoint, his computer screen serves as a digitized piano keyboard he "plays." Dissertations may be defended in a second-life environment with study participants animated, perhaps acting out crucial themes or findings of the scholarly work.

Relevant to your transition is the advent of creative opportunities for self-directed, tutorless and mentorless learning experiences, as in the teacherless learning scenario just described. Some of these are dissolving boundaries and uniting people, others are separating and insulating them. Experiment. Set the bar and be a resource to others.

E-networks and innovations work hand-in-glove. Create the very opportunities you are awaiting. You are living in the midst of an open-source movement that enables, from your personal living space, communication, collaboration with learning communities, and access to materials and products worldwide. Prepare yourself, as entrepreneurial thinking is everywhere and is rewiring the academy, our workplaces, and the very core of ourselves.

Ruth's story offers a particular type of grounding in this vision. It is a window into the struggles and breakthroughs of academics undergoing major shifts in their professional development as online entrepreneurial educators. Adjusting to online platforms for crucial communications is *not* optional for academically motivated digital immigrants. Thus, this case was selected because of its potential for role modeling—it is not a "fish to water" account of digital e-learning. Ruth's learning resembles that of many of the contributors to this book and, by way of extension, some readers. She is not a highly adaptive digital immigrant who generates educative networks with ease and finesse. Instead, her focus is on the substance of ideas, quality interchanges with colleagues energized by networked learning, and collective goals toward which progress is made.

A snapshot of her generation, Ruth naturally "computes" in terms of the physicality of space and place. She translates digital tools (and icons) into their known conventions, such as microphones that get turned on and pages instead of screens; furthermore, the notes she takes are scribbled in longhand on paper *beside* the computer. Similarly, in the advent of the automobile, people saw the car as a horseless buggy. For Ruth and those of her generation, technology-based communication is a necessary source of support for which stress and discomfort are tolerable only because of the benefits. Computers are strictly a functional tool for her, not a source of generative outreach or meditation, inspiration, and enjoyment like they are for some digital natives.

What is Ruth's network? This committed group of tenured professors, a few digitally self-taught but most not, work in higher-education institutions across the United States. These executive leaders have challenged each other to work smarter and do more by adapting to unfamiliar technology environments. They had no one to guide them, so they taught themselves. They share a purpose, to help their organization thrive by forging a productive, governance-led **microcollaborative network**. The organization itself is in transition. It is simultaneously an established association with a history that conducts business using governance protocols *and* an evolving advocacy think-tank of scholars and practitioners. A primary goal of this organization involves impacting public education and school systems. Its influence and voice are represented by a strong online presence, branding or imaging process, and worldwide dissemination of works. The interface with the membership itself, that broader network of members who likely include graduate students, is implied. The governance team generates academic services for the association's membership.

Established organizations in education will likely be evolving more in this direction. Organic networks with a strong ethic of critique have the potential to outstrip and outpace undesirable boundaries between membership and governance. Visionary entrepreneurial students and graduates push the boundaries of the status quo by fostering diversity and monitoring dynamics of power, authority, and distance to include otherwise excluded groups. Become the ambassador of the very opportunities you want to come your way.

ACADEMIC ENTREPRENEURISM IN SOCIALLY MEDIATED CONTEXTS

The days of classic scholarship may belong to an era gone by. Scholarship of this ilk tends to be attached to causes articulated in the abstract. There is a call to action and benefit for people and society. Educational, social, and political activism is sweeping all disciplines from the social sciences to the humanities to the behavioral sciences. Students and professors are being persistent about exerting influence on their home institutions, in their societies, and in the world at large. Breakthrough ideas fueled by passion and expressed as new forms of e-mentoring in digital environments are examples of creative people and groups investing in themselves. Thankfully, factory-model environments do not always hold entrepreneurism back.

As academic entrepreneurs, high-performing graduate students are developing into networked collaborators and leaders. They are impacting areas of high interest. At the same time, though, graduate students who are seeking jobs in academia are being challenged to compete more vigorously than ever. In a globalized economy, hundreds of people have the same skills and can do what any one of us can do. Commonly shared skills include producing high-quality surveys for schools or conducting evaluative assessments of formal (mentoring) programs.

In order to stand out, graduate students, new graduates, and academics must exhibit what Hoffman calls **competitive differentiation** (or positioning) (as cited in Hoffman and Burnett [2012]). Translated from the business lens into an academic one, this idea refers to such capacities as developing and improving systems and infrastructure for learning; generating databases for analyzing areas of interest and making informed decisions; establishing value and worth through ethical and reliable behaviors that reduce risk and increase synergy; building and strengthening interpersonal bonds; and creating agencies, organizations, and think-tanks.

Ask yourself: What is my value or worth? How can I "market" myself? How do others, such as faculty mentors and employers, perceive my worth and value? Dispositions that academic employers in the field of leadership tell me they care about when scrutinizing applicants for jobs in higher education include reliability and timeliness, organizational skills, collegiality as a team player, and quality of work produced. What experience can I gain with building the infrastructure for networks to flourish?

Paradoxically, you will move ahead to the extent that you successfully cooperate and collaborate with peers, leaders, and others in learning networks (see chapters 5 and 8). To set yourself apart, you will find it necessary to constantly teach yourself new skills, market yourself, and take your profession seriously. As you adjust to digital learning, stretch to become a platform of innovation and inspiration in service to a cause.

Academic entrepreneurism is the name I have given to innovation that is proliferating in public education and other domains. Academics are articulating visions of social learning, some by modeling collaborative teamwork and a cross-fertilization of ideas. Comentoring, as defined previously in this book, means that collaboration is mutual, reciprocal, and student centered, and that activism forces change in antiquated, as well as corrupt, systems and societies. Academic entrepreneurism is highly conducive to comentoring whereby the parties are teaching and learning with a commitment to the ethics of justice, critique, and care and to the profession itself (Shapiro and Stefkovich 2010; see chapter 6). Intentionally enact these ethics in your relationships, groups, and networks, and you will make a lasting difference.

All around you is a rich array of academic entrepreneurism. Develop an **influence repertoire** that you can harness for establishing your success in academia. Forge relationships with official and unofficial leaders and peers; manage upward so strong leaders will have less burden on them while you move ahead; immerse people in structured mentoring or learning activities so they can connect, engage, and transform; generate data-based reports to identify situations that can improve; and organize information and be your own living/breathing reference librarian and teacher.

In support of innovation and in cooperation with those who are leading the vision and work are associations of educational research and critical scholarship within specific fields (e.g., teacher education, educational leadership, special education, cultural studies).

Academic entrepreneurism in public education and schooling is at times broad in vision and other times specific in purpose (see preface). Reflecting this spectrum, here are some real-world examples of academic entrepreneurism:

- Committing to a vision of education that empowers future generations to confront and resolve the ecological, social, economic, and political challenges of the day.
- Advancing critical social communities that address a changing national and global context using social constructs in education—democracy, community, equity, justice, responsibility—forcibly in research and scholarship.
- Working in the areas of research, policy, and advocacy in education intended to benefit underserved children and families.
- Focusing on the new political economy for preparing educators in schools facing changing rules of engagement and challenging moral conditions.
- Creating partnerships to transform high-needs schools with twenty-first-century technology.
- Coordinating initiatives to resist the dissolution of tenure and collective bargaining and the instability of teachers', students', and citizens' lives.

- Taking on the challenges faced by educational practitioners, policy makers, researchers, and teachers working with children and young people with special educational needs and disabilities.
- Engaging the public in learning how to work with adults, youth, and children in struggling communities using multimedia and multisensory approaches to learning.
- Protesting the aggressive actions of some countries to censor Internet content.
- Taking a humanitarian stand against child exploitation and violence, specifically the suffering of children living in war zones.
- Joining communities in a spiritual effort to serve as role models and generate resources for disadvantaged populations.
- Spearheading innovation by developing new technologies for combating cancer and other life-threatening diseases, and for monitoring early detection.

Academic entrepreneurism defies easy description. A life force, it is happening everywhere, deep within networks you may not know about, or maybe those you will generate yourself. Some students and their professors are rechanneling academies that are resistant and outmoded. Instead of waiting for permission or desirable opportunities to come to them, they are initiating peer-led and collaborative networks. New roles are emerging for mentors and mentees engaged in simultaneous creative renewal. Academic entrepreneurs endeavor to direct growth, development, and advancement for targeted and special populations, such as citizens disenfranchised by war and storms, locally and worldwide.

Academic entrepreneurism, then, is not about investing financially in a start-up, as an entrepreneur would in a new business, but rather in yourself—*you* are the start-up initiative. Digital immigrants might say that they study and have expertise in a certain topic. Take, for example, the overlapping areas of ecology and education. Consider the effects of ecological changes on indigenous peoples and schooling. Digital natives might say that they *are* ecologists who advocate for the protection of indigenous communities and their natural schooling processes. They have a strong stake in their own personal, professional, and political identity.

Some digital natives, like some digital immigrants, might be entering into or even accepting a different kind of selfhood, a **freefall identity**. This includes people facing retirement or joblessness after decades of working and knowing themselves only in a particular way. As a conscious choice, freefall identity is a creative alternative to default identity, the latter of which is manifest in preestablished role identities, such as tenure-earning faculty titles that have the lure of relative stability and comfort. Those who embrace freefall identity approach such academic positions differently, such as by pioneering new projects, theories, or methods at the outer edges of their profession.

On the Internet you can get a sense of freefall identity through such projects as think-tanks that track the activity of mining companies, with activists forcing global awareness of human damage and rights, as well as a calling for action. Another example is online resource centers that generate high-quality services for children, youth, and families in areas of destitution not equitably resourced by taxpayers. What ideas do you see in books, articles, blogs, and elsewhere that need to be translated into action?

Entrepreneurism, though, has an ugly underbelly. Applying the ethic of critique to the notion of academic entrepreneurism, the idea that anyone can simply invest in themselves because they choose to is overstated. Not everyone has access to the same level of educational resources, including teachers and mentors, and the support of others. Darling-Hammond (2010), Ladson-Billings (2006), and other leading education researchers concluded that "educational opportunity" is neither the same for all students or schools nor is it equally distributed for particular races, classes, and cultures.

Children living in impoverished environments do not have the same type or quality of opportunities as affluent families, with stark differences in educational resources and experiences as examples. Disparity occurs for graduate students who do not have social support, are self-supporting without full-time jobs, and, unlike their affluent or well-positioned counterparts, do not have access to crucial resources, such as high-quality curriculum, focused attention from mentors, and financial support (e.g., scholarships). Poverty is like the Earth's tectonic plates, mostly invisible (i.e., under the ocean) but constantly in play, informing action on the surface.

About our corporate-driven lives today for which entrepreneurism is a source of customer marketing, we're making bedeviled deals, knowing and not knowing it. Each of our demographics is collected when we make purchases and do searches online, and in ways unknown to us. Customer profiles and consumer heuristics are generated for academics and others who do searches online reflecting our recent history (for example, of books and audio CDs previously searched).

Not always detectable, service-sector micromultinationals like Facebook (Facebook.com) and Alibaba (Alibaba.com) are ubiquitous entrepreneurial megaproducers of financial trade that sometimes make human contact (English et al. 2012). These dispersed virtual corporations, some originating as small businesses, are capturing global markets and capitalizing on Internet tools like Amazon and Google, shaping the consciousness of all users, especially digital natives. It is naïve to say that academic entrepreneurs are in control of their own marketing strategies for investing in themselves and their dreams.

With widespread popularity, Facebook, for example, attracts students and faculty with the nostalgia of long-ago cherished villages resurrected as global communities through friendly peer communication and social inclusion. Facebook is a hugely popular, worldwide marketing tool that taps into people's need for belonging, friendship, and community. It relies on peer influence and pressure for impact. We are colluding, knowingly or unknowingly, in pressuring each other and in violating privacy for which trickery is a covert mechanism for gaining access to people's private worlds translated into vast but targeted databases of consumer patterns, interests, and tastes. Investment and entrepreneurism are loaded with connotations like these.

A push back is that language and concepts—such as worth, investment, entrepreneurism, and marketing—can be mindfully used on our own terms. The willingness of children, youth, and young adults to commit to their education and future is "interwoven" with whether others "believe they are worthwhile investments—perceptions that enable them to invest in themselves," which "can leverage strong achievement" (Darling-Hammond 2010, 30). Graduate students, too, who experience a gap in educational opportunity, face deficits that make the difference between failure and success. Their belief in themselves is inextricably linked to others' belief in their worth.

Individuals can engage in high-leverage networking to embolden themselves and their learning and leadership. Networks have an indelible influence in and on graduate school and academic careers. Networking in the digital entrepreneurial age has amplified just how crucial collegial learning relationships are. The global reach of technology has paradoxically allowed for and created distance between and among individuals and groups, while bringing people closer together with countless virtual travelers on the digital highway.

Graduate students can excel through high-quality relationships offline and online, and these can be generated through mentoring mosaics that combine electronic and personal contacts. These robust scholarly networks compensate for differences in people's style, skills, and values: while some mentors and protégés eat and breathe technology, others have clear boundaries or monitor their involvement—when it comes to mentoring, technology can draw us closer or push us further apart.

For many people, experiences of involvement and connection, aloneness and isolation change, even daily. The academic digital entrepreneur will want to seek environments that have healthy spaces for learning and psychosocial and career benefits. The fact that "cyberbullying" and "cyberwellness" have bubbled up on the Internet underscore that online relationships and networks are not somehow magically exempt from having strong, influential psychosocial and emotional elements.

Just as digital immigrants can learn to adapt to various e-platforms for increasing the capacity to mentor and be mentored, digital natives can teach each other in ways that are beneficial, such as by developing appropriate connections and friendships. Importantly, digital natives can also translate or balance the styles of the technology-reluctant older generation (e.g., tolerance only for face-to-face meetings with their graduate students, who may prefer online chats and texting).

The digital native, however, could mistakenly judge graduate mentors as not having value when, in fact, many faculty members are sophisticated in complex areas of adult learning such as professional socialization, critical thinking, and problem solving, in addition to their disciplinary knowledge and scholarly excellence. Digital natives will need to internalize the lifelong sensibility of the ethics of justice, critique, care, and of the profession. Mistakes might include making public (via screen captures) their own email inboxes with the assumption that their electronic exchanges can be put on display for audience viewing, with the digital immigrants to whom they are e-mailing surprised to see their personal and private communication "captured" and rendered public. Another example is creating cumbersome or non-intuitive surveys for digital immigrants to take.

Entrepreneurial and tech-savvy students doing dissertations/theses will need to dig down deep into their repertoire to navigate the politics of education. Peer networks of your own making are crucial for compensating for sporadic mentoring and assisting with multiple tasks, such as critiquing and editing drafts and preparing for presentations for job interviews. It takes entire communities of faculty experts and peer synergists and months or years of applied discipline and sacrifice on the part of students to meet standards of excellence and to succeed as graduates.

Areas of the thesis/dissertation that may play out in subsequent studies are significance and clarity of the problem; development of the research questions; quality of reviews of theoretical and research literature; appropriateness and rigor of methodology; thick databases of information; clarity of reporting findings/results; sophisticated interpretation of the value of what has been discovered; and quality of writing in the abstract and throughout the work (Thomas and Brubaker 2008). Add to the list visual, graphic, and multimedia renderings or augmentations of your text for different readers and viewers.

DIGITAL IMMIGRANT–DIGITAL NATIVE COLLABORATIONS

When a digital immigrant mentors a digital native, the latter, usually younger, will learn how to navigate the academy from start to finish in knowledge-building, professional networks. Politics of education are deeply nuanced. This is not simply a subject that can be memorized and for which being in relation to others, such as professors and educated peers, affects graduate student success. Learning through a generation other than one's own is a cultivated art. Learning within an academy that is changing into a hybrid of online/offline worlds is a daunting challenge for all involved. The protégé, in turn, could be teaching the mentor how to accomplish this goal through skillful and clever use of software. The protégé can introduce the mentor to completely new ideas, not just intriguing ways of communicating, such as blogs and podcasts, or ways of translating what is known in their virtual forms, reaching new audiences, worldwide.

As an example of generational differences, while I print out work to be revised and edited, my thirty-something graduate assistant reads from digital devices. Also, he does not just use the Internet to gather information—he lives on the Internet. With ease, he creates his own online library repositories, invites others to contribute or use them, and darts in and out of online learning communities. After discussion together, he changed our department's newsletter, *Organic Unity*, from an online electronic file into a live e-platform (a digital blog). This medium solicits contributions from students and broad audiences, extending the vision of just and equitable education. His peers now have more ownership of the news they think is important. They are exerting influence in the otherwise elusive landscape of publishing and function as publisher, editor, and reviewer.

This graduate student leader is also blending technology and art into a creative hybrid, as in Elsewhere, a creative idea he launched. Known as CoLAB, this platform for interactive media and learning brings together youth, who explore a downtown area with mobile media devices that capture images, video, and sounds in the neighborhood. He is teaching them how to edit and make small films, record and mix music, broadcast live on the radio, and conduct interviews with local community members. His pioneering idea is to create an interactive project, a "living museum," that shares creative findings online. He is working closely with digitally oriented and resistant peers alike, guiding them while incorporating their concerns into his creative vision. His initiatives are collaborative, inclusive invitations that help address the gaps in opportunity for youth and peers. I wouldn't be surprised if his dissertation ends up being digitally innovative, grounded in youth-based learning communities that generate opportunities of value for themselves.

Go forth. Open doors.

POINTS TO REMEMBER

Learning to network as a digital entrepreneur is already a fundamental part of the academy and beyond in such domains as schools and corporations (English et al. 2012). As you think about your future, what technological trends, shifts, and possibilities might help focus your continued learning and digital readiness for the careers you will move into or create?

If you're in graduate school or getting ready to graduate from a master's or doctoral program, you will be joining midcentury leaders whose work and widespread technological advances heavily influence lives. At the same time, you will see opportunity deficits for populations of students living in poverty. How can you help?

Digital immigrants who are insiders in the academy and digital natives who are entering higher education institutions will experience a generation gap. However, they will also encounter a unique opportunity for learning differently than many of their predecessors. As cross-generational collaborators, they can make global connections and model interdisciplinary outreach; uplift student populations from diverse cultures and backgrounds; and design and deliver education to reach remote communities.

SUMMARY

Here, mentoring, learning, and collaboration were explored as related to two academic trends: academic entrepreneurism in socially mediated contexts and digital immigrant–digital native collaborations. New doors or possibilities are available for readers interested in knowing more about creative forms of learning during their graduate studies, their transition to careers in academe, and their lifespan. Diversity issues are explored relative to such concepts as opportunity gap, professional identity, and global activism. Mentoring is closely linked to innovative, entrepreneurialism, creativity, renewal, and new possibilities for leadership. These foster active learning for executive leaders within established organizations and organic networks that coalesce around social projects and humanitarian causes. New terminology is introduced to reflect some of the emerging demographics in society, as well as newer practices of teaching and learning.

Navigational Prompts

- Reflect on the examples in the bulleted list in the section "Academic Entrepreneurism in Socially Mediated Contexts" (this chapter). What do you believe in? What will you try to improve, even transform, through your personal–professional pursuits and career in academia? Articulate your focus of influence and change in a few sentences. Then create a blog post, wiki, or applet and see what response your Internet presence generates.
- List your primary skills of influence (e.g., association with influential peers) and those you have yet to develop (e.g., working relationship with insiders who are official leaders); consider how you can go about developing each skill.
- Create a brand, logo, or image that captures who or what you stand for, one that you can use as an identity signifier when you tweet or post something.

GLOSSARY

academic entrepreneurism (my term). The spirit of innovation manifested or expressed by academics who initiate new enterprises and invite others to belong or benefit.

competitive differentiation. A business concept (see Hoffman and Burnett 2012) that refers to customizing products and making service delivery noticeably different or better than the competition's and using technology as a driver (Oracle Corporation 2010).

digital immigrant. People who were born before the Internet and whose generation is adjusting to or coping with unfamiliar technology in everyday life (Prensky 2001a, 2001b).

digital native. The younger generation born in the digital world, having grown up with the prevalence of technology and the Internet (Prensky 2001a, 2001b).

freefall identity (my term). Contrasting with the need for established, predictable, and stable identities, freefall identities are underway when entrepreneurs experiment and take risks, testing comfort zones and working against the norms of professional stability, comfort, and career progression.

influencer. A person who exerts influence in daily living, does not get bogged down by merely coping with unsatisfactory situations, and works closely with groups in an effort to effect desirable or necessary change (Patterson et al. 2008).

influence repertoire. Skills that a person intentionally leverages for becoming successful and making a difference, for surpassing their personal limits, and for creating new opportunities and changing environments (Patterson et al. 2008).

microcollaborative network (my term). Network led by a small group of remarkable leaders who constitute the governance body of an established organization or association for which a broader membership belongs.

networked soloist (my term). People who have the resources to live alone and who are choosing to do so, particularly within urban centers in different countries; they communicate as solitary but connected beings within select online talent pools and some have influential roles in workplaces (see, e.g., Klinenberg 2012).

open-source movement. Free access to materials and products on the Internet fosters networked learning and organizational development; the decentralized platforms of production enable grassroots initiatives to spring up and assume greater control over distribution and dissemination.

Postscript

CLOSING THE ACADEMY'S DOOR

This book is a doorway through which you got a sneak-peek at the academy—its exterior, interior, and life activity. Once you pass through the academy's doorway, much within can invite or obstruct entry. With this text some doors have been pried open for novice scholars and new faculty, maybe even for experienced academicians and administrators. Each chapter has an aperture on important mentoring issues that, together, provide windows for viewing the professoriate. Student and faculty readers have been guided through becoming successfully mentored and mentoring effectively, largely by entering into viable mentoring relationships and learning the art of giving and receiving.

What have you learned from this book? If you have sought a deeper or extended understanding of mentoring, you have at your fingertips intriguing concepts and proven practices. Faculty members and administrators gain from new ideas for supporting diverse student populations. Students have been guided to develop self-directed networks. Test the ideas and tips in your own context. Maybe you have perceived something in a fresh way or made entirely new discoveries.

Some faculty respondents shared that my study had raised their awareness about mentoring and their own roles as mentors. In the words of one doctoral supervisor from California, "After having read the preliminary version of your book, I was reminded of how much time and energy I put into mentoring my doctoral students, as well as those who take my course on qualitative research design and methods, although, funny enough, I rarely use the term *mentoring*."

Indeed! Try consulting graduate handbooks to look up the responsibilities of the program advisor, dissertation chair, and committee member. You will quickly see that the complex role of mentorship is not captured; instead, it is overshadowed by the administrative functions of advising and mentoring. Universities and colleges focus on procedural elements, such as the approval of key documents, the graduate student's supervisory-committee form and admission-to-candidacy form, specification of the style manual to be used for the thesis/dissertation, working knowledge of format requirements, and approval of the thesis/dissertation for content and format prior to signing the certificate of approval.

For those of us who guide thesis/dissertation writers, such emphases are flat and strictly technical. If taken to an extreme, they would not allow mentoring relationships to flourish, "starving" even the most talented and independent candidates of the necessary time, attention, and care. For committed faculty supervisors, the weight placed on our mentoring function therefore far outweighs our managerial function, a reality that, though invisible to parties outside the mentoring relationship, has formed the backbone of this book.

Remember Dr. Goya from chapter 2, the faculty mentor who wrote about his budding relationship with a talented new advisee? Dr. Goya wrote me again after his initial e-mail, sharing that reflection on the mentor–mentee exchanges sent to me inspired further thought on how he might improve his own doctoral supervisory work. He requested statistics on graduate completion rates in education relative to cohorts, which I forwarded, noting these were rough estimates only. He also asked to see the table of contents for my book, in addition to the entire text in draft form.

The outcome was that Dr. Goya felt inspired to organize his doctoral candidates into an informal cohort. His explanation, communicated privately, was that he did "not want to give so much personal time and focus to [his] students not yet in candidacy, should any of them drop out, and besides, the advanced students really need the attention." Sent to his doctoral candidates, his Evite was for participation in the new group, complete with practical, individualized attention for job searching:

> Dear doctoral candidates:
>
> I think it would be useful for us to meet as a group on a regular basis, say, once a month for an hour or more. Since you're all at the critical phase of your degrees, such a meeting might provide the mutual inspiration and support that will enhance your chances for completion. Remember, the statistics on PhD completion are not good; within colleges of education roughly half fail to graduate. The good news is that those who participate in the type of cohort I'm proposing have a significantly higher chance of completion.
>
> In addition to the encouragement derived from our proposed meetings, I envision them as opportunities for professional preparation for those of you seeking careers in academe. I'd like to share my experience, for example, in crafting a vita, writing a job application letter, going for a campus interview, and negotiating a job offer. There are also aspects to being a new faculty member that they don't teach you in Professor 101. Having served in several research institutions for twenty years, I have experience you'll find useful.
>
> Maybe once a month will not be enough. But I'll leave that decision, as well as the one to accept or decline my invitation, up to you. If your inclination and schedules permit, I'd like to start next week. Please let me know either way.
> R.G.

Writing *From Student to Professor: Translating a Graduate Degree into a Career in Academia* has allowed me to get closer to the experiences of different agents and recipients of mentorship. Dr. Goya is one such agent. With a forthrightness revealing investment in the subject at hand, graduate students, beginning and seasoned faculty members, and higher-education administrators have all reinforced the message that mentoring—and its related functions of advising, counseling, and so forth—greatly matters to the quality of degrees and candidates. Proactively mentored and entrepreneurially networked students and graduates have a greater capacity for translating their degree into a career in academia. The many contributors, along with differences in outlook and even remarkable confessions, shared unique perspectives on learning, leading, and succeeding.

Readers have access to guarded secrets about graduate school, not only concerning cultural norms that set the standards for academic success but also mentors' unspoken values and rituals. As one such example, faculty mentors often expect students to create or contribute to support systems by assisting peers and receiving assistance, thus engaging in genuine partnerships. Digitally minded students push past even this standard of excellence, creating opportunities for themselves that they want to generate in a globally networked world.

The contributors and I have tested the mentoring-and-learning approaches described in real-life and virtual contexts. The familiar and unfamiliar formats of mentoring covered offer a wide range of options: go ahead and customize individualized approaches. These encompass broad interdisciplinary programs on national and global scales, as well as personalized relationships with mentors and peers. Each chapter's cases and analyses are supported with data from documents, surveys, and interviews, including outcomes from long-standing graduate networks, such as the Writers in Training (WIT).

Learning how to communicate well with others about one's interests and needs, professional-development goals, and career issues is one theme of this book. Another is the need to change outmoded organizational systems in higher education that are seemingly unresponsive to committed students, faculty mentors, and underrepresented groups, as well as underemployed faculty in part-time positions and undervalued administrative support staff. Such core values have been translated into scenarios featuring student and faculty characters in a variety of situations, with extrapolations to principles about responsive relationships and systems.

Developing a professional identity as a scholar, someone who draws heavily upon his or her inner resources and makes the best of external resources, is also highlighted. Such an individual demonstrates the "smarts" of being self-aware, ethical, politically astute, highly resourceful, deeply connecting, independent as a problem solver, and interdependent as a synergist in the journey of others.

Take good care of yourself. Do not neglect your physical well-being and health or your personal support systems because of your aspirations or the academic demands placed on you. Invest in yourself so you can invest in others.

Finally, in our graduate programs and life we are not always simply positioned on the inside or outside. Our worlds are dynamic and fluid, and we will find ourselves constantly moving back and forth between these two localities. The doors we encounter in academe open onto more doors, inviting ritual, meditation, and gathering.

Ending with a door *behind* you, what possibilities can you imagine *in front*?

Appendixes

Nine appendixes follow that I developed based on my experience as a doctoral supervisor and department chair. My hope is that students, faculty members, and administrators will use or adapt them in support of their work. The forms can be used in live instructional settings, such as dissertation/thesis defenses and courses; in consultation with others; or alone.

These documents are specifically intended to aid in the development of doctoral students, particularly those seeking knowledge of procedures, expectations, and strategies that guide success in graduate programs. Additional documents are for those providing information to reference writers in support of their job applications; initiating communications with graduate faculty for the purposes of constituting their thesis/dissertation committees; documenting recommended changes in defense of their work; listing the actual changes to their thesis/dissertation on a review form; producing cover letters that accompany manuscripts for publication review; summarizing changes accompanying a reworked manuscript for publication review; reviewing someone else's paper that is in review with a journal or another type of publication; and preparing a cover letter for an assistant professor position. In this final scenario, the writers of such a cover letter are typically doctoral graduates, students in an advanced stage of candidacy, and nontenure faculty members, as well as assistant professors.

A

Program Dos for Thesis/Dissertation Writers

Apply the following generic procedures and expectations to your own institutional context and graduate-program stages (in no particular order):

- *Policies*. Follow all policies to a T. If you require an exception (e.g., residency waiver) that has been approved, get it in writing with a signature and date. Locate, read, and save all policies relevant to your doctoral program, including candidacy. Place these in a repository, such as a notebook (e.g., "personal policy" record), and consult them regularly. Internalize the information; educate professors and students about the policies in situ. Be sure that any changes in policy or new understandings about the existing policies are reflected in your personal repository (or shared drive).
- *Registration*. Register for courses and candidacy hours on time. Penalties include late fees and even a statement to the effect of "academic dismissal" on your transcript. Keep the reminder dates for registration each semester in a handy place—avoid relying on memory or others' reminders.
- *Duplicates*. Scan/retain all signed and approved documents (e.g., programs of study) before officially submitting them. Do not assume that you can get by without a backup copy, as important documents can go astray and slip through the cracks. In such cases, students are required to obtain all of the relevant signatures once again. Avoid using the department (e.g., advisor, secretary) for obtaining signatures, unless such individuals should offer to do so, as this is usually the student's responsibility.
- *Samples*. From your advisor or supervisor, request access to approved samples of student work throughout your program. This will give you an immediate appreciation for the expected scholarly standards and writing forms in your discipline. In each case, you may need the student writer's permission. Programs of study, concept papers, proposals, and dissertations are some of the most salient products to review. Obtain dissertations of interest from digital databases, including your library, and read them avidly. Take the initiative to answer your questions by reading and talking with students. Avoid asking advisors questions that can be resolved by learning what other writers have done.
- *Listservs*. Join helpful listservs, and when these are not established, request that they be set up. For example, if your dissertation chair has more than one assigned mentee, he or she could establish a listserv for sharing materials, files, and news. Graduate-student associations offer another venue for peer-based information sharing. Offer to assist by either establishing the listserv yourself or keeping it updated.

- *Associations*. Join select graduate-student associations in your college and nationally and internationally, as well as professional associations in your state and region. Student fees make membership more affordable. (For leading associations, institutes, and more, see "References and Resources.")
- *Read*. Do not just read—read extensively. Notably, your literature reviews, completed at the midpoint in a given year, should reflect any sources that have been published that same year. Avoid being informed that your literature citations are out of date, too few, or random.
- *Format*. Access the expected formatting manual in your field (e.g., the American Psychological Association manual). Use the most current edition. Consult this source each time you prepare academic material for circulation; identify and fix your own formatting errors. You can also obtain easy-to-consult sources online, such as crib sheets. Check that they are accurate and consistent with the official version of the manual in your field.
- *Presentations*. Present your preliminary and finished work at conferences in your discipline. Copresent with your advisor, dissertation chair, coach, committee members, or peers. Or go solo. Every year present at at least one conference and seek professional-development enrichment from conference venues. Make gains from participating in vibrant networks, developing public-speaking skills, and listening and responding to audiences.
- *Defenses*. Attend public defenses of students' dissertations. Give particular attention to those that reflect the next stage in your programmatic development, such as proposal writing, and those that will lend insight for your own defenses. Take notes and talk with the student afterward. To obtain notices, join listservs, search websites, or contact the graduate school (or another official entity) for the scheduled defenses. Defenses may be posted as YouTube videos, but many institutions keep these in-house.
- *Acknowledgments*. Prepare a thoughtful dedication and acknowledgments page for your thesis or dissertation. Avoid omitting or rushing these important statements. Take the chance to thank the people (e.g., doctoral committee, administrators, colleagues, friends, and family) who have "packed your parachute" and contributed to your success. Also consider any networks or other sponsorships that provided support.
- *Organization*. Bring copies of the essential defense forms to the hearing (hard copy and/or e-copy). Examples include the defense form and certificate of approval. Become familiar with your graduate school system and the necessary forms (usually posted online). By going over the official forms ahead of time, you can see what is expected and when. When your committee signs a form and prepares to submit it, request a duplicate. Keep all such items in your program notebook.
- *Leadership*. Manage upward—organize your defenses as though you are the advisor. For example, schedule or check that all committee members will be ready at the appointed time and that they have the final documents. Confirm that the room/space for the defense has been scheduled and contains any necessary technology. Bring backups.
- *Timeliness*. The timely submission of your proposal and thesis/dissertation to the committee and graduate school is crucial. Be sure to give yourself plenty of time to follow the university's guidelines for properly formatting your text and for communicating with individuals for this purpose. Go over completed theses and dissertations that have been produced at your own college and university for formatting ideas. You may see variances and discrepancies, though, so adhere to the most current official guidelines.
- *Dissemination*. Prepare your work for electronic upload and worldwide availability. Be sure that your committee members can access the e-version of your final work (don't assume they can). You may also want to share a bound copy, at least with your advisor, even

though this ritual has been going out of style. Consult with your advisor on how best to disseminate your work to the committee and possibly the unit as well. Communicate pride in your amazing accomplishment and appreciation for good mentoring.

B

Reflecting Student Input in a Faculty Supporting Letter

[POSTAL ADDRESS]
[DATE]
[ADDRESSEE]

In her four years of teaching, Tabitha Smith has proven to be a dedicated, ambitious, and compassionate educator. Her disposition, capabilities, and skills would make her a stellar candidate for the [anonymous] education leadership program.

Tabitha was a student in my Foundations of Curriculum and Instruction course last spring. Her intellectual curiosity was evident in classroom discussions and her analysis of curriculum issues. Tabitha examined a local high school and made a discovery that mirrors national trends: racial inequality in the enrollment of minority students in honors and advanced placement courses, which has been correlated with future college success. This assignment showed her ability to tackle a serious educational issue by examining the causes and implications for American public education. She worked closely with peers, guiding their overall contribution.

Since the time Tabitha took my course, she has completed the certification track for education leadership and passed the Florida Education Leadership Examination. She now holds certification in education leadership (all grades) and social sciences (grades 6–12). In September 2012, Tabitha passed the assistant principal screening process in [anonymous county] and will soon be interviewing for vacant positions.

In the classroom, Tabitha's extensive knowledge of subject matter and ability to motivate students have earned her the coveted position of advanced placement teacher. Her students continuously outperform national averages on the advanced placement psychology exam. Because of this achievement, she was asked by the [anonymous] county school district on two separate occasions to facilitate professional study workshops. As a facilitator, she guided colleagues through best practices in the teaching of advanced placement psychology and strategic reading across the curriculum. The collected evaluations show how well these sessions went.

This past spring, Tabitha's commitment to her profession was recognized, as she was selected to mentor teachers at [a high school] under Florida's Better Educated Students and Teachers legislation. Chosen by a panel of administrators and teachers, she has since worked with new teachers in developing classroom management and best practices for the continuous improvement of student achievement. Furthermore, Tabitha has reviewed the Florida Comprehensive Assessment Test data for her school and collaborated with the school improvement team to develop goals for the 2012–2013 school-improvement plan.

Beyond the classroom, Tabitha has headed numerous positions, again demonstrating her leadership ability. She coordinates school-wide activities, including homecoming, teacher and student incentive programs, charity events, and pep rallies. Her eagerness to plan and execute these daunting tasks while not compromising her commitment to high expectations in the classroom credits her decision making, prioritizing, and organization—all crucial leadership abilities.

Tabitha's professional accomplishments attest to her commitment to education. She has worked diligently to build her credentials as a leader and eagerly awaits the next challenge as a doctoral student in the educational leadership program at the [anonymous] university.

I strongly recommend Tabitha Smith's admittance to this program and can be reached for further information at the contact numbers provided.

Sincerely,

[FIVE LINE SPACES]

[NAME, DEGREE ABBREVIATION (IF APPLICABLE)]

C

Initiating Communications with Graduate Program Committee

What follows is a synthesis of forty-five written reports of students' communication with doctoral committees. The reports span two semesters. The first-person pronoun is used to personalize this collective statement; no one person or individual statement has been cited, and all points are paraphrased. These may serve as helpful pointers for readers:

- I asked established, reputable people I know for recommendation letters for the doctoral program and talked with the program advisor before and after my acceptance.
- I selected a dissertation chair after consultation with peers and faculty in my college.
- I consulted with my new chair about selecting courses for upcoming semesters.
- After closely reading the graduate handbook, I e-mailed my chair questions about the program and received responses and direction—we regularly e-mail and text now.
- I developed the individualized program/plan of study by the end of my first semester. I used the electronic forms and solicited the advice of my dissertation chair. I wanted to make informed choices and select an appropriate sequence for my courses (my committee form with the signatures of faculty will not be complete until I know who will be serving on my committee).
- In the first semester, I talked with my dissertation chair about the selection of a cognate area—I learned that I would need commitment from a faculty member in the corresponding program (i.e., social and cultural foundations) to serve on my doctoral committee, so I sought and secured one.
- In the third semester of my program, I met with my chair to select the committee members—she made most of the suggestions due to her experience serving on many committees and personal knowledge of the faculty body. She also recommended which professor I should approach in the social and cultural foundations program to serve as the content expert in my cognate area.
- At my chair's suggestion, I asked the professor in social and cultural foundations to serve on my committee.
- I obtained the commitment of three faculty members in order to meet the minimum policy requirements for the number of faculty serving on a doctoral committee.

- I took advantage of the insights I gleaned from a professor wherein a great deal of information was shared about the doctorate as a part of the hidden curriculum of her course. This required reporting updates and asking informed questions of my faculty coordinator, which in turn influenced the frequency and quality of communication I received from my personal advisor, faculty members, and potential committee members.
- As a new member of my chair's dissertation group of students, I met with her cohort, consisting of all of her mentees, after receiving an agenda and papers to read via e-mail.
- I attended the meeting and found it motivational and inspirational; my professor shared completed dissertations with her group, and we discussed their structural features, as well as similarities and differences in topic, philosophy, methods, findings, and more.
- At the next study meeting, each member of the group presented insights on one of the dissertations, and by so doing, we became more knowledgeable of different styles and approaches to research problems, including thoughtful criticisms of what we studied.
- I continued to attend all of the study-group meetings and prepared by reading the assigned student draft writings, handouts, and textbook readings. I took prolific notes at each session, sought clarification by asking questions, and gradually shared my thoughts.
- I e-mailed my dissertation chair a brief outline of ideas and methods that may potentially lay fertile ground for my own dissertation topic.
- I investigated the qualifying/comprehensive examination that will follow my coursework in one year. I would like to begin preparing—for information, I first checked the graduate handbook for the relevant policies. Then I talked with my dissertation chair and members of my study group, some of whom have already passed their quals/comps. Following this, a session of our study group was devoted to the qualifying exam process, along with planning tips and test-taking strategies. The chair circulated a list of research studies and scholarship in our field for ongoing study. We decided to take ownership of the exam process, approaching the reading list as a live encounter, making additions to it as we read and dialoguing about the texts and comparing our reactions.
- We selected a book by a renowned educator to read in our study group, and we alternated reading and analyzing high-quality articles.

D

Documenting Changes on a Graduate Defense Form

Proposal Defense (check): __
Dissertation Defense (check): __
Rehearsal with Study Group (or other) (check): __
Name: _____
Date: _____
Document Version Number/Date: _____

Outside/External Visitor

Page	Question	Page	Change

Positive Statement:
Overview Comments:

Dissertation Chair

Page	Question	Page	Change

Positive Statement:
Overview Comments:

Committee Member

Page	Question	Page	Change

Positive Statement:
Overview Comments:

Committee Member

Page	Question	Page	Change

Positive Statement:
Overview Comments:

Committee Member

Page	Question	Page	Change

Positive Statement:
Overview Comments:

Listing Amendments on a Dissertation Review Form

Name: _____

Date: _____

E-mail: _____

Phone: _____

Draft #: _____

Submitted to (i.e., chair only, all members, etc.): _____

Revisions table: Organize the table from page 1 of your document, or you may cluster revisions by type and order them by page number.

Page #	Paragraph Number(s)	Revision Type*	Suggested by (Name Committee Member or N/A)	Description/Explanation	Page # in Previous Draft (If Applicable)

*Revision types:

Addition—add new information

Deletion—delete information

Expansion—greater detail and explanation of a point

Editing—tightening the writing or improving the flow

Correction—changing incorrect information or fixing a typo or grammatical error

Additional chapters since the last draft (i.e., chapter 4):

Other additions (i.e., table of contents, executive summary):

General changes since the last draft (i.e., put everything in chapters 1 and 3 in the past tense):

Other: _____

Deadline you are trying to meet with this draft (if applicable): _____

Estimated graduation date: _____

Is there any suggestion from a committee member(s) regarding the previous draft that you did not address? If yes, please explain.

_____

_____

_____

F

Cover Letter Accompanying Manuscript Submission

[DATE]
[EDITOR'S NAME AND ADDRESS]

Dear [INSERT NAME OF PERSON, PUBLISHER, OR DESIGNEE]:
Please accept the submission of my [or our coauthored] manuscript, ["TITLE"], [if relevant, give order of coauthors' name] to [JOURNAL NAME] for publication review.

This paper addresses the aims and scope [OR PHILOSOPHY] of [JOURNAL NAME] by focusing on [THEME OR FOCUS]. [IF THIS SUBMISSION IS FOR REVIEW IN A SPE-CIAL ISSUE, MENTION THIS AND GIVE THE NAME OF THAT VOLUME.] Your readers should find this work of value because [REASON]. [OR START DIFFERENTLY, WITH ANOTHER BIG-PICTURE STATEMENT, SUCH AS THAT WHICH FOLLOWS.] The specific themes addressed in the manuscript are [BRIEFLY ELABORATE HERE AND GIVE ANY OTHER RELEVANT OR UNIQUE DETAILS ABOUT YOUR WORK, SUCH AS ITS INTERNATIONAL APPEAL AND RESEARCH SIGNIFICANCE OR THE PAR-TICIPANT POPULATION INVOLVED, METHODS USED FOR COLLECTING AND INTERPRETING DATA, AND MEANING OF THE RESULTS].

This manuscript conforms to your journal's guidelines [SUCH AS THE REQUIRED LENGTH OF THE ABSTRACT AND MANUSCRIPT, AS WELL AS THE FORMATTING OF THE TEXT AND REFERENCES]. [IDENTIFY WHAT HAS BEEN UPLOADED TO THE PUBLISHER'S CENTRAL MANUSCRIPT SYSTEM, SUCH AS YOUR MANU-SCRIPT, IDENTIFYING COVER PAGE, THIS LETTER OR A MORE INFORMAL ONE ENTERED INTO A TEXTBOX, AND ANY FIGURES OR TABLES. LESS LIKELY, YOU WILL BE REQUIRED TO SUBMIT THE FILES DIRECTLY TO THE EDITOR'S E-MAIL ADDRESS OR DESIGNATED PARTY'S]. This document has been prepared for blind peer review [IF APPROPRIATE].

If you have any questions, I can be reached at my office number [NUMBER], cell phone [NUMBER], or home number [NUMBER], or at this e-mail address: [FUNCTIONING E-MAIL ADDRESS]. [COMMUNICATE ANY RESTRICTIONS ON YOUR AVAILABIL-ITY OR ALTERNATE CONTACT INFORMATION FOR SUMMER MONTHS OR HOLI-DAYS.] I [or we] would appreciate receiving an acknowledgment of receipt and look forward to receiving the reviews.

Kindly forward all correspondence to the following e-mail address:

[ADDRESS—THE CONTACT PERSON FOR ALL CORRESPONDENCE IS ALSO SPECIFIED ON THE IDENTIFYING COVER PAGE IF THERE IS MORE THAN ONE AUTHOR.]

Thank you for your time and consideration.

Sincerely,

[FIVE LINE SPACES]

[NAME, DEGREE ABBREVIATION (IF APPLICABLE)]

G

Summary of Changes Accompanying Reworked Paper

[DATE]
[EDITOR'S NAME AND ADDRESS]

RE: Revised version of manuscript [MS CODE IF YOU KNOW IT] for [JOURNAL NAME]

Dear [INSERT NAME OF PERSON, PUBLISHER, OR DESIGNEE]:
Thank you for the helpful reviews of my [coauthored] manuscript, ["TITLE"]. Enclosed [or attached] please find the revision of the original work and [NUMBER OF ENCLOSED COPIES IF POSTAL MAILED]. I [or we] have carefully addressed the substantive and encouraging feedback and significantly shortened the paper. The revised version is less than half the length of the original. Your editorial letter provided an overview of the changes and practical ways for approaching the revision, which proved invaluable. Also, I [or we] have made many additional changes in order to strengthen the work. The major changes are listed below. I [or we] hope the paper is now ready for publication but would be pleased to make any further improvements.
Summary of Changes
Editor's Comments

1. The paper has been reworked, targeting the practice section of the journal. Toward this end, the discussion of the literature has been refocused on the nature of the principal-ship. (The principal has been renamed Paula, which is her real name.)
2. Relevant literature has been introduced to highlight the successful practice (e.g., [SPECIFY, IF RELEVANT]).
3. The manuscript has been rewritten to highlight more relevant examples of the principal's practice.
4. Notably, the principal's self-report does not exist in a vacuum or solely from our reviewer field notes. Even in the original document, we had drawn upon a number of sources (e.g., school-generated data) that gave weight to her claims. However, in this new version we have clarified this undertaking, without making this a research-based case study. Indeed, multiple sources of information (school and student achievement

data) have been highlighted; new data have been retrieved and interpreted. School data for the 2012–2013 school year have been forthcoming since the submission of the original paper. The results are included in the new version.

Reviewer [CODE SPECIFICATION, IF PROVIDED] Comments

1. The conflict/tension between the state of Florida and the Career Academy model on page 10 of the original was not expanded upon, as suggested. It was believed to have been a marginal point that could not be developed in a shorter paper.
2. The "democratic value" connection that was implied in the original has been thoroughly addressed, as recommended.
3. A tentative set of claims regarding positive results (e.g., correlation between higher test scores and increase in student learning) has been streamlined throughout.
4. The implications section has been developed related to the school's practice and future.

Reviewer [CODE SPECIFICATION, IF PROVIDED] Comments

1. Evidence and examples of consistency between the principal's claims and data have been provided (see, e.g., section called "The Principal's Autobiographical School Report" [12–14]). However, with the heightened emphasis on practice, the new version is not weighted with research-based evidence.
2. As a piece that has been rewritten for the practice section of the journal, the views of stakeholders are no longer needed (as endorsed by editor's letter).
3. A shift has occurred in the rewrite from attention on the principal to the whole team. Wherever the principal is the focus, an explanation is given (e.g., this school is in the process of becoming a learning organization, so the principal's leadership-driven, decision-making process has at times been more pronounced than the whole-school team effort; however, the emphasis on change at the school highlights the team effort, as reflected in the paper).
4. The information on the modified block schedule has been eliminated, thus the reviewer's concerns have been handled.
5. Telecasting of what is to follow in the writing (e.g., "as will be discussed") has been eliminated.
6. The few writing errors have been fixed.

In addition, as previously noted, we have carefully proofread and revised the entire paper.

Thanks once again for your time and consideration. I [or we] look forward to hearing from you soon.

Sincerely,

[FIVE LINE SPACES]

[NAME, DEGREE ABBREVIATION (IF APPLICABLE)]

H

Brief Review of a Paper Submitted to a Journal

This manuscript is basically a proposal for an online mentoring format involving teacher-education students, cooperating teachers, and a university professor. The article is well structured and well written. The construction plan for the website is clearly conceptualized, and the strategy for evaluating it is thorough. But I find the manuscript ultimately unsatisfying in the lack of detail—it does not get into the kinds of issues that might be attended to in this type of mentoring, nor does it discuss how interactions surrounding a student's predicament might play out.

The discussion needs to be more grounded in specificity to make the notion of e-mentoring more compelling. The editors have asked contributors to this issue to include the processes of learning and the products of learners. This is precisely what is missing from this manuscript. The reader would benefit from a detailed scenario and explicit treatment of situations that indicate a need for this type of mentoring and what a sample interaction might accomplish.

I realize that this paper is a proposal at this stage, but even if the full format has not been activated, the authors need to include more examples that have given rise to this idea or some interactions that mimic the results of such a setup. If the authors could provide such grounding through rich examples, then I think the manuscript would be appropriate for the special issue.

In sum, the notion of developing an online mentoring program among teachers, student teachers, and university teaching supervisors is convincing. To merit publication, though, the idea needs more specifics and greater detail.

I

Cover Letter for an Assistant Professor Position

[DATE]

Dear [INSERT NAME OF PERSON, PUBLISHER, OR DESIGNEE]:
This application is for the position of assistant professor in [DISCIPLINE] at [UNIVERSITY], which appeared in [TITLE OR NAME OF THE MOST FORMAL SOURCE, e.g., *The Chronicle of Higher Education*]. [Next, establish your rationale for applying for this position. For example, "As a new PhD graduate committed to the agenda of reforming schools and preparing leaders for this purpose, I am drawn to the quality and prestige of your university and especially to the commitment to social justice, equity, and high performance within the School of Education. Commensurate with my qualifications, I am seeking consideration for this position."] [Here or elsewhere, give a few relevant details about the department or unit in which the line will be held, as well as the college and university.]

As background information, [HERE, ESTABLISH YOUR CREDENTIALS RELATED TO THE POSITION AND THE EMPHASES IN THE AD, SUCH AS ON TEACHING EDUCATION PROFESSIONALS—PROVIDE RELEVANT HIGHLIGHTS FROM YOUR VITA]. For example, at [INSERT THE NAME OF THE UNIVERSITY YOU GRADUATED FROM] I have gained teaching experience, specifically in [NAME COURSE AND PROGRAM]. [Provide specifics, such as whether you taught solo and the type of delivery—face-to-face classroom learning, hybrid teaching, or a distance-delivery format, and the outcomes of the student reviews, peer assessments, and the annual review from your unit head.]

[Using the priority placed on qualifications in the advertisement, structure your letter accordingly, emphasizing "required" qualifications followed by "preferred." Give examples in each of the major areas, such as "awards or scholarships received or peer-reviewed conference presentations or publications produced" in the generic area of "demonstrated exemplary academic performance."]

[From numerous real-world academic ads for an assistant professor in educational leadership, the following major areas were derived; each would need to be firmly addressed by the job candidate, preferably using headings so search committees can easily spot your key points and, importantly, be able to note their evaluation of your record of accomplishments on their candidate ranking sheet.]

1. Doctorate in education, relevant to a specific discipline
2. Past teaching or administrative experience (e.g., in public schools)

3. A record demonstrating promising scholarship (appropriate to rank)
4. Commitment to working collaboratively with colleagues and advising and mentoring students
5. Experience with classroom teaching, including technology context and skills
6. Record of collaboration with schools and school systems (e.g., urban, rural)
7. Experience working with diverse populations and developing interventions
8. Progress with grant development and networks, with seed studies under way

[End with a comment that is not simply generic and show your enthusiasm for the position using professional language. Go beyond such conventionalism as "In summary, I look forward to hearing from you. Thank you for your time and consideration."]

    Sincerely,

[FIVE LINE SPACES]

[NAME, DEGREE ABBREVIATION (IF APPLICABLE)]

Attached [whatever is requested, typically the vita and contact information for references, and maybe representative work, publications, or reports]

[ADDENDUM]:

CONTACT INFORMATION FOR REFERENCES:

[NAME]

[ADDRESS]

[E-MAIL, OFFICE/CELL/HOME PHONE, FAX]

References and Resources

PRINT RESOURCES

Apps, J. W. (1996). *Teaching from the heart*. Malabar, FL: Krieger.

American Association of University Women (AAUW). (2004). *Tenure denied: Cases of sex discrimination in academia*. Washington, DC: AAUW Educational Foundation and the AAUW Legal Advocacy Fund.

Andrews, J. (1965). *Climb every mountain*. http://olddreamz.com/midway/quoimage/CLIMB.html/.

Banks, C. (2000). Gender and race as factors in educational leadership and administration. In Jossey-Bass Publishers (Ed.), *The Jossey-Bass reader on educational leadership* (pp. 217–56). San Francisco, CA: Jossey-Bass.

Barkham, J. (2005). Reflections and interpretations on life in academia: A mentee speaks. *Mentoring & Tutoring, 13*(3), 331–44.

Bauerlein, M. (Ed.). (2011). *The digital divide*. New York: Jeremy P. Tarcher/Penguin.

Bell, D. A. (2010, May 13). The intricacies of spousal hiring. *The Chronicle of Higher Education, 56*(35), A33–A35. chronicle.com.

Bennouna, S. (2003). *Mentors' emotional intelligence and performance of mentoring functions in graduate doctoral education*. Unpublished doctoral dissertation, University of South Florida, Tampa.

Beyene, T., Anglin, M., Sanchez, W., and Ballou, M. (2002). Mentoring and relational mutuality: Protégés' perspectives. *Journal of Humanistic Counseling, Education and Development, 41*(1), 87–102.

Bolles, R. N. (2011). *What color is your parachute? A practical manual for job-hunters and career-changers 2012* (40th ed.). Berkeley, CA: Ten Speed Press.

Bolton, G. (1994). Stories at work: Fictional–critical writing as a means of professional development. *British Educational Research Journal, 20*(1), 55–68.

Brown II, M. C., Davis, G. L., and McClendon, S. A. (1999). Mentoring graduate students of color: Myths, models, and modes. *Peabody Journal of Education, 74*(2), 1–8.

Browne-Ferrigno, T., Barnett, B., and Muth, R. (2003). Cohort program effectiveness: A call for a national research agenda. In F. C. Lunenburg and C. S. Carr (Eds.), *Shaping the future: Policy, partnerships, and emerging perspectives* (pp. 274–90). (Yearbook of the National Council of Professors of Educational Administration.) Lanham, MD: Scarecrow.

Brubaker, M. D., and Brubaker, D. L. (2011). *Advancing your career: Getting and making the most of your doctorate*. Lanham, MD: Rowman & Littlefield Education.

Caffarella, R. S., and Barnett, B. G. (2000). Teaching doctoral students to become scholarly writers: The importance of giving and receiving critiques. *Studies in Higher Education, 25*(1), 39–52.

Cahn, S., and Van Heusen, J. (1959). *Discogs*. http://www.discogs.com.

Chickering, A. W., and Reisser, L. (1993). *Education and identity* (2nd ed.). San Francisco, CA: Jossey-Bass.

Clark, R. A., Harden, S. L., and Johnson, W. B. (2000). Mentor relationships in clinical psychology doctoral training: Results of a national survey. *Teaching of Psychology, 27*(4), 262–68.

Clutterbuck, D. (2001). *Everyone needs a mentor: Fostering talent at work* (3rd ed.). London: CIPD Enterprises.

Connelly, F. M., and Clandinin, D. J. (1988). *Teachers as curriculum planners: Narratives of experience*. New York: Teachers College Press.

Damrosch, D. (2000, November 17). Mentors and tormentors in doctoral education. *The Chronicle of Higher Education, 47*(12), B24. chronicle.com.

Darling-Hammond, L. (2010). *The flat world and education: How America's commitment to equity will determine our future*. New York: Teachers College Press.

Darion, J. (1972). *Reel classics.* http://reelclassics.com.

Darwin, A. (2000). Critical reflections on mentoring in work settings. *Adult Education Quarterly, 50*(3), 197–211.

Dewey, J. (1938). *Experience and education.* New York: Macmillan.

Dinham, S., and Scott, C. (2001). The experience of disseminating the results of doctoral research. *Journal of Further and Higher Education, 25*(1), 45–55.

Dorn, S., and Papalewis, R. (1997). *Improving doctoral student retention.* Paper presented at the American Educational Research Association, Chicago.

Dorn, S. M., Papalewis, R., and Brown, R. (1995). Educators earning their doctorates: Doctoral student perceptions regarding cohesiveness and persistence. *Education, 116*(2), 305–10.

Dreher, G. F., and Chargois, J. A. (1998). Gender, mentoring experiences, and salary attainment among graduates of an historically black university. *Journal of Vocational Behavior, 53,* 401–16.

Eisner, E. W. (2004). What does it mean to say a school is doing well? In D. J. Flinders and S. J. Thornton (Eds.), *The curriculum studies reader* (2nd ed.) (pp. 297–305). New York: RoutledgeFalmer.

Enelow, W. S., and Kursmark, L. M. (2010). *Cover letter magic: Trade secrets of professional resume writers* (4th ed.). Indianapolis, IN: JIST Works.

English, F. W., Papa, R., Mullen, C. A., and Creighton, T. (2012). *Educational leadership at 2050: Conjectures, challenges and promises.* Lanham, MD: Rowman & Littlefield Education.

Engstrom, C. M. (1999). Promoting the scholarly writing of female doctoral students in higher education and student affairs program. *NASPA Journal, 36*(4), 264–77.

Fields, D., and Kern, J. (1936). *Filmsite.* http://www.filmsite.org/swin.html.

Fletcher, S., and Mullen, C. A. (Eds.). (2012). *The SAGE handbook of mentoring and coaching in education.* Thousand Oaks, CA: Sage.

Formo, D. M., and Reed, C. (2011). *Job search in academe: How to get the position you deserve* (2nd ed.). Sterling, VA: Stylus.

Freeman, K. (1999). No services needed? The case for mentoring high-achieving African American students. *Peabody Journal of Education, 74*(2), 1–6.

Freire, P. (1997). A response. In P. Freire, with J. W. Fraser, D. Macedo, T. McKinnon, and W. T. Stokes (Eds.), *Mentoring the mentor: A critical dialogue with Paulo Freire* (pp. 303–29). New York: Peter Lang.

Gallimore, R. G., Tharp, R. G., and John-Steiner, V. (1992). *The developmental and sociocultural foundations of mentoring.* Columbia University, New York: Institute for Urban Minority Education. www.eric.ed.gov.

Geisler, C. (2004). *Analyzing streams of language.* New York: Pearson Education.

Glatthorn, A. A. (1998). *Writing the winning dissertation: A step-by-step guide.* Thousand Oaks, CA: Corwin.

Goodlad, J. I. (1994). *Educational renewal: Better teachers, better schools.* San Francisco, CA: Jossey Bass.

Greene, M. (1971/2004). Curriculum and consciousness (pp. 135–47). In D. J. Flinders and S. J. Thornton (Eds.), *The curriculum studies reader* (2nd ed.). New York: RoutledgeFalmer.

Griffin, K. A., and Reddick, R. J. (2011). Surveillance and sacrifice : Gender differences in the mentoring patterns of Black professors at predominantly White research universities. *American Educational Research Journal, 48*(5), 1032–57. doi:10.3102/0002831211405025.

Groban, J. (2004). *You raise me up.* http://www.financial-inspiration.com.

Gross, R. A. (2002, February 28). From 'old boys' to mentors. *The Chronicle of Higher Education,* 1–5. chronicle.com.

HarperCollins Publishers. (2003). *Harold and his friends: A Harold and the purple crayon treasury.* New York: HarperCollins Publishers. (Crockett Johnson, original creator).

Healy, C. C. (1997). An operational definition of mentoring. In H. T. Frierson (Ed.), *Diversity in higher education: Mentoring and diversity in higher education, 1.* Greenwich, CT: JAI Press.

Heiberger, M. M., and Vick, J. M (2001). *The academic job search handbook* (3rd ed.). Philadelphia, PA: University of Pennsylvania Press.

———. (2002, April 22). Learning the lingo. *The Chronicle of Higher Education.* chronicle.com.

———. (2003, July 3). Learning the lingo: Part II. *The Chronicle of Higher Education.* chronicle.com.

Henson, K. T. (1999). *Writing for professional publication: Keys to academic and business success.* Needham Heights, MA: Allyn & Bacon.

Hoffman, R., and Burnett, E. (2012, February 16). *CNN: Investing in start-ups pay off.* (CNN interview with Reid Hoffman, cofounder of LinkedIn, with Erin Burnett, interviewer). www.cnn.com/video/#/video/bestoftv/2012/02/17/erin-i-d-e-a-reid-hoffman.cnn.

Horn, Jr., R. A. (2001). Promoting social justice and caring in schools and communities: The unrealized potential of the cohort model. *Journal of School Leadership, 11,* 313–34.

Jenkins, R. (2011, November 11). The teaching–experience paradox. *The Chronicle of Higher Education, 58*(12), A39. chronicle.com.

Johnson, W. B. (2007). *On being a mentor: A guide for higher education faculty.* Mahwah, NJ: Erlbaum.

Johnson, W. B., and Huwe, J. M. (2003). *Getting mentored in graduate school.* Washington, DC: American Psychological Association.

Johnson, W. B., and Mullen, C. A. (2007). *Write to the top! How to be a prolific academic.* England: Palgrave.

Johnson-Bailey, J. (2012). Effects of race and racial dynamics on mentoring. In S. Fletcher and C. A. Mullen (Eds.), *The SAGE handbook of mentoring and coaching in education* (pp. 155–68). Thousand Oaks, CA: Sage.

Johnson-Bailey, J., and Cervero, R. M. (2004). Mentoring in black and white: The intricacies of cross-cultural mentoring. *Mentoring & Tutoring, 12*(1), 7–21.

Kealy, W. A. (2000). Full circle: Lessons from my mentor's heroes. In C. A. Mullen, M. B. Cox, C. K. Boettcher, and D. S. Adoue (Eds.), *Breaking the circle of one: Redefining mentorship in the lives and writings of educators* (pp. 175–88) (2nd ed.). New York: Peter Lang.

Klinenberg, E. (2012). *Going solo: The extraordinary rise and surprising appeal of living alone.* New York: Penguin Press.

Kowalski, T. J. (2005). *Case studies on educational administration* (4th ed.). New York: Pearson.

Krathwohl, D. R. (1994). A slice of advice. *Educational Researcher, 23*(1), 29–32.

Ladson-Billings, G. (2006). From the achievement gap to the education debt: Understanding achievement in U.S. schools. *Educational Researcher, 35*(10), 3–12.

Laing, P., and Bradshaw, L. K. (2003). The use of cohort models in preparation programs for school leaders. In F. C. Lunenburg and C. S. Carr (Eds.), *Shaping the future: Policy, partnerships, and emerging perspectives* (pp. 262–73). Lanham, MD. Rowman & Littlefield Education.

Lamb, M. E. (Ed.). (1999). *Parenting and child development in "nontraditional" families.* Mahwah, NJ: Erlbaum.

Lee, W. Y. (1999). Striving toward effective retention: The effect of race on mentoring African American students. *Peabody Journal of Education, 74*(2), 1–9.

Maslow, A. (1962). Toward a psychology of being. New York: Van Nostrand.

McClain, L. T. (2003, September 29). Working part-time by choice. *The Chronicle of Higher Education,* 1–6. chronicle.com.

Mendis, P. (2001). Teaching in the information age: Leadership aspects of integrated learning with technology in democratic environments. *Academic Leadership, 1*(2), 1–5. www.academicleadership.org.

Merriam, S. B. (2001). Andragogy and self-directed learning: Pillars of adult learning theory. *New Directions for Adult and Continuing Education,* (89), 3–13.

Merriam-Webster. (2012). Merriam-Webster, Incorporated. nws.merriam-webster.com/opendictionary/new-word_display_recent.php.

Michaelsen, L. K., Knight, A. B., and Fink, L. D. (Eds.). (2002). *Team-based learning: A transformative use of small groups.* Westport, CT: Praeger.

Miller, J. W. (1999). Foreword from the leadership. In C. A. Mullen and D. W. Lick (Eds.), *New directions in mentoring: Creating a culture of synergy* (pp. 79–86). London: Falmer.

Miller, K. J., Pearl, C. E., and Wienke, W. D. (2004). Florida universities address the need for special education professoriate: Considerations and crucial supports for doctoral students. *Florida Educational Leadership, 5*(1), 59–62.

Mullen, C. A. (2001). The need for a curricular writing model for graduate students. *Journal of Further and Higher Education, 25*(1), 117–26.

———. (2005). *The mentorship primer.* New York: Peter Lang.

———. (2007a). Naturally occurring student–faculty mentoring relationships: A literature review. In T. D. Allen and L. T. Eby (Eds.), *The Blackwell handbook of mentoring: A multiple perspectives approach* (pp. 119–38). Malden, MA: Wiley-Blackwell.

———. (2007b). Trainers, illusionists, tricksters, and escapists: Changing the doctoral circus. *The Educational Forum, 71*(4), 300–15.

———. (Ed.). (2008). *The handbook of formal mentoring in higher education: A case study approach.* Norwood, MA: Christopher-Gordon Publishers.

———. (Ed.). (2009). *The handbook of leadership and professional learning communities.* New York: Palgrave Macmillan.

———. (2011a). Facilitating self-regulated learning using mentoring approaches with doctoral students. In B. Zimmerman and D. H. Schunk (Eds.), *Handbook of self-regulation of learning and performance* (pp. 137–52). New York: Routledge.

———. (2011b). The paradox of change in public schooling and education leadership. In F. W. English (Ed.), *The SAGE handbook of educational leadership: Advances in theory, research, and practice* (2nd ed.). Thousand Oaks, CA: Sage.

———. (2012). Mentoring: An overview. In S. Fletcher and C. A. Mullen (Eds.), *The SAGE handbook of mentoring and coaching in education* (pp. 7–23). Thousand Oaks, CA: Sage.

Mullen, C. A., Cox, M. D., Boettcher, C. K., and Adoue, D.S. (Eds.). (2000). *Breaking the circle of one: Redefining mentorship in the lives and writings of educators.* New York: Peter Lang.

Mullen, C. A., Creighton, T., Dembowski, F. L., and Harris, S. (Eds.). (2007). *The handbook of doctoral programs in educational leadership: Issues and challenges.* Rice University Connexions collections: NCPEA Press. my.qoop.com.

Mullen, C. A., Papa, R., Kappler Hewitt, K., Eadens, D., Schwanenberger, M., Bizzell, B., and Chopin, S. (2012, August). *The future as we see it: Junior faculty's envisioning of mid-century leadership.* Paper presented at the National Council of Professors of Educational Administration, Kansas City, MO.

Murray, B. (1998). Flexibility is key to a successful career (pp. 1–8). *The APA Monitor Online.* [American Psychological Association]. www.apa.org/monitor/jun98/homepage.html.

Nafisi, A. (2003/2004). *Reading Lolita in Tehran: A memoir in books.* New York: Random House.

National Academic Advising Association (NACADA) (2012). *The global community for academic advising*. Kansas State University, Manhattan, KS. www.nacada.ksu.edu/search.htm?btnG=Search+NACADA.

Nyquist, J. D., and Woodford, B. J. (2000). *Re-envisioning the PhD: What concerns do we have?* Seattle, WA: Center for Instructional Development and Research and the University of Washington.

Ogden, E. H. (1993). *Completing your doctoral dissertation or master's thesis in two semesters or less* (2nd ed.). Lancaster, PA: Technomic Publishing.

Oracle Corporation. (2010, January). *Competitive differentiation: An Oracle white paper*. Redwood Shores, CA: Oracle Financial Services. (report). www.oracle.com/us/industries/financial-services/045681.pdf.

Pajares, F. (2007). *The elements of a proposal*. www.emory.edu/education/mfp/proposal.html.

Patterson, K., Grenny, J., Maxfield, D., McMillan, R., and Switzler, A. (2008). *Influencer: The power to change anything*. New York: McGraw-Hill.

Payne, R. K. (2003). *A framework for understanding poverty* (3rd ed.). Highlands, TX: Aha Process.

Phillips, E. M., and Pugh, D. S. (1994). *How to get a PhD: A handbook for students and dissertation supervisors*. Milton Keynes, UK: Open University Press.

Piantanida, M., and Garman, N. B. (1999). *The qualitative dissertation: A guide for students and faculty*. Thousand Oaks, CA: Corwin.

Pinar, W. F., Reynolds, W. M., Slattery, P., and Taubman, P. M. (1995/1996). *Understanding curriculum: An introduction to the study of historical and contemporary curriculum discourses*. New York: Peter Lang.

Pratt, D. D. (1998). Ethical reasoning in teaching adults. In M. W. Galbraith (Ed.), *Adult learning methods* (2nd ed.) (pp. 113–25). Malabar, FL: Krieger.

Prensky, M. (2001a, September/October). Digital natives, digital immigrants. *On the Horizon, 9*(5), 1–6.

———. (2001b, November/December). Digital natives, digital immigrants, part 2: Do they really think differently? *On the Horizon, 9*(6), 1–6.

Previn, A., and Previn, D. (1965). *Song lyrics from around the world*. http://lyricsplayground.com.

Rendina-Gobioff, G., and Watson, F. (2004). *Faculty/student collaboration: Mentoring in graduate school*. Unpublished paper.

Richardson, L. (1994). Writing: A method of inquiry. In N. K. Denzin and Y. S. Lincoln (Eds.), *Handbook of qualitative research* (pp. 516–29). Thousand Oaks, CA: Sage.

Roberts, A. (2000). Mentoring revisited: A phenomenological reading of the literature. *Mentoring & Tutoring, 8*(2), 145–64.

Robinson, C. (1999). Developing a mentoring program: A graduate student's reflection of change. *Peabody Journal of Education, 74*(2), 1–8.

Rodgers, C. (2002). Defining reflection: Another look at John Dewey and reflective thinking. *Teachers College Record, 104*(4), 842–66.

Rohrer, P. (2004, December 10). Not exploited. *The Chronicle of Higher Education*, 1–5. chronicle.com.

Rosen, C. (2011). Virtual friendship and the new narcissism. In M. Bauerlein (Ed.), *The digital divide* (pp. 172–88). New York: Jeremy P. Tarcher/Penguin.

Rowland, A. Z. (1982). *Handcrafted doors and windows*. Emmaus, PA: Rodale Press.

Scardamalia, M., and Bereiter, C. (1986). Research on written composition. In M. C. Wittrock (Ed.), *Handbook of research on teaching* (3rd ed.) (pp. 778–803). New York: Macmillan.

Schneider, A. (1998, March 13). More Professors are working part time, and more teach at 2-year colleges. *The Chronicle of Higher Education*. chronicle.com.

Shapiro, J. P., and Stefkovich, J. A. (2010). *Ethical leadership and decision making in education: Applying theoretical perspectives to complex dilemmas*. New York: Routledge.

Shaw, G. B. (1903). *Dedicatory letter. Man and superman: A comedy and a philosophy*. Cambridge, MA: The University Press.

Sigismund Huff, A. (1997). *Writing for scholarly publication*. Thousand Oaks, CA: Sage.

Smallwood, S. (2005, January 14). "The scary place': Thousands who flocked to the MLA meeting scored interviews and jobs. Thousands more did not. *The Chronicle of Higher Education, 51*(19), A11. chronicle.com.

Spanky and Our Gang. (1967). YouTube. http://www.youtube.com.

Sternberg, D. (1981). *How to complete and survive a doctoral dissertation*. New York: St. Martin's Press.

Stripling, L. (2004). *All-But-Dissertation non-completion of doctoral degrees in education*. Unpublished doctoral dissertation, University of South Florida, Tampa.

Styles, I., and Radloff, A. (2001). The synergistic thesis: Student and supervisor perspectives. *Journal of Further and Higher Education, 25*(1), 97–106.

Tareilo, J., and Bizzell, B. (Eds.). (2012). *NCPEA handbook of online instruction and programs in education leadership*. Rice University Connexions collections: NCPEA Press. my.qoop.com.

Thomas, R. M., and Brubaker, D. L. (2008). *Theses and dissertations: A guide to planning, research, and writing* (2nd ed.). Thousand Oaks: Corwin Press.

Thorpe, J. (2005, January). *APS Observer, 18*(1), 1–3. Published interview with Robert Zajone, Stanford University. (Association for Psychological Science). www.psychologicalscience.org/observer.

Toor, R. (2004, September 10). Back to school. *The Chronicle of Higher Education, 51*(3), B5. chronicle.com.

Waterman, H. (2004, November 5). Graduate students and mentors. *The Chronicle of Higher Education, 60*(11), B18. chronicle.com.

Watts, A. (1957/1985). *The way of Zen.* New York: Vintage Books.

Weinstein, J. R. (2004). Aliens, traitors, and elitists: University values and the faculty. *The NEA Higher Education Journal, 20*(1), 95–106.

Weis, L., and Fine, M. (2000). *Speed bumps: A student-friendly guide to qualitative research.* New York: Teachers College Press. Wikipedia.org.

Wilson, P. P., Pereira, A., and Valentine, D. (2002). Perceptions of new social work faculty about mentoring experiences. *Journal of Social Work Education, 38*(2), 317–33.

Wilson, R. (2004, December 3). Where the elite teach, it's still a man's world. *The Chronicle of Higher Education, 51*(15), A8–A12. chronicle.com.

Wisker, G., and Braun, R (2004). *Making a difference: The doctoral enterprise and afterwards.* Unpublished interview. www.adkidum.com/APU/Rose%20Braun.htm.

Young, J. P., Alvermann, D., Kaste, J., Henderson, S., and Many, J. (2004). Being a friend and a mentor at the same time: A pooled case comparison. *Mentoring & Tutoring, 12*(1), 23–36.

Zimmerman, S. (2004). From ABD to EdD: Musings of a dissertation committee chair. *The AASA Professor, 26*(3), 26–29. www.aasa.org.

Zinn, L. M. (1998). Identifying your philosophical orientation. In M. W. Galbraith (Ed.), *Adult learning methods* (2nd ed.) (37–56). Malabar, FL: Krieger.

Zuckerman, H. (1977). *Scientific elite: Nobel laureates in the United States.* New York: The Free Press.

NONPRINT RESOURCES

Academic Career Websites and Job-Seeking Tools

See free appendix "Finding News about the Academy and the Academic Job Market and Locating Jobs across the Disciplines" (www.styluspub.com/resrcs/user/jsappendix.pdf) (for an elaboration, see chapter 8, this book).

More essential websites for job applicants follow.

- LinkedIn (www.linkedin.com) is a global platform for professional networking that subscribers configure to their needs.
- *The Chronicle of Higher Education* (chronicle.com) is a widely established academic career resource.
- New York Times Company (gradschool.about.com/lr/curriculum) provides specific guidance on how to write an academic vita, complete with samples.
- Academic Careers Online (www.academiccareers.com) is a global marketplace of activity where job applicants search for jobs and submit materials, and employers search jobs and post materials.
- *Education Week* (www.edweek.org/ew/index.html), sponsored by Editorial Projects in Education, focuses on the top school and district jobs in public education for teachers, leaders, directors, and others.
- HigherEdJobs (www.higheredjobs.com) is an online company that offers a suite of tools ranging from job notices in higher education to the contact information for people the user is seeking.
- H-Net: Humanities and Social Sciences Online (www.h-net.org; sponsor, Michigan State University) is an open community that fosters discussion networks, provides access to databases that include peer-reviewed materials, and enables users to receive announcements for job openings.

Academic Mentoring Networks and Mentoring-Friendly Associations

The networks and associations listed below offer explicit mentoring through multiple venues, both formal and informal, governance driven and student initiated. These provide a vibrant sample of diverse national and international communities of academics, including education professionals committed to mentoring, coaching, learning, innovation, and the success of all members, specifically students, graduates, and emerging scholars and professionals.

Student benefit is channeled across the platforms of these networks and associations. Examples vary widely and include mentoring programs; special interest groups, academies, and venues; professional development; diversity-oriented goals; mentoring roundtables, workshops, and panels with experts and specialists; dissertation, research, and professional awards; scholarships, fellowships, and grants; special funding allocations; newsletters, blogs, webinars, advice from influential mentors/scholars/researchers, graduate-led networks, talk radio, blogs, and socials; refereed and invited publications; calls for papers for conferences and publication in special issues, books, yearbooks, and more; graduate-student publications; self-authored publications; custom-designed works; personal collections created out of resources searched (such as books, articles, modules, courses, and lessons); career advice, resources, and opportunities, including job postings for postdocs, assistant professors, and much more.

Some of these associations also have e-mentoring communities dedicated to comprehensive mentoring programs that link students with personal mentors and peer groups, often in guided, one-to-one mentoring relationships and/or small groups. These also model vision and renewal through diversity task forces committed to the preparation of new professionals for employment and leadership in equitable workplaces.

In addition to networks, associations, councils, and academies in different countries and states/provinces, graduate students and new professors can search for opportunities within universities and colleges. These mentoring initiatives overlap with what some networks and associations offer. Needs-identified opportunities facilitated at some campuses range from scholarships for specified and eligible populations to support for innovative and electronic theses/dissertations to guidance with research ethics. Labor-intensive mentoring support is geared toward graduate student writing, presenting, teaching, publishing, as well as job placement and promotion.

Search these and other websites of interest using key words (e.g., "mentoring," "networks," "awards"). Also peruse the website's home page for initiatives that include special events and current opportunities. Follow some of these venues (e.g., associations) through LinkedIn, Facebook, Twitter, and more. To navigate further, find out which associations, institutes, centers, and academies your campus subscribes to/is accredited with, and seek out opportunities and value-added benefits for members (e.g., professional relationships, mentoring programs, publications, directories, proceedings, postings).

- American Association of Colleges for Teacher Education (AACTE) - aacte.org

  Holmes Scholars Program, part of AACTE
  aacte.org/pdf/Programs/Holmes-Scholars/holmes-scholars-brochure.pdf

- American Association of School Administrators - www.aasa.org
- American Educational Research Association (AERA) - www.aera.net

  Mentorship and Mentoring Practices Special Interest Group, part of AERA

- American Educational Studies Association (AESA) - www.educationalstudies.org
- American Psychological Association (APA) - www.apa.org
- Association for Career and Technical Education (ACTE) - www.acteonline.org/awards.aspx
- Association for Educational Communications and Technology (AECT) - www.aect.org/newsite/
- Association for the Study of Higher Education (ASHE) - www.ashe.ws
- Association for Supervision and Curriculum Development (ASCD) - www.ascd.org
- American Educational Research Association (BERA) - www.bera.ac.uk
- American Library Association (ALA) - www.ala.org
- Australian Association for Research in Education (AARE) - www.aare.edu.au/offserv.htm
- Austrian Society for Research and Development in Education (ASRDE) - www.oefeb.at
- Bergamo Conference on Curriculum Theory and Classroom Practice - jctonline.org
- Canadian Society for the Study of Education (CSSE) - www.csse.ca
- Council for Accreditation of Counseling and Related Educational Programs (CACREP) - www.cacrep.org/template/index.cfm
- Council for Exceptional Children (CEC) - www.cec.sped.org
- Educational Studies Association of Ireland (ESAI) - www.esai.ie
- Hong Kong Educational Research Association (HKERA) - www.hkera.edu.hk/eng/index.html
- International Association of Special Education (IASE) - www.iase.org
- International Conference on Education & E-Learning (EeL) - e-learningedu.org
- International Institute of Qualitative Inquiry (IIQI) - www.iiqi.org
- International Mentoring Association (IMA) - www.mentoring-association.org
- International Society for Technology in Education (ISTE) - www.iste.org/welcome.aspx
- Interuniversity Association of Education Research (AIDIPE) - www.uv.es/aidipe
- Japanese Educational Research Association (JERA) - wwwsoc.nii.ac.jp/jsse4/index-e.html
- MentorNet, the National Electronic Industrial Mentoring Network for Women in Engineering and Science - www.mentornet.net
- Mexican Council for Educational Research (MCER) - www.comie.org.mx
- National Academic Advising Association (NACADA) - www.nacada.ksu.edu
- National Association of Elementary School Principals (NAESP) - www.naesp.org
- National Association of Secondary School Principals (NASSP) - www.nassp.org/awards-and-recognition
- National Association of Special Education Teachers (NASET) - www.naset.org/conferences.0.html
- National Council of Professors of Educational Administration (NCPEA) -www.emich.edu/ncpeaprofessors

    NCPEA Member Research Directory
    NCPEA Mentoring Mosaic Program

- Nordic Educational Research Association (NERA) - www.nfpf.net
- Phi Delta Kappa International (PDK) - www.pdkintl.org
- Scottish Educational Research Association (SERA) - www.sera.ac.uk
- Society of Research Administrators International (SRA International) - www.srainternational.org
- University Council for Educational Administration (UCEA) - www.ucea.org
    David L. Clark National Graduate Student Research Seminar in Educational Administration & Policy

UCEA Barbara L. Jackson Scholars Network

Index

About the Author

Carol A. Mullen, PhD, is professor and chair of Educational Leadership and Cultural Foundations in the School of Education at The University of North Carolina at Greensboro, USA, having been in this position since 2007. She specializes in mentoring innovations and democratic approaches to professional development in education across university and K–12 settings. She mentors graduate students and new professionals and collaborates with scholars and practitioners. She is coauthor of *Educational Leadership at 2050: Conjectures, Challenges, and Promises* (Rowman & Littlefield Education 2012), a practical, bold, no-holds-barred look at challenges facing educational leaders and the university programs that prepare them through midcentury.

She has taught in higher education (universities and colleges) in the United States and Canada since 1985. She teaches doctoral courses on successful approaches to mentoring and scholarly writing. She was editor of the *Mentoring & Tutoring: Partnership in Learning* journal (Routledge). Her authorships encompass more than two hundred refereed journal articles and book chapters, fourteen special issues of journals, and fifteen other books. Other recent books include the coedited volume *The SAGE Handbook of Mentoring and Coaching in Education* (SAGE 2012), and awards for scholarship include AERA's Award for *Breaking the Circle of One*, a University President's award for faculty excellence, a women's leadership award, and doctoral mentoring and teaching awards. She has founded, coordinated, and researched numerous mentoring and writing networks and programs for professional associations and universities. She served as president of the National Council of Professors of Educational Administration (NCPEA) from 2012 to 2013. She is a plenary session representative for the University Council for Educational Administration (UCEA). She earned her PhD from The Ontario Institute for Studies in Education of the University of Toronto, Canada.